Lawrence Clavering

by

A. E. W. Mason

Double9
BOOKS

Lawrence Clavering
by A. E. W. Mason

ISBN: 978-93-68091-63-9

Published by

DOUBLE 9 BOOKS

2/13-B, Ansari Road
Daryaganj, New Delhi – 110002
info@double9books.com
www.double9books.com
Tel. 011-40042856

ABOUT THE AUTHOR

A. E. W. Mason, born Alfred Edward Woodley Mason on January 7, 1865, was a distinguished English author and playwright, best known for his contributions to detective fiction and adventure novels. His works often feature intricate plots and compelling characters, showcasing his versatility and creativity. "At the Villa Rose" (1910): This novel features Inspector Hanaud and is renowned for its engaging plot and suspenseful storytelling. It remains one of Mason's most celebrated works. "The Four Feathers" (1902): An adventure novel set, during, the Sudanese campaign of the late 19th century. The story follows a young British officer's quest for redemption after resigning from his regiment. The novel was later adapted into several films and remains a classic of adventure literature. "The House of the Arrow" (1924): Another notable detective novel featuring Inspector Hanaud, known for its clever plot and strong character development. Mason's works have left a lasting impact on the genres he wrote in, and his novels are still enjoyed by readers today. A. E. W. Mason passed away on November 22, 1948, but his legacy endures through his classic novels and plays.

CONTENTS

CHAPTER I
TELLS OF A PICTURE

The picture hangs at my lodgings here at Avignon, a stone's throw from the Porte de la Ligne, and within the shadow of Notre Dame des Doms, though its intended housing-place was the great gallery of Blackladies. But it never did hang there, nor ever will; nor do I care that it should—no, not the scrape of a fiddle. I have heard men circumstanced like myself tell how, as they fell into years, more and more their thoughts flew homewards like so many carrier-pigeons, each with its message of longing. But Blackladies, though it was the only home I ever knew in England, did not of right belong to me, and the period during which I was master there was so populous with troubles, so chequered with the impertinent follies of an inexperienced youth raised of a sudden above his station, that even now, after all these years, I look back on it with a burning shame. And if one day, perchance, as I walk in the alleys here beyond the city walls, the wind in the branches will whisper to me of the house and the brown hills about it—it is only because I was in England while I lived there. And if, again, as I happen to stand upon the banks of the Rhone, I see unexpectedly reflected in the broken mirror of its waters, the terraces, the gardens, the long row of windows, and am touched for the moment to a foolish melancholy by the native aspect of its gables—why, it is only because I look out here across a country of *tourelles*.

However, I come back to my lodging, and there is my picture on the wall—an accountant, as it were, ever casting up the good fortune and the mishaps of my life, and ever striking a sure balance in my favour.

I take the description of it from a letter which Mr. George Vertue wrote to a friend of mine in London, and that friend despatched to me. For, since the picture is a portrait of myself, it may be that an account of it from another's hand will be the more readily credited. Mr. Vertue saw it some years since at a dealer's in Paris, whither, being at that time hard pressed for money, I had sent it, but was lucky enough not to discover a purchaser.

"I have come across a very curious picture," he wrote, "of which I would gladly know more, and I trust that you may help me to the knowledge. For more than once you have spoken to me of Mr. Lawrence Clavering, who fought for the Chevalier de St. George at Preston, and was out too in the Forty-five. The picture is the bust of a young gentleman painted by Anthony Herbert, and with all the laborious minuteness which was distinctive of his earlier methods. Indeed, in the delicacy with which the lace of the cravat is figured, the painter has, I think, exceeded himself, and even exceeded Vandermijn, whom at this period he seems to have taken for his model. The coat, too, which is of a rose-pink in colour, is painted with the same elaboration, the very threads of the velvet being visible. The richness of the work gives a very artful effect when you come to look at the face, which chiefly provokes my curiosity. In colour it is a dead white, except for the lips, which are purple, as though the blood stagnated there; the eyes are glassy and bright, with something of horror or fear staring out of them; the features knotted out of all comeliness; the mouth half opened and curled in the very sickness of pain; the whole expression, in a word, that of a man in the extremity of suffering—a soul's torture superimposed upon an agony of the body; and all this painted with such circumstantial exactness as implies not merely great leisure in the artist, but also a singular pleasure and gusto in his subject...."

After a few more remarks of a like sort, he continues: "I made it my business to inquire of Mr. Herbert the history of the picture. But he would tell me no more than this: that it was the portrait of Mr. Lawrence Clavering, painted in that gentleman's youth, and that if I would have fuller knowledge on the matter, I must get it from Mr. Clavering himself; and Mrs. Herbert, a very gentle woman, now growing old, but I should say of considerable beauty in her prime, warmly seconded him in his reticence. Therefore I address myself to you to act as an intermediary between Mr. Clavering and myself."

The information I did not think it fitting at that time to deliver. But both Mr. Herbert and his wife are dead these three years past; and so I write out the history of my picture, setting down, as my memory serves, the incidents which attach to it in the due order of their sequence. For if the picture is a strange one, it has, I think, a history to match.

CHAPTER II
I TAKE A WALK AND HEAR A SERMON IN THE COMPANY OF LORD BOLINGBROKE

That history I take to have begun on the 28th day of March at Paris in the year 1715. I was sitting in my room at the Jesuit College in the Rue St Antoine, with the "De Imitatione" at one elbow, and Marco Polo's travels at the other; and, alas! I fear that I gave more attention to the adventurer than I did to the theologian. But, in truth, neither author occupied the chief place in my thoughts. For the spring sparkled in the air, its music was noisy among the budding trees, and something of its music, too, seemed to be singing in my blood. From my window I looked down across the roof-tops to the Île St. Louis, and I could see a strip of the Seine flashing in the sunlight like a riband of steel. It was on the current of the river that my thoughts floated, yet they travelled faster than the current, seeing that while I still looked they had reached the bar where the river clashes with the sea. I had the tumble of its waters in my ears when the door was opened, and one of the lay coadjutors entered with a message that the rector wished to speak with me.

I followed him down the stairs, not without a guilty apprehension as to the nature of the interview in store for me, and found the rector pacing backwards and forwards across one end of the hall, with his hands folded behind his back. As I made my reverence, he stopped and eyed me for a moment thoughtfully.

"Twelve months since," said he, "you received from the Duke of Ormond in England the offer of a cornetcy in the Horse Guards."

"Yes, Father," I replied, taken aback by his unexpected commencement; and I replied hastily, "I refused it."

"You refused it!" he repeated very deliberately; and then, suddenly bending his eyebrows, "And without reluctance?"

I felt my face flush as he asked the question. "Father," I stammered, "I refused it;" and so came to a stop.

He nodded his head once or twice, but pressed me no further upon the point. Instead—

"You know at whose instance the commission was offered to you?" he asked.

"I have no certain knowledge," I replied, with considerable relief; "but I can think of but one person in the world with the power and inclination to do me that service."

"Ah," broke in the rector, sharply, "you count it a service, then?"

"He would count it a service," I answered, with a clumsy effort to retrieve the mistake. "For my part, Father, I refused it."

"Precisely," said he. "He would count it a service he was doing you. There are no fine feathers in our army, and there is no leisure to parade them were there any. Yes, Lord Bolingbroke would count it a service he was doing you."

Now, although the relationship between Lord Bolingbroke and myself was the merest thread—my father having married a niece of Lady Joanna St. John—I was well enough acquainted with his diligence to know that the sneer was unjust; and I was preparing to make some rejoinder in a proper spirit of humility when the rector continued—

"It is of Lord Bolingbroke that I wish to speak to you. He is in Paris."

"In Paris, Father!" I exclaimed incredulously.

"In Paris. He came last night, and asks permission of me this morning that you should wait on him."

"Father," I cried, "you will give that permission?"

He shook his head over my eagerness and resumed his walk.

"Very well," he said at length, and he gave me Lord Bolingbroke's address. "You can go now," he added.

I waited no longer than sufficed to utter a brief word of thanks, and hurried towards the door.

"My son."

I turned back towards the rector, with a doleful thought that he would revoke his permission. But as I approached him reluctantly enough, I saw something of a smile brighten upon his rigorous face.

"My son," he said, without a trace of his former severity, "you have taken no vows as yet, and will not for eight months to come. Think, and think humbly, during those months! Our Order, thank God, is not so poor in service that we need to reckon obstinacy as devotion."

I stood abashed and shamefaced at his words. "Father," I said, "I have chosen."

"But it is for us to ratify the choice," he answered, with a cast back to his former sternness, "or to annul it as unworthy." With that he dismissed me; but this time, being somewhat stung by his warning, I retired with a more decorous step. Once in the street, however, I made up for the delay. For, in truth, I was at some trouble to account for my kinsman's sudden arrival in France; for, although Walpole had publicly declared his intention of bringing both Bolingbroke and the Earl of Oxford to trial for their work in compassing the Peace of Utrecht, it was common rumour that Bolingbroke and his colleague awaited the impeachment in all confidence as to its issue. This hasty departure, however, bore to my thinking all the appearance of a desperate flight, and I hurried to his lodging in no small anxiety of spirit. My Lord Bolingbroke makes but a slight figure in this story of my picture, compared with that he made upon the wider field of a nation's chronicle; and it is very well for me that this is so. For, indeed, I never understood him; although I held him in a great liking and esteem, and considered him to have confronted more adversity and mischance than commonly falls to any one, I never understood him. He was compacted of so many contradictions, and in all of them was so seemingly sincere that a plain man like Lawrence Clavering was completely at a loss to discover the inward truth of him. But as he was a riddle to my speculations, so was he a cherished object to my affections. For even during those last years of Queen Anne's rule, when his life was at its busiest and his fortunes at their climax, he still found time to show kindness to one whose insignificance was only rivalled by his poverty. He was "Harry St. John" to me as to his equals and my betters, and in spite of the difference of our years; and when I found myself in company with Dr. Swift and Mr. Congreve and Mr. Prior and the little crook-back poet whose "Windsor Castle" had brought him into a sudden reputation, he was ever at pains to distinguish me in his conversation, so that I might suffer no shame from my inferiority. Doubtless it was to the natural courtesy of the man rather than to any special inclination that his behaviour was due, but I was none the less grateful to him on that account.

He had just finished dinner, and was still at the table over his wine, when his footman introduced me into his apartment.

"Ah," said he, "I expected you would come;" and he drew a chair to the table, and filled a second glass, "It is not the welcome you have had from me at Bucklersbury, but philosophers"—and he made a polite flourish of the hand to include me in the phrase—"will ever be content with a makeshift. For my part," he continued, "I do not know but what the makeshift is the better. A few trustworthy friends, a few honest books and leisure wherein to savour their merits—it is what I have chiefly longed for these last five years;" and he threw up his arms with a long breath of relief, as though he had been unexpectedly lightened of some burdensome load. I had heard him talk often enough in this way before, and was disinclined to set great value upon his contentment.

"What brought you in this scurry to Paris?" I asked.

"They meant to pursue me to the scaffold," he returned. "I had sure information of that. No testimony would have helped me or thwarted them. It was my blood they needed—Marlborough told me so—my blood and Oxford's." And he flashed out into a sudden passion. "There's the point. Alone I would have faced them. These whimsical Tories are the frailest of reeds, the Whigs the most factious and vindictive opponents. Still, I would have faced them had I stood alone. But to make common cause with Oxford! No, I abhor him to that degree, I cannot. It were worse than death. However, let's talk no more of it!" and he recovered himself with an effort, and sat for a little, silent, fingering his glass. "Oxford!" he exclaimed again with a bitter laugh of contempt. "Soft words, and never a thing done! To live till to-morrow was the ultimate of policy to him. And jealous, too! The bubble of his own jealousy! Had he cared to act, or had he been dismissed but a few weeks earlier, I tell you, Lawrence, the Tories would now be cemented to such a solidity of power that——" He stopped abruptly, and leaned over to me: "For whom are you?" he asked, "the Hanoverian, or the"—and he paused for the briefest space—"the Chevalier de St. George?"

"I am for King James the Third," I replied promptly.

"Oh," says he; and, rising from his chair, he took a turn across the room. "I rather fancied," he resumed, with a queer smile, "that discretion was amongst the lessons taught at the Jesuit Colleges."

"We are taught besides," I answered, "to distinguish between the occasion for discretion and the occasion for plain speaking."

"Then," said he, "I fear me, Lawrence, the teaching is faulty, if I am to judge from the instance you have given me. I had some talk with my Lord Stair this morning, and the talk was of the friendliest."

"Lord Stair?" I cried, rising in some confusion, for I knew the Chevalier to possess no more redoubtable opponent than the English ambassador.

"Yes," replied Bolingbroke. "And I leave Paris for the Dauphiné—mark that, Lawrence—not for Lorraine, though I have been invited thither. But, in truth, I have had my surfeit of politics." Even while he spoke, however, a serving-man was ushered into the room with a letter to deliver.

"I was bidden, my lord, to give it into your hands," he explained.

"Very well," replied Lord Bolingbroke, something hastily; and I noticed that he dropped his hand over the superscription of the letter. "I will send the answer;" and he added, correcting himself, "if one be needed."

The servant bowed, and went out of the room. I began to laugh, and Bolingbroke turned an inquiring glance at me.

"There is some jest?"

"It is of your making, my lord. I fancy those few honest books will not be opened yet awhile."

He flushed a little. "I don't understand," he said.

"That is because you cover so closely the handwriting of your letter that you have not as yet perceived from whom it comes."

"That is very true," he replied immediately; and he glanced at the cover of it. "The hand is strange to me. Perchance you recognize it;" and he frankly held it out to me.

"No," I replied; "but I recognized the servant who brought it. Marshall Berwick has sent him more than once with messages to the rector of my college."

"Oh," said he, with a start of surprise, "Marshall Berwick, the Chevalier's minister?" He opened the letter with a fine show of indifference. "I think I mentioned to you that I had already been invited by the Chevalier to Bar. Doubtless this is to second the invitation." He read it through carelessly, and tore it up. "Yes. But I travel south, not east, Lawrence. I go to Dauphiné, not Lorraine;" and as if to dismiss the subject, he diverted his speech from the Chevalier to myself.

"And so, Lawrence," he said, "it is to be the soutane, and not the red-coat; the rosary, and not the sword."

It seemed to me that there was a hint of wonder and disappointment in his voice; but, maybe, I was over-ready at that time to detect a slight, and I answered quickly—

"I have to thank you for the cornetcy. The offer was a-piece with the rest of your kindness; but I was constrained to refuse it."

"And what constrained you? Your devotion to the priesthood?"

He glanced at me shrewdly as he spoke, and I knew that my face was hot beneath his gaze. Then he laughed. The laugh was kindly enough; but it bantered me, and if my face was hot before, now it was a-flame.

"You come of an obstinate stock, Lawrence," he continued; "but I was misled to believe that you had missed the inheritance."

"It was out of my power to accept the cornetcy," I returned, "even had I wished it For I am a Papist."

"You would not have found yourself alone," he said, with a laugh. "The Duke of Ormond prefers Papists for his officers. He showed me a list not so long ago of twenty-seven colonels whom he had a mind to break, and strangely enough they were all Protestants, with never a fault besides to their names."

"Moreover," I went on, "I was too poor;" and there I think I hit the true and chief reason, though I would not acknowledge it as such even to myself.

"But you have an uncle in Cumberland," said Bolingbroke.

"He is a Whig and a Protestant," I replied. "He can hardly hold me in that esteem which would give me warrant to approach him."

My kinsman nodded his head as though he approved the argument, and sat for a little silent over his wine, while my fancies went straying over imagined battle-fields. It is strange how a man will glorify this business of cutting throats, the more particularly if he be of a sedentary life. Most like it is for that very reason. I have seen something of a war's realities since then; I have seen men turned to beasts by hunger and thirst, and the lust of carnage; I have seen the dead stripped and naked upon the hillside of Clifton moor white like a flock of sheep. But at the time of which I write I thought only of a battlefield as of a place where life throbbed at its fullest to a sound of resonant trumpets and victorious shouts; and the smoke of cannon hid the trampled victims, even from my imaginings.

"Come!" said Lord Bolingbroke, breaking in upon my reflections of a sudden; "if your afternoon is not disposed of, I would gladly take a turn with you. I have it in my mind to show you a picture."

I agreed willingly enough to the proposal, and together we went down into the street.

"This will be our way," he said; and we walked to the monastery of the Chartreux. Then he stopped.

"Perhaps you know the picture."

"No," I replied. "This is the first time that ever I came hither."

He took me forthwith to the wonderful frescoes of Le Sœur, and, walking quickly along them, stopped at length before the most horrid and ghastly picture that ever I set my eyes on. It was the picture of a dead man who spoke at his burial, and painted with such cunning suggestion and power that, gazing at it, I felt a veritable fear invade me. It was not merely that his face expressed all the horror, the impotent rage, the pain of his damnation, but there was also conveyed by the subtlest skill a certain consciousness in the sufferer that he received no more than his merits. It was as though you looked at a hypocrite, who knew that his hypocrisy was discovered.

"Well, what think you of it?" asked my companion. "It does credit to the painter's craftsmanship;" and his voice startled me, for, in my contemplation of the picture, I had clean forgotten his presence. The painting was indeed so vivid that it had raised up alert and active within my breast a thought which I had up till now, though not without effort, kept resolutely aloof from me.

"But yet more to his imagination," I replied perfunctorily, and moved away. Lord Bolingbroke followed me, and we quitted the monastery, and walked for some way in silence.

I had no mind for talk, and doubtless showed my disinclination, for my companion, though now and again he would glance at me with an air of curiosity, refrained from questions. To speak the truth, I was fulfilled — nay, I overbrimmed with shame. The picture lived before my eyes, receding in front of me through the streets of Paris. It seemed to complete and illustrate the rebuke which the rector had addressed to me that morning; it pointed a scornful commentary at my musings on the glory of arms. For the figure in the picture cried "hypocrite," and cried the word at me; and so insistently did the recollection of it besiege me that I came near to thinking it no finished painting limned upon the wall, and fixed so until such time as the colours should fade, but rather a living scene. I began almost to expect that the figures would change their order and disposition, that the dead man speaking would swerve from his attitude, and, as he spoke, and spoke "hypocrite," would reach out a bony and menacing finger towards me. So far had my fancies carried me when my kinsman touched me on the arm.

"It is as you say, Lawrence," he said, as though there had been no interval of silence since my last words — "it is the imagination, not the craftsmanship, which fixes the attention. It is the idea of a dead man speaking — no matter what he speaks."

There was a certain significance in his tone which I did not comprehend.

I stopped in the street.

"You were anxious to show me the picture," I said.

"Yes," he replied.

"Why?"

"Does it tell you nothing concerning yourself?"

I was positively startled by the question. It seemed incredible that he could have foreseen the effect which it would produce on me.

"What do you mean?" I exclaimed.

He gave an easy laugh, and pointed across my shoulder.

"There is a church," said he, "and moult and moult people entering it. Let us go in too."

I looked at him in increased surprise, for I had not believed him very prone to religious exercises. However, he crossed the road, with me at his heels, and went up the steps in the throng.

The church was dim, and because I came into it out of the April sunshine, it struck upon my senses as dank besides.

The voices of the choir beat upwards through an air blue and heavy with incense; the tapers burning on the altar at the far end of the nave over against us shone blurred and vague as though down some misty tunnel; and from the painted windows on the right the sunshine streamed in slanting rods of light, vari-coloured, disparting the mist.

At the first, I had an impious thought, due partly may be to my unfamiliarity with the bustle of the streets, and partly no doubt to the companionship of my kinsman, who ever brought with him, as it were, a breath of that wide world wherein he lived and schemed, that I was returning to a narrow hemisphere wherein men had no manner of business. But after a little a Carmelite monk began to preach, and the fire of his discourse, as it rose and fell, now harsh with passion, now musical with tenderness, roused me to a consciousness of the holy ground on which I stood. I bent forward, not so much listening as watching those who listened. I noted how the sermon gained upon them, how their faces grew expectant. Even Lord Bolingbroke lost his indifference; he moved a step or two nearer to the preacher. His attitude lost the lazy grace he was wont to affect; he stood satisfied, and I knew that there was no man on earth so critical in his judgment of an orator.

I was assured then of the sway which the monk asserted over his congregation, and the assurance pierced to my very soul.

For I knew the cause of his power; one had not to listen long to realise that. The man was sincere. This was no pleasurable discourse waved delicately like a scented handkerchief to tease the senses of his auditors. Sincerity burnt like a clear flame kindling his words, and compelled belief. Of the matter of his sermon I took no note. Once or twice "the Eve of St. Bartholomew" came thundering at my ears, but for the most part it seemed that he cried "hypocrite" at me, until I feared that the congregation would rise in their seats in that dim church, and a mob of white faces gibber and mow the accusation. I stood fascinated, unable to move, until at last Bolingbroke came back to me, and, taking my arm, led me out of church.

"You study late of nights?" he asked, looking into my face.

"The preacher wrought on me."

"He has eloquence," he agreed; "but it was a dead man speaking."

I stopped in the street, and stared at him.

"Yes," he continued; "he warns, he exhorts, like the figure in the picture there, but the man himself—what of him, Lawrence? He is the mere instrument of his eloquence—its servant, not its master. He is the priest—dead to the world in which he has his being, a shadow with a voice, a dead man speaking."

"Nay," I broke in, "the words were born at his heart. He was sincere, and therefore he lives. The dead man speaking is the hypocrite."

I cried the words in a very passion of self-reproach, and without thought of the man I addressed them to.

"Well, well," said he, indulgently, "he has, at all events, a live advocate. I did not gather you were so devoted to the vocation;" and he laughed a little to belie the words, and so we parted company.

It was in no complacent mood, as you may guess, that I returned to the college, and, indeed, I loitered some while before the gates or ever I could make up my mind to enter them. The picture weighed upon my conscience, and seemed like to effect my Lord Bolingbroke's evident purpose, though by means of a very different argument. It was not the priest, but myself, the hypocrite, who was the dead man speaking; and thus, strangely enough, as I had reason to think it afterwards, I came to imagine the picture with myself as its central figure. I would see it at nights as I lay awake in my bed, painted with fire upon the dark spaces of the room, and the face that bore the shame of hypocrisy discovered, and with that shame the agony of punishment was mine. Or, again, a word of reproof; the mere sight of my Marco Polo was sufficient to bring it into view, and for the rest of that day it would bear me company, hanging before my eyes when I sat down to my books, and moving in front of me when I walked, as it had moved in front of me through the streets of Paris on that first and only occasion of my seeing it. For, though many a time I passed and repassed the monastery of the Chartreux, I never sought admittance. I saw the picture no more than once; but, indeed, I was in no danger of forgetting it, and within the compass of a few months events befell me which fixed it for ever in my memory. I have but to shut my eyes, and I see it after this long interspace of years, definite in every detail. I have but to open them, and, sitting at this table at which I write, I behold, actually painted, the second picture into which my imagination then transformed the first—the picture of myself as the dead man speaking.

CHAPTER III
MY KINSMAN AND I RIDE DIFFERENT WAYS

Two days later, being deputed upon some errand, the import of which I have forgotten, I chanced to pass by the barrier of the Rue de Grenelle, and a travelling-carriage drew up at my side. My eyes were bent upon the ground, so that I took no heed of it until I heard my name cried. I looked up, and there was my Lord Bolingbroke at the window.

"You see, Lawrence," he said, "I leave Paris as I promised Stair, and I travel into Dauphiné."

"But by a roundabout road," I answered eagerly. "It is possible that you might take St. Germains on the way;" for it had reached my ears that Queen Mary of Modena was desirous to try her persuasions upon him.

"No," he returned, with a shake of the head; "I have my poor friends in England to consider. I should provide a fine excuse for ill-using them if I made common cause with the Chevalier. They have served me; it is my turn to serve them; and I shall be better employed that way than in weaving fairy-stories with Queen Abdicate.—But what's the trouble?" he continued, with a change of tone. "You walked as though the world had withered at your feet."

"Nay," I answered, with a laugh, "there is no trouble. I was merely wondering——" and I hesitated.

"At what?" he asked curiously.

"At the rule which bids me sleep with my chamber-window closed," I returned, with a laugh. And, indeed, it was a question you had reason to put during this hot spring, when from behind your stifling panes you looked out at night across Paris lying cool and spacious beneath a purple sky. But the truth is that all these regulations which were instituted to discipline the novice to a habit of obedience, were beginning to work me into a ferment of irritability; and through the months that followed, April, May, and June, the irritability increased in me to a spirit of rebellion. At times I felt a mad desire to rise in my seat and hurl defiance, and with that defiance my books, at my tutors' heads. The desire surged up within my veins, became active in every limb, and I had to set my teeth until my jaws ached to repress it. At times sick and dispirited, I counted up the years to come; I passed them through my thoughts even as I passed the beads of my rosary beneath my thumb, and even as the beads of my rosary, they were monotonously alike one to the other.

Doubtless, too, the recollection of the picture I had seen at the monastery of the Chartreux helped to intensify my unrest. For it abode vividly in my memory, and the menace I drew from it grew more and more urgent as the days slipped on. I should note, however, that a certain change took place in the manner in which it presented itself. I could still see, I could still hear the figure speaking. But it did not so much cry "Hypocrite!" as thunder out, in the very lines of the Carmelite preacher, "The Eve of St. Bartholomew — the Eve of St. Bartholomew."

Of course, as the rector had declared, I was under no vows or obligation to persist in my novitiate. But I felt the very knowledge that I was free to be in some way a chain about my ankle constraining me. I took a cast back to the period of my boyhood when enrolment amongst the priests of the Jesuit order had been the aim of a fervid ambition; when the thought of that body, twenty thousand in number, spread throughout the earth, in Japan, in the Indies, in Peru, and working one and all in a consonant vigilance for the glory of their order, had stirred me with its sublimity; and I sought — with what effort and despair! — to recreate those earlier visions. For to count them fanciful seemed treachery; to turn deliberately aside from them was evident instability.

So much I have deemed it necessary to set down concerning my perplexities at this time, since they throw, I think, a light upon the events which I am to relate. For I was shortly afterwards to depart from this safe corner, and wander astray just as I wandered when I lost myself in the labyrinth of Blackladies. And the explanation I take to be this — for it is merely in explanation and not at all in extenuation that I put this forward — I had clean broken from the one principle by which, however clumsily, I had hitherto guided my life, and had as yet grappled to no other with sufficient steadiness of faith to make it useful as a substitute.

It was on the Saturday of the first week of July that I left the Jesuit College. I was standing at my window about two of the afternoon, and looking down at the river and the bridge which crossed it. I had a clear view of the bridge from end to end betwixt the gables of a house, and I noticed that it was empty, save for one man, who jogged across on horseback — or rather, so it seemed at the height from which I looked, for when I saw the horse close at hand a short while afterwards, I found reason to believe that the man had galloped. I stood watching him idly until he crossed out on to the quay; and I remember that the refectory bell rang just as he turned the corner and passed out of my sight. Towards the end of dinner, a message was brought to me that the rector desired to see me in his study as soon as we were risen from table. This time, however, it was in no hesitancy or trepidation that I waited on him, but rather with a springing heart. For let him but dismiss me from the college, and here was an end to all the torture of my questionings—an unworthy thought, you will say, and, indeed, none knew that more surely than myself.

On the contrary, however, the rector received me with a benevolent eye. "I have strange news for you, my son," said he, with a glance towards a stranger who stood apart in the window; and the stranger stepped forward hurriedly, as though he would have the telling of the news himself. He was a man of middle height and very close-knit, though of no great bulk, dark in complexion, and possessed, as far as I could judge, of an honest countenance.

"Mr. Clavering," he began, with a certain deference, and after these months of "brother" and "my son" the manner of his address struck upon my ears with a very pleasant sound, "I was steward to your uncle, Sir John Rookley, at Blackladies in Cumberland."

"Was?" said I.

"Until Monday was se'nnight," says he.

"Then what may be your business with me?" I asked sharply. For there was throughout England such a division of allegiance as set even the members of a family on opposite sides the while they maintained to the world an appearance of concord, so that many a dismissed servant carried away with him secret knowledge wherewith to make his profit. I was therefore pretty sharp with the steward, and quickly repeated the question.

"Then what may you have to ask of me?"

"That you will be pleased to continue me in the office," he returned humbly.

I stood cluttered out of my senses, looking from the servant to the rector, and from the rector again to the servant, with I know not what wild fancies choking at my throat.

"It is true," said the rector. "Your uncle died of an apoplexy a fortnight back."

"But he has a son," I gasped out

"Sir John quarrelled with Mr. Jervas two days before he died," answered the steward. "Blackladies comes to you, Mr. Clavering, and I have travelled from Cumberland to acquaint you of the fact."

It was true! My heart so throbbed and beat that I could not utter a word. I could not so much as think, no, not even of my uncle or my cousin. It is true that I had seldom seen the one, and never the other. I was conscious only of an enlarging world. But my eyes chanced at the moment to meet the rector's. His gaze was fixed intently upon my face, and with a sudden feeling of shame I dropped my eyes to the ground.

"My son," he said, drawing me a little on one side and speaking with all kindliness, as though in answer to my unspoken apology, "it may be well that you can do better service as the master of Blackladies. You will have the power and the means to help effectually, and such help we need in England;" and as I still continued silent, "If you become a priest, by the laws of your country you lose that power, and surely the Church will share in the loss. And are you fitted for a priest?" He looked at me keenly. "I spoke my doubts to you some while back, and I do not think they went much astray."

I did not answer him, nor did he wait for an answer, but took me by the arm and led me back to the steward.

"My cousin quarrelled with his father. Then what has become of him?" I asked, still in an indecision.

"I do not know, sir. Most like he is in France."

"In France?" I cried with a start. For the answer flashed a suspicion into my mind which—prove it true, and it was out of my power to accept the inheritance! "In France? And the substance of the quarrel?"

"It is not for me, sir, to meddle in the right or wrong of it," he began.

"Nor did I ask you to," I cut him short "I ask you for the bare fact."

He looked at me for a second like one calculating his chances.

"Mr. Jervas sided with the Jacobites," and the words struck my hopes dead. My world dwindled and straitened as swiftly as it had enlarged.

"Then I can hardly supplant him," I said slowly, "for I side with that party too."

The steward's eyes gleamed very brightly of a sudden.

"Ah!" said I, "you, too, have the cause at heart"

"So much, sir, that I make bold to forget my station and to urge you to accept the bequest. There is no supplanting in the case. For if you refuse Blackladies it will not fall to Mr. Jervas." He drew from his pocket a roll of paper fastened with a great seal, and held it out to me. I broke the seal, and opened it. It contained a letter from Sir John's attorney at Appleby, and a copy of the will which set out very clearly that I was to possess the house and lands of Blackladies with all farms, properties, and rents attached thereto, upon the one condition, that I should not knowingly divert so much as the value of a farthing into the pockets of Mr. Jervas Rookley.

So far I had read when I looked up at the steward in a sudden perplexity.

"I do not understand why Sir John should disinherit his son, who is, at all events, a Protestant, because he is a Jacobite, in favour of myself, who am no less a Jacobite, and one of the true faith besides."

The steward made a little uneasy movement of impatience. "I was not so deep in my master's confidence that I can answer that."

I held out the will to him, though my fingers clung to it. "I cannot," I said, "take up the inheritance."

It was not, however, the steward, but the rector who took the paper from me. He read it through with great deliberation, and then—

"You did not finish," he said, and pointed his finger to the last clause.

"I saw no use in reading more, Father," I replied; but I took the will again and glanced at the clause. It was to this effect: that if I failed to observe the one condition or did not enter into possession from whatsoever cause, the estate should become the property of the Crown.

"I cannot help it," I said. "To swell the treasury of the Hanoverian by however so little, is the last thing I would wish to do, but I cannot help it. Mr. Jervas Rookley suffers in that he is what I pride myself on being. I cannot benefit by his sufferings," and I folded up the will.

"There is another way, sir," suggested the steward, diffidently.

"Another way?" I asked.

"Which would save the estate and save Mr. Jervas too from this injustice."

"Explain!" I cried. "Explain!" For indeed it grieved me beyond measure that I should pass these revenues to one whom I could not but consider an usurper.

"I do but propose it, sir, because I see you scruple to——" he began.

"Nay, man!" I exclaimed, starting forward, "I need no apologies. Show me this way of yours!"

"Why, sir, the will says the Crown. It names no names. If you infringe the condition or refuse the estate, Blackladies goes to the Crown. But," and he smiled cunningly, "it is not likely that King James, did he come to the throne, would accept of a bequest which comes to him because the rightful owner served his cause so well."

I nodded my head. "That is true. King James would restore it," I said.

"To the rightful owner," said he.

"So be it, then!" I cried. "I will hold Blackladies in trust for Jervas Rookley," and then I stopped. "But meanwhile Mr. Jervas Rookley must shift for himself," I added, bethinking me of the condition.

The steward smiled again. "If you knew him, sir, you would not fear for him on that account;" and he continued, "You will return with me to England?"

"Yes, but not now," I exclaimed, for all at once a new resolve had taken shape within my mind. There was no word in the will about my politics. Sir John was acquainted with them when he made the will. I was free to use Blackladies as I chose.

"Wait you here in Paris," I cried to the steward, and came of a sudden to an awkward pause. "You brought money with you?" I asked.

"I have an order upon Mr. Waters the banker," he replied.

"Good," I said, my spirits rising with my voice. "Get it cashed—now, at once, and bring the money back to me. But be quick, be quick. For I have business in Lorraine."

"In Lorraine?" exclaimed the steward, and his face flashed to an excitement equal with my own.

"In Lorraine," I repeated, "and at Bar-le-Duc."

He waited for no further explanation, but made his reverence to the rector, a low bow to me, and departed on his errand. I began to pace impatiently about the room, already looking for his return, even as I heard him pass beneath the window.

"Was I not right, my son?" asked the rector. "You walk, you speak, like a man refreshed. And yet—and yet——"

He came over to me and laid a hand upon my shoulder, while a great gravity overspread his face, and somehow at the touch of his hand, at the mere sight of his face, my overweening confidence burst like a bubble. For looking through my eyes he seemed to search my soul, and in his eyes I seemed to see, as in a mirror, the naked truth of all the folly that he noted there.

"These are the last words," he went on, "which I shall speak to the pupil, and I would have you bear them as the crest and motto of your life. I would have you beware of a feverish zeal. To each man I do solemnly believe there comes one hour of greatness, and only one. It is not the hour of supreme happiness, or of a soaring fortune, as worldlings choose to think, but the hour when God tries him upon His touchstone. And for that hour each man must watch if he would not fail. Indeed, it brings the test which proves—nay, makes—him man, and in God's image, too, or leaves him lower than the brutes; for he has failed. Therefore watch! No man knoweth the hour of God's coming. Therefore watch! But how shall he watch"—and his voice to my hearing had in it some element of prophecy—"how shall he watch who swings ever from elation to despair, and knows no resting-place between them?"

He spoke very quietly, and so left me alone. I do not know that I am inclined now to set great store upon the words. They seem almost to present some such theory as children and men over-occupied with book-learning are wont to fondle. But after he had left me alone, I sat with his discourse overlaying me like an appalling shadow. The sunlight in the court without lost its brightness; the very room darkened within. I saw my whole life before me, a procession of innumerable hours. Hooded and cloaked, they passed me with silent feet. I sought to distinguish between them. I chose at random from amongst them. "This," I cried, in a veritable fear—"this is the hour;" and even as I spoke, one that had passed threw back the hood and turned on me a sorrowing face. So would the hour come, and so unready should I be to challenge it! My fear swelled to a panic; it bore me company all that day as I made my purchases in the streets, as I took leave of my companions, as I passed out of the Porte St. Antoine. It was with me, too, in the quiet evening long after the spires of Paris had vanished behind me, when I was riding with my steward at my back across that open country of windmills and poplar trees on the highroad to Lorraine.

CHAPTER IV
AND MEET. I CROSS TO ENGLAND AND HAVE A STRANGE ADVENTURE ON THE WAY

For the steward rode with me, though I barely remarked his presence until we had ridden some ten miles. Then, however, I called him to my side.

"I bade you wait at Paris for my return," I said, and I reined in my horse. He followed my example, but with so evident a disappointment that I forgave him his disobedience on the instant.

"You left no word, sir, as to the date of your return, or where I should look for you," he explained, readily enough.

"Besides," I added, with a laugh, "I ride to Bar-le-Duc, is it not so?" and I allowed him to continue with me, bethinking me at the same time that I might inform myself the sooner concerning Blackladies and the politics of the county. Upon these points he gave me information, which inclined me in his favour. The northern counties, as far south as Derbyshire, were so much tinder. It needed but a spark to set them ablaze from one coast to the other. I was ready to listen to as much talk of that kind as he could pour into my ears, and indeed he did not stint me of it; so that, liking his story, I began in a short while to like the man who told it, and to hold myself lucky that I was possessed of a steward whose wishes so jumped with his service.

He had been born on the estate, he told me, some thirty years since, and had been reared there, though, thanks to the kindness of his late master, my uncle, he had received a better schooling than his father before him. He spoke, indeed, very correctly for a servant, but with a broadish accent and a clipping of his *the's*, as the natives of that district are used to do. But for my part I never got the tang of it, and so make no effort to reproduce it here. He was called Leonard Ashlock.

In his company I journeyed, then, the fifty-eight leagues to Bar-le-Duc, where I seemed all at once to have come into my own country without the trouble of crossing over seas. For as I rode through the narrow streets, it was the English tongue that I heard spoken on every side, though more often with a Scotch or an Irish accent. But the one whom I came to seek I did not find. The Chevalier, they told me, had gone to Commercy. So to Commercy we travelled eastwards after him for another eight leagues or so, and arrived there towards the close of the afternoon on the next day.

We rode straight to the Toison D'or, the chief inn of the town, and while I was dismounting in the courtyard, I noticed a carriage, which was ranged, all dirtied and muddy, against an angle of the wall. I stepped over and examined it. There was a crest upon the panels.

I turned to the ostler.

"When did the carriage come?"

"This morning."

"And monsieur?"

"He is within, I think."

I ran up the steps into the house and fell plump against a girl who was carrying some glasses and a jug upon a tray. She gave a little scream; the tray struck me on the chest; there was jingle of broken glass, and a jugful of claret was streaming down my breeches and soaking about my knees.

"Monsieur is in?" I asked.

"Stupid!" she said, with a stamp of the foot.

"Monsieur is in?" I asked again.

"Booby," says she, and caught me a swinging box on the ears.

"I beg your pardon," said I, and I ran up the stairs. A footman stood beside the door on the landing, and I knew the man.

"Ah," said I, "he is here."

The footman advanced a step towards me.

"My lord is busy."

"He will see me."

"I have the strictest orders, sir."

I pushed past the fellow and hammered at the door. It was thrown open from the inside, and Lord Bolingbroke stood anxiously in the door.

"Good morning," said I, airily. "It is a roundabout journey, this of yours to Dauphiné;" and while he stared and frowned at me I stepped past him into the room. In the window opposite there stood a man with his back towards me—a man of a slender and graceful figure, plainly dressed in a suit of black velvet. He turned hastily as I stumbled across the threshold, and in a twinkling I knew what I had done. There was no mistaking the long, melancholic features, the gentle aspect of long-suffering. His race was figured in the mould of his lineaments, and the sad history of his race was written in his eyes.

I dropped upon my knees.

"Your Majesty," I stammered out; and again, "your Majesty."

He took a step eagerly towards me. I felt the claret trickling down my legs.

"You bring pressing news," he exclaimed; and then he checked himself and his voice dropped to despondency. "But it will be bad news. Not a doubt of that! 'Tis always bad news that comes in such hurry;" and he turned to Bolingbroke with the saddest laugh. "Bad news, my lord, I'll warrant."

"Nay, your Majesty," I answered, "I bring no news at all;" and I glanced helplessly at Bolingbroke, who, having closed the door, now stood on one side, midway between King James and myself. How I envied him his easy bearing! And envying him thus I became the more confused.

"It is a kinsman of mine," he said, in some perplexity—"Mr. Lawrence Clavering, and a devoted servant of your Majesty."

"A kinsman of yours," said the King, affably. "That makes him doubly welcome."

And then the most ridiculous thing occurred, though I perceived nothing of its humour at the time. For of a sudden the King gave a start.

"He is wounded, my lord," he cries. "He shall have my surgeon to attend to him. Tell Edgar; he is below. Bid him hurry!" and he came a little nearer towards me, as though with his own hands he would help me to rise. "You were hurt on your journey hither. How long—how long must blood be the price of loyalty to me and mine?"

The poignant sadness of his voice redoubled my confusion.

"Quick!" cried the King. "The poor lad will swoon." And, indeed, I was very near to swooning, but it was from sheer humiliation. I glanced about me, wishing the floor would open. But it was the door that opened, and Lord Bolingbroke opened it. I jumped to my feet to stop him.

"Your Majesty," I exclaimed, "it is no wound I would to my soul that it were!"

"No wound!" said the King, drawing back and bending his brows at me in a frown.

"What is it, then, Lawrence?" asked Bolingbroke as he closed the door.

I looked down at my white buckskin breeches, with the red patches spreading over them.

"It is," said I, "a jugful of claret."

No one spoke for a little, and I noticed the King's face grew yet sterner and more cold. He was, in fact, like so many men of a reserved disposition, very sensitive to the least hint of ridicule upon all occasions, and particularly so when he had been betrayed into the expression of any feeling.

"Your Majesty," I faltered out ruefully, "the Rector of the Jesuit College in Paris warned me before I set out, of the dangers which spring from overmuch zeal, and this is the second proof of his wisdom that I have had to-day. For now I have offended your Majesty by stumbling impertinently into your presence; and before, the maid boxed my ears in the passage for upsetting her claret."

The speech was lucky enough to win my pardon. For Bolingbroke began to laugh, and in a moment or two the King's face relaxed, and he joined in with him.

"But we have yet to know," said he, "the reason of your haste."

I explained how that, having come into an inheritance, I had ridden off to Bar-le-Duc, to put it at his disposal, and from Bar-le-Duc to Commercy; and how, on the sight of Lord Bolingbroke's carriage in the courtyard, I had rushed into his presence, without a thought that he might be closeted with the King. I noticed that at the mention of Blackladies the King and Bolingbroke exchanged a glance. But neither interrupted me in my explanation.

"You give me, at all events, a proof of your devotion to your kinsman," said the King; "and I am fain to take that as a guarantee that you are no less devoted to myself."

"Nay," interposed Lord Bolingbroke; "your Majesty credits me with what belongs to yourself. For I doubt if Lawrence would have shown such eagerness for my company had he found me in the Dauphiné instead of in Lorraine."

The King nodded abstractedly, and sat him down at the table, which was littered over with papers, and finally seized upon a couple of letters, which he read through, comparing them one with the other.

"You can give me, then, information concerning Cumberland," he said, changing to a tone sharp and precise; and he proceeded to put to me a question or two concerning the numbers of his adherents and the strength of their adhesion.

"Your Majesty," I replied, "my news is all hearsay. For this inheritance has come to me unexpected and unsought. The last year I have lived in Paris."

He drummed with his fingers upon the table, like one disappointed.

"You know nothing, then, of the county?"

"I have never so much as set foot in it. I was born in Shropshire."

"Then, your Majesty," Lord Bolingbroke interrupted, "neither is he known there. There is an advantage in that which counterbalances his lack of information."

The King raised his eyes to my face, and looked at me doubtfully, with a pinching of the lips.

"He is young for the business," he said, "and one may perhaps think" — he smiled as he added the word — "precipitate."

My hopes, which had risen with a bound at the hint that some special service might be required of me, sank like a pebble in a pool. I cudgelled my brains for some excuse, my recollections for some achievement, however slight, which might outweigh my indiscretion. But I had not a single deed to my name: and what excuse could acquit me of a hot-headed thoughtlessness? I remained perforce silent and abashed; and it was in every way fortunate that I did, for my Lord Bolingbroke tactfully put forward the one argument that could serve my turn. Said he quite simply —

"His grandfather fell at Naseby, his father in the siege of Deny, and with those two lives, twice were the fortunes of the family lost."

The King rose from his table and came over to me. He laid a hand upon my shoulder.

"And so your father died for mine," he said, and there was something new, something more personal in the kindliness of his accent, as though my father's death raised me from a unit in the aggregate of his servants into the station of a friend; "and your grandfather for my grandfather."

"Your Majesty sees that it is a privilege which I inherit," I replied. From the tail of my eye I saw my kinsman smiling appreciation of the reply.

"Lawrence has the makings of a courtier, your Majesty," said he, with a laugh.

"Nay," I interrupted hotly, "this is honest truth. Let the King prove me!"

It was the King who laughed now, and he patted my shoulder with a quite paternal air, though, in truth, he was not so many years older than myself.

"Well," he said, "why not? He is a hawk of the right nest. Why not?" and he turned him again to Bolingbroke. "As you say, he is not known in Cumberland, and there is, besides, a very natural reason for his presence in the county." He stood looking me over for a second, and then went back abruptly to his papers on the table. "But I would you could give me reliable news as to those parts."

"News I can give your Majesty," I answered, "though whether it is reliable or not I cannot take it upon oath to say. But the man who passed it to me was the steward of Blackladies, and he spoke in that spirit wherein I would have all men speak." And I told him all that Ashlock had recounted to me.

"Oh," said the King, when I had ended, and he made the suggestion eagerly to Bolingbroke. "Perhaps it were best, then, that I should land upon the coast of Cumberland in England. What say you?"

I saw Bolingbroke's eyebrows lift ever so slightly.

"I thought," he answered, with the merest touch of irony in his tone, "that your Majesty had determined some half an hour since to land at Montrose?"

"I know," said the King, with something of petulance; "but these later advices may prove our best guide."

"But are they true?" said Bolingbroke, spreading out his hands.

"They tally with the report of Mr. Rookley," said the King.

I started at the mention of the name, and the King remarked the movement. He looked towards me, then again at the letter in his hand, which was written in a round and clumsy character. I caught sight of a word in that letter, and I remembered it afterwards, because it chanced to be misspelt.

"Oh," said he, "Mr. Jervas Rookley signs himself of Blackladies? I fancied that the name was familiar to me, when first you uttered it."

I repeated all that Ashlock had related to me concerning the man, and how I was to hold his estate in trust for him until the King came to his throne.

"We will see to it," said he, "that Mr. Clavering shall not be the loser."

I felt the blood rush into my face.

"It was with no thought of that kind that I spoke," I declared earnestly. "I pray your Majesty to believe me."

But Lord Bolingbroke broke in upon my protestations.

"This steward is with you at Commercy? Then, if it please your Majesty, I would advise that we see the man here, and question him closely face to face. For Mr. Jervas Rookley——" And he filled the gap of words with a shrug of significance.

"You distrust him?" asked the King; "yet it appears his loyalty has cost him an estate."

"It is that perplexes me; for I know these country gentlemen," and his voice sharpened to the bitterest sneer. "At night, over their cups, they are all for King James; then they consult their pillows, and in the sober morning they are all for King George. Oh, I know them! A sore head makes a world of difference in their politics."

The words seemed to me hot and quick, with all the memories of his defeated labours during those last six years of Queen Anne's reign, and I fancied the King himself was inclined to discount their value on that account.

"Yet," he urged, "these letters speak in no uncertain terms."

"They speak only of a disposition towards your Majesty," rejoined his minister. "It is a very tender, delicate, and unsatisfactory thing, a disposition. What we would have is their resolve. Are they resolved to drive on with vigour, if matters tend to a revolution? Will they support the revolution with advantage, if it spins out to a war? It is on these points your Majesty needs to be informed; and it is on these points they keep so discreet a silence. We ask them for their plan, as Marshall Berwick asked them time out of mind, and we get the same answer that he received. How many troops will his most Christian Majesty land? How many stands of arms? how many thousand crowns? Not one word of a definite design; not one word of a precise statement of their resources."

He walked about the room as he spoke, with every mark of discouragement in his gestures and expression, while the King listened to him in an uneasy impatience, as though he was rather irritated than impressed by Bolingbroke's doubts.

"Very well," said the King, tapping his foot on the floor, "we will examine Mr. Clavering's steward;" and he bade me go and fetch Ashlock into the room. But search as I might, nowhere could I find a trace of him. He had stayed no more than five minutes in the house, the people of the inn informed me. I hurried to the stables, thinking perchance to find him there. I questioned the ostlers, the drawers, even the wench who had boxed my ears. No one had knowledge of his whereabouts, and since it would be an idle business to go hunting for him through the unfamiliar streets of Commercy, I left a sharp word that he should come up the moment he returned, and so got me back chapfallen to Lord Bolingbroke's apartment.

The King's secretary, Mr. Edgar, was now in the room, gathering together the papers which overspread the table.

"It is no great matter," said the King, when I explained how that I had failed in my search, "for I doubt me that I could have heard him out. Besides, Mr. Clavering, I have had some talk concerning you with your kinsman here, and since your inheritance and your journey hither fit so aptly with our needs, it were a pity to miss the occasion."

"Your Majesty," I cried, and I felt my heart swell and leap within me, and my head spin with exultation. Here was the very thing of which I had dreamed hopelessly so often during those weary months at Paris, letting my fancies dally with it as with some bright and charming fairy tale, and, lo! it had come true. It had come true! The words made a silent music at my heart, and animated all my blood. It had come true! and then, of a sudden, there shot through me, chilling me to the centre, the rector's warning, and the forebodings that had flowed from it. Did this mission, which the King assigned to me, harbinger the hour of trial? Should I fail when it came? I set my teeth and clenched the nails into the palms of my hands. My whole body cried No! No! but underneath I seemed to hear a voice, very low, very persistent, speaking with full knowledge, and it said Yes! Yes!

"Then this will be your charge," continued the King, recalling me to myself. "You will journey with all speed to London, and bear with you a letter in my hand to the Duke of Ormond, at Richmond," and he paused upon the words. "It must pass from your hand into the Duke's. You will then go north to your estate, and collect knowledge for our use as to what help we may expect from Cumberland, and, so far as you can gather, from the counties adjoining. Lord Bolingbroke will inform you more of the particulars. Your errand, of course, you will keep secret—locked up from all—from our supporters, no less than from our opponents. It would be of detriment to us if they came to think that we distrusted them. Nor do we—it is their judgment, not their loyalty, about which we wish to be assured. We think, therefore, that it would be prudent in you to make no parade of your convictions. Hear both sides like one that holds the balance evenly. For, if you take one side openly, you will hear from our friends just what we hear so far away as Bar-le-Duc; and so God speed you!" and he held out his hand to me, and I kissed it. Then Mr. Edgar opened the door, and the King walked to it. He was already across the threshold, when he stopped and turned back, pulling a silver medal from his fob.

"This," said he, "is the fac-simile of that medal which the Duchess of Gordon presented to the Faculty of Advocates in Edinburgh, seven years back," and he gave it into my hand. "It may serve to keep me in your heart and memories. Moreover, a day may come when it will be necessary for you to convince our friends in the North, on whose side you stand; and this will help you to the end. For there is no other copy."

I knelt down and kissed the medal reverently. On the one side was struck the head of King James—very true and life-like—with the words "cujus est;" on the other a picture of the British Islands, with this motto inscribed beneath it, "Reddite."

"It is a text," I said, and indistinctly enough, for that simple word "Reddite," so charged was it with a sad and pitiful significance, brought the tears welling to my throat "It is a text I would have every man in England preach from."

"You will act on it," said the King; and I flattered myself with the thought that I noted something of a veritable tenderness in his accent "You will act on it; that is better;" and so he went out of the room.

Lord Bolingbroke closed the door, flung himself into a chair, and yawned prodigiously.

"Lawrence," he said, "I am very thirsty."

A bottle of Rhenish wine was standing on a sideboard at one end of the room. He went over and opened it, and filled two glasses.

"Let us drink," said he, and handed one to me "Let us drink to ourselves," and he raised the glass to his lips.

"Nay," I cried, "to the King first"

"Very well, to the King first, if you will, and to ourselves next. What matters the toast, so long as we drink it?" and he drained his glass to the bottom. I followed his example.

"Now to ourselves," said he; and he filled them again. "It is a good fashion," he continued, in a musing tone, "that of drinking to the King. For so one drinks double, and never a word can be said against it." I noticed, however, that he drank triple and quadruple before he had come to an end. Then he looked at my breeches and laughed.

"And so the wench boxed your ears," he said, and, becoming quite serious, he took me by the arm. "Lawrence, let's drink to her!"

"I should reel in my saddle if I did," said I, drawing back.

"Then don't sit in it!" he replied. "Let's drink to her several times, and then we'll go to bed."

"I trust to go to bed a good twenty miles from Commercy."

He shook his head at me.

"Lawrence, it is plain that you are new to the service of kings."

"You have a letter for me," said I.

"To the Duke of Ormond," and he looked at me in surprise. "You mean to start to-night?"

"Yes."

"Very well," and he sat himself down to the table, transformed in a second to a cool man of business. "The letter is in the chevalier's hand"— he drew it from his pocket as he spoke—"and there are many ships in the Channel. You had best charter a boat at Dunkirk, the smaller the better, and set sail at nightfall, so that you may strike the Downs before sunrise." Thereupon he proceeded to instruct me as to the precise details concerning which I was to inform myself in Cumberland—such as the number of troops they could put into the field, and how competent they were to face well-drilled and disciplined squadrons, their weapons, the least assistance from France they would hazard the rising upon, and such-like matters. Then he rose and prepared to accompany me downstairs. I was still holding the medal in my hand, and now and again fingering it, as a man will what he holds most precious. "And, Lawrence," he said, "I would hide the medal, even from yourself, if that be possible. You may find it a very dangerous gift before you have done."

He spoke with so solemn a warning as even then did something to sober my enthusiasm.

"It was a wise word that the Chevalier spoke when he bade you beware how you sided openly with the Jacks."

"Oh!" said I, as the thought struck me. "It was you, then, that prompted that advice—and for my sake."

"Not altogether."

"But in the main, for my sake."

"Lawrence," said he, leaning across the table, with his eyes fixed upon my face and his voice lowered to a whisper, "I misdoubt me, but this is a fool's business we're embarked upon. You heard the Chevalier. He has no fixed design," and he brought his hand down upon the table with a dunch. "One day he will land at Montrose, the next in Devonshire, the next in Cumberland, and, God knows, but the most likely place of all is the Tower steps."

"No!" I cried. "I'll not believe that. He has you to help him now."

Bolingbroke smiled, but shook his head.

"He has six other ministers besides myself, with Fanny Oglethorpe and Olive Trant at the head, and all of them have more power than I. He will concert a plan with me, and the hour after give a contrary order behind my back. It was the same when Berwick had the disposing of his affairs. No, Lawrence, I would have you be prudent, very prudent."

He came down the stairs with me and stood in the courtyard repeating ever the same advice, the while I mounted my horse. Of my steward I still could see no sign, and, leaving another direction that he should follow with all speed, I rode off towards the village of Isoncour, where Ashlock caught me up some two hours after I came there. I rated him pretty soundly, being much contraried by the melancholy forebodings of Lord Bolingbroke.

Ashlock made his excuses, however, very submissively, saying that he had dined at an ordinary in the town, and thereafter, being much fatigued with the hurry of our travelling, had fallen fast asleep. And I, bethinking me that, in spite of his gloomy forecast, Lord Bolingbroke would none the less serve the King with unremitting vigour, began to take heart again, and so pardoned Leonard Ashlock.

We came then to Dunkirk in the space of four days, and I was much put to it how I should get safely over into England with the King's letter. For the English warships were ever on the watch for the King's emissaries, and one of them, a sloop, was riding not so far out in full view of Dunkirk. In this difficulty Ashlock was of the greatest service to me, discovering qualities which I should never have suspicioned in him. For, espying a little pinnace drawn up on the beach, he said:

"The two of us could sail that across, sir."

"No doubt," said I, "if one of us could steer a course and the other handle the sails."

"I can do the first, sir, by myself, and the second with your help," he replied.

I went down the sands to the boat, and discovering to whom it belonged from a bystander, sought the owner out and forthwith bought it at his own price. For thus we need confide our business to no one, but waiting quietly till nightfall, we might slip past the big ship under cover of the dark. And this we did, launching the boat and bending the sails by the light of a lantern, which we kept as nearly as we could ever turned towards the land. The moon was in its fourth quarter and not yet risen when we started, so that the night, though not so black as we could wish, was still dark enough for our purpose. We had besides the lights from the port-holes of the warship to guide us, which gleamed pure and bright across the water like a triple row of candles upon an altar. We ran cautiously, therefore, for some distance to the west close under the shadow of the coast, and then fetching a wide compass about the ship, set our course straight for England. It was a light boat we were in, rigged with a lug-sail and a jib, and we slipped along under a fine reaching wind that heeled us over till the thwart was but an inch from the froth of the water.

"If only the wind hold!" said Ashlock, with a glance at the sail, and there was a lively ring of exultation in his voice. And, indeed, it was an inspiriting business this flight of ours across the Channel, or at all events this part of it I lay forward in the bows with a great coat atop of me, and my face upturned to the spacious skies, which were strewn with a gold-dust of stars and jewelled with the planets. The wind blew out of the night sharp and clean, the waves bubbled and tinkled against the planks as the prow split them into a white fire, and we sped across that broad floor of the sea as if licensed to an illimitable course. Now and again the lights of a ship would rise to the right or left, glimmer for a little like an ocean will-o'-the-wisp and vanish; now and again we would drive past a little fleet of fishing-smacks lying to for the night with never so much as a candle alight amongst them all, and only the stars, as it were, entangled amongst their bare poles and rigging; and, after a little, the moon rose.

I thought of my crib in the Rue St Antoine and the months of confinement there as of something intolerable. The wide freedom of the sea became an image of the life I was entering upon. I felt the brine like a leaven in my blood. And then of a sudden the sail flapped above me like the wing of a great bat, the strenuous motion of the pinnace ceased, and we were floating idly upon an even keel.

I looked towards Ashlock; he sat motionless in the stern with the tiller in his hand and the moonlight white upon his face. Then he took a turn about the tiller with a rope, glanced along the boat with his body bent as though he was looking forward beneath the sail, and came lightly stepping across the benches towards the bows. I lay still and watched him in a lazy contentment. Midway betwixt bow and stern he stopped and busied himself with tightening a stay; then again he crouched down and looked forwards, but this time it seemed to me that he was not looking out beyond the bowsprit, but rather into the bows to the spot where I lay huddled under my coat in the shadow of the thwart I could see his face quite plainly, and it appeared to me to have changed, in some way to have narrowed. It may have been a fancy, it may have been the moonlight upon his face, but his eyes seemed to glisten at me from out a countenance suddenly made trivial by cunning.

After a second he crept forward again, and I noticed how lightly—how very lightly he stepped. Would he stop at the mast, I asked myself? Was his business the tightening of a sheet even as he had tightened the stay? He stooped beneath the sail and still crept forward, running his hand along the top of the gunwale as he came; and it broke upon me as something new that he and I were alone in mid-channel, cabined within the planks of a little boat, he the servant,—but whose servant?—I not so much the master as the master's substitute and tripper-up.

I felt for my sword, but I remembered that I had loosed it from my belt when we had put to sea. From the spot where I lay I could see the scabbard shining by the tiller. At all events, Ashlock had not brought it with him. I watched him without a movement as he approached, but underneath the coat, every nerve and muscle in my body was braced to the tightness of a cord.

He bent over me, holding his breath, it seemed; his hands came forward hovering above my chest, but they held no weapon; his face sank out of the moonlight, dropped beneath the gunwale lower and lower down upon mine. Meanwhile I watched him, looking straight into his eyes. His face was but a few inches from mine when he drew back with a little quivering cry—it was, indeed, more of a startled in-drawing of the breath than a cry—and crouched on his hams by my side. Still I did not move, and again his face came forward over mine, very slowly, very cautiously, and down to where I lay in the dark, with my eyes open watching his. I could endure the suspense no longer.

"What is it, Ashlock?" I asked quietly, and in asking the question that moment, made a very great mistake, the importance whereof I did not discover until long afterwards.

Ashlock sprang back as though I had struck him in the face, I raised myself on one elbow and thrust the other outside the covering.

"I could not tell, sir, whether you waked or slept," he said; and I thought his voice trembled a little.

"I was awake, Ashlock. What is it?"

"The wind has shifted, sir," and now he answered confidently enough, "and blows dead in our teeth. We must needs tack if we are to reach the coast by daybreak."

"Well?"

"I cannot do it, sir, without your help. It needs two to tack if you sail with a lug-sail."

And that I found to be true. For the sail being what is called a square-sail with a gaff along the top of it, each time the pinnace went about it was necessary to lower it, and hoist it again on the other side of the mast. The which it fell to me to do, while Ashlock guided the tiller. So that I knew there was good reason for his waking me. However, I had little time for speculation upon the matter one way or another, since we sailed into a mist shortly afterwards, and were on the stretch, both eyes and ears, lest we should be run down by some vessel, or ever we could see it.

I was much exercised, too, what with the stars being hid, and our constant going about, whether Ashlock would be able to keep the boat in a course towards England. I need not, however, have troubled my head upon that score, for it was as though he had some sixth sense which found its occasion upon the sea, and when the day broke and the mist rolled down and massed itself upon the water, we were within five miles of the white cliffs with Dover Castle upon our starboard bow. The mist, I should say, was at that time about chin high, for standing up in the boat we looked across a grey driving floor, above which the smaller vessels only showed their masts.

"Shall I run her into the harbour?" asked Ashlock, and he turned the boat's head towards land.

"No!" I cried vehemently. For now that we were come within sight of England the letter that I carried began to burn in my pocket, and I felt the surest conviction that if we disembarked at Dover, we should be surrounded, catechised, and finally searched, upon the ground of a tell-tale face, which face would assuredly be mine. "No!" I said; "let us take advantage of the mist, and creep along the coast till we find some inlet where we can beach the boat."

This we did, and running now with a freer sail, we came in little more than an hour to a cove some four or five miles to the north-east of Dover, the cliffs breaking off very sharp at each side with a line of thin rocks jutting out at the south corner, and the walls of the cove steep all round and thickly wooded as low as we could see. Towards this cove we pointed, intending to run in there and abandon the boat. But when we were within half a mile of land the sun blazed out in the sky and the fog shredded like so much gauze burnt up in a fire. It was a fortunate thing for us that we had come no nearer to the shore. For there, low down on the beach, and but a yard or two from the water's edge, on a tiny strip of level ground, were four little cottages with the British ensign afloat. Ashlock rapped out an oath and thrust the tiller across to its further limit, meaning to go about and run back out of sight of the cove.

"The sail, sir!" he cried in great excitement, "Oh! damn it, sir, the sail!"

I sprang to the mast, loosed the sheets, lowered the sail, and of course must needs in my hurry get the spar entangled amongst the stays a foot above the thwart. Ashlock rose in a passion, and leaving the tiller to shift for itself, came leaping towards me.

"There, there, sir," he sneered, "leave it to me!" and losing at once his air of deference, he was for wresting rather than taking the spar out of my hands. "Did ever man see?" he exclaimed. "O Lord, did ever man see— —"

"Such a fool-master and such a clever servant," said I, finishing the sentence for him. But the words were hardly out of my mouth when I let go of the spar. He staggered back, holding the one end of it in his hands, the other caught me a crack in the joint at the knees, and the next moment I was sprawling on my back at the bottom of the boat. I heard Ashlock mutter, "Lord send us less pride and a ha'porth of common sense," the while he busied himself with getting the sail into position, and then he turned to me.

"You'll find, sir, the Preventive men will make little difference between master and servant when they discover the pretty letter you are carrying."

"The Preventive men!" I cried, scrambling to my feet.

"Ay, sir, the Preventive men," said he with a glance at the beach.

Now Ashlock was standing with his back to me bowsprit, whereas I faced him, and looking across his shoulder, I saw a sheer face of white cliff, topped with a thatch of grass, glide, as it were, behind him. I turned me about. The boat was swinging round with the tide now that it had neither sail nor a hand at the rudder to direct it. Before, it had been pointing for the beach midway in the cove; now it was heading for the rocks at the south corner of the bay; and each moment it moved faster, as I could judge from the increasing noise of the ripple at the bows. I jumped across the benches to the rudder.

"Hoist the sail!" I said in a low, quick command.

Ashlock looked from me to the rocks.

"The tide is running round the corner like a mill-race," said he, doubtfully, and he made a movement as though he would take my place.

"Hoist the sail!" said I, and he obeyed, and again prepared to come astern.

"No, stay where you are," I ordered sharply. He looked at me sharply, shrugged his shoulders, and sat him down by the mast. I brought the boat's head up until the wind against which we had been tacking was directly astern of us, and the tiller kicked in my hand as we drove through the water. We were now within the line of rocks, and I saw Ashlock give a start as he noticed the point I was making.

"You must round the corner of the reef, sir," he cried.

"We have no time for that. The tide runs in shore. There's a gap in the reef; we'll make for the gap."

The gap was, in fact, in a bee-line with the tip of the bowsprit. I had wind and tide to quicken my speed, and I felt the boat leap and pulse beneath me like a live thing. Ashlock looked at me in surprise, and then gave a little pleased laugh, as though my action chimed in with his nature.

Doubtless the plan was foolhardy enough; but the day was clear, and we were within full sight of the cottages upon the beach. More, our boat was the only boat in this secluded bay. I thought, indeed, only of the latter point, and not at all of the narrowness of the passage, and maybe it was that very oblivion which kept my hand steady. So engrossed was I, in truth, in my one idea, that I could not forbear from glancing backwards now and then in a mortal dread, lest I should see the sun flash upon the disc of a perspective glass or mark a boat splash out through the surf into the sea. Upon one such occasion I heard Ashlock rise to his feet with a muttered "God save us!" and a second later we grazed past a tooth of chalky rock some half a foot below the surface.

"Sit down!" I cried sharply, for the fellow obscured my vision. He dropped into his seat; I bent forward, peering out beneath the sail. We were within twenty yards of the gap in the reef, and the water converging on it from right and left, foamless and oily like a rapid in the Severn. The boat gave a great spring, and then slid with a swift, easy motion like a sledge.

I heard the waves burst over the rocks and patter back upon the sea; I felt the spray whipping my forehead; and then the cliffs fell away from my eyes and closed up behind my back. Ashlock lowered the sail and dropped the kedge from the bows. We were floating in still water, just round the point and close in to shore under the shadow of an overhanging cliff.

"Now, Ashlock!" said I, "you can come astern."

He came reluctantly, and in his coming began to babble an apology for the disrespect he had shown me. I cut him short at the outset of it.

"I am not concerned with your insolence," I said. "It is too small a thing. I am willing to believe, moreover, that you were hurried into it through devotion to a higher master than myself. I have forgotten it. But how came you to think that I carried a letter?"

"Your hand, sir," he replied readily, "was ever at your pocket on the road if we galloped—on the sea if we passed a ship."

It was truth that he said—every word of it—and it caused me no small humiliation. For here was I entrusted with a mission of some consequence, and I had betrayed a portion of my business at the outset.

"There is another thing," I continued sharply. "How comes it that you, Cumberland-born and Cumberland-bred, have so much knowledge of the sea?"

I looked at him steadily as I spoke, and I saw his face change, but not to any expression of suspicion or alarm. Rather it softened in a manner that surprised me; a look, tender and almost dreamy, came into his eyes, a regretful smile flickered on his lips. It was as though the soul and spirit of a poet peeped out at you from a busy, practical countenance.

"I should have been a sailor," he said, in a low, musing voice. "All my life I have longed for that one thing. The very wind in the branches for me does no more than copy the moan of the surf. But my parents would not have it so, and I live inland, restless, unsatisfied, like a man kept out of his own." He checked himself hastily, and continued in a flurry, for no reason which I could comprehend, "Still, I made such use as I could of the opportunities that presented. At Whitehaven and at Workington I learnt the handling of a boat."

"But," I interrupted him, "this is not the first time you have sailed from Dunkirk to England."

"No, sir," he answered, and his face hardened at my questioning. It was as though a lid had been slammed down upon an open box. "I have crossed more than once with young Mr. Rookley."

"That will do," I said; and he drew a breath of relief.

The explanation, I assured myself, was feasible enough, but—but—I could not get from before my eyes the vision of him creeping stealthily from the tiller to the bows. As he lay sleeping just where I had lain—for all that day we remained hidden within the cliffs—I saw him continually stoop beneath the sail; I saw his face sink out of the moonlight down and down to mine, and his hands hover above my breast. And with that a light flashed in on me. He knew of the letter I was carrying! He knew of the pocket I carried it in! I sat staring at him dumfounded. Was this the link? Was he playing me false?

"If I had only closed my eyes!" I cried, and in my perturbation I cried the words aloud.

Ashlock woke up with a start.

"What is it, sir?" he asked, in a whisper. "The Preventive men?" and the eagerness of his voice gave the lie to my suspicion. Yes, I reasoned, he had shown an anxiety equal with my own to escape from their clutches, was showing it now, and his anxiety was due to this very knowledge that I had the letter in my possession. I relapsed into perplexity, and in a little my fears took another and engrossing shape. Doubtless it was Ashlock's startled whisper set my thoughts particularly that way, and from minute to minute I lay expecting the Preventive men to row round the point and discover us. There was no possible escape for us if they did. The more I searched and searched the cliffs, the more clearly I saw how impossible they were to scale. It would, I think, have made the strain and tension of this waiting more tolerable had I been able to reach some point whence I could command a view of the bay, though it would have served no other end. But that too was denied to me. I lay the livelong day the impatient hanger-on of chance. No sound came to me but the ceaseless lapping of the waves beneath me, the ceaseless screaming of the gulls above my head, in a single monotonous note, sharp and clean like the noise that a large pebble makes hopping over ice. To add to my discomfort, we had no water in the boat, nothing, indeed, but a few hard biscuits, which served to choke us. And the sun was pitiless all day in a shadowless sky. The very colour of the sky seemed to have faded so that it curved over our heads, rather grey than blue, hot and hard—a cap of steel.

However, the day wore to sunset in the end, and the Preventive men had not come. We set sail as soon as it was dark, and coasting along, landed shortly after two in the morning, at a spot in the Downs a few miles from Deal. Thence, after setting our pinnace adrift, we made what haste we could to London.

Ah me! that ride through the night to London! I remember it as if I had ridden along that road yesterday. It was so long since I had been in England. I remember the homely little inn at which we roused a grumbling landlord and hired our horses. His very grumbles were music to my ears. I laughed at them, I remember, with such enjoyment that we had much ado to persuade him to part with the horses at all, and it was because of his grumbles that I paid him double what he asked. I remember, too, the hedgerows a-glimmer with wild-roses as with so many pale stars. To ride ever between hedgerows! It seemed the ultimate of happiness. And the larks in the early morning—never since have I heard larks sing so sweetly as they sang that morning over the Kentish meadows. We passed a little whitewashed church, I remember, with its mossy gravestones nestling in deep grass about its walls. Well, well, this is Avignon, and my old bones, I take it, will sleep just as easily under Avignon soil.

CHAPTER V
BLACKLADIES

I wasted no long time in London, you may be sure, but leaving Ashlock at the Hercules' Pillars in Piccadilly, went down with my letter to Richmond. On my return I supplied myself with a wardrobe better suited to my present state and set out for the north.

The mansion of Blackladies lies off Borrowdale upon the flank of Green Comb. I got my first view of it from the top of Coldbarrow Fell; for on coming to Grasmere, Ashlock had informed me of a bridle-path leading by Harrop Tarn and Watendlath, which would greatly shorten the journey, and since my impatience had grown hotter with every mile we had traversed, I despatched my baggage by the roundabout high-road through Keswick, and myself took horse in company with Ashlock.

It was noonday when we came to the ridge of the fell, and the valley lay beneath us shimmering in a blue haze, very lonely and very quiet. Now and again the thin sharp cry of a pee-wit came to our ears. Now and again our voices waked a sleepy echo. A little hamlet of white cottages— Stonethwaite they called it—was clustered within view, and towards the centre of Borrowdale, but so small was it and so still that it seemed not so much a living village as a group of huts upon some remote island which a captain, putting in by chance for water, may discover, long since built by castaways long since perished.

"Look, sir!" cried Ashlock, pointing downwards with his whip. "That is your house of Blackladies."

It lay in the hollow at my feet, fronting Langstrath and endwise to me; so that I only saw the face of it obliquely, and got no very clear idea of that beyond that it was pierced with an infinity of windows, for a score of mimic suns were ablaze in the panes. It was a long house with many irregular gables, built in three stories, of grey stone, though this I could hardly make sure of at the time, for the purple bloom of a wisteria draped the walls close and clambered about the roof. What attracted my eyes, however, far more than the house, was the garden, of which I had the plainest view, since it was built up from the slope at the east end of Blackladies, and not so much on account of its beauty as because of the laborious care which had been bestowed upon it. It was laid out in the artificial fashion of half a century ago, with terraces and stone staircases, and the lawns cut into quincunces and etoiles, and I know not what geometrical figures. The box-trees, too, were fashioned into the likeness of animals; here and there were statues. I could see the spray of a fountain sparkling in the sun, and on the level below the first terrace, a great white grotto and an embroidered parterre like a fine lady's petticoat. Nature sprawls naked hereabouts; only at this one point had it been trimmed and dressed, and that with so quaint an extravagance as to make me conjecture whether I had not been suddenly translated within sight of some fairy pleasaunce of the Arabian Nights.

I sat in my saddle, gazing at the house silently, and bethinking me of what service it might prove in the enterprise on which I was embarked.

"It is a handsome property, sir," said Ashlock, from just behind my elbow, and he spoke in a tone of anxious inquiry, as though he would fain discover what effect the glimpse of it had wrought in me.

"With a handsome rent-roll to match?" I asked no less eagerly, as I looked downwards.

A shadow fell sharply along the neck of my horse. I turned and saw Ashlock's face stretched forward, and peering into mine with startled eyes.

"A very handsome rent-roll, sir," he replied; "so handsome that a plain man finds it difficult to understand how the heir could sacrifice it for any cause." He dropped the words very slowly one after the other.

I understood the fellow's suspicion, and I swung my horse round with a jerk, so as to look him squarely between the eyes. He drew himself straight on the instant, and it seemed to me that his hand tightened insolently upon his whip.

"Ashlock!" I exclaimed, "before we go down to Blackladies, I will say a word to you. In Paris you showed me a way by which I could hold this estate fairly and honourably."

"It was at your own wish, sir, that I spoke," he interrupted hurriedly, "and because I saw that you meant to refuse it."

"Yes, yes," I went on. "But I thanked you then for the readiness of your wits, and there was an end of your concern in the matter. I hold Blackladies in trust for this cousin of mine, Mr. Jervas Rookley. I have said so, and I need no mentor at my elbow to remind me of a pledge I gave to myself. Least of all will I permit my servant"—and in my heat I threw an ungenerous scorn into the term—"to take that office on himself. If he does, his first word sends him packing."

The man bent his head so that I could no longer see his face, and replied with all the confidence gone from his voice and manner.

"I came to Paris with no thought but of serving you as faithfully as I endeavoured to serve Sir John before you. But it was your reluctance that put the thought of Mr. Jervas into my head; and once it was there, it stayed and grew; for I loved Mr. Jervas, sir. It was Mr. Jervas I served in my heart, and not Sir John."

The fellow spoke with such evident contrition, and a devotion so seemingly sincere, that I felt reproved for the severity I had used, and I began to admire what sort of man my cousin must be who could leave so clear an image of himself in the hearts of his dependents. I was for saying something of the sort, when a movement which Ashlock made arrested me. It was an insignificant movement—just the reaching out of his hand to the snaffle of his bridle—but it woke all my distrust of him; for I noted the quick play of his long, sinuous fingers, and I recalled his stealthy advance from the tiller of the pinnace to the bows, and the hovering of his hands above my chest.

"Get down from your horse!" I cried suddenly.

He looked in surprise at me, as well he might. I repeated the order; he obeyed it.

"Are you Catholic or Protestant?" I asked.

Ashlock's surprise increased.

"Catholic, sir," he answered.

"Good! Now, understand this. Of the journey to Bar-le-Duc, of the passage from Dunkirk, you must never speak, you must never think. So much hangs on your silence and mine as you can have no notion of. You came to Paris, and from Paris I returned with you. That is all you know. Of the rest, whisper so much as a hint to the deafest yokel in the valley, and it will go very ill with you."

"I promise," he answered.

"But I need more than a promise; I need an oath. You are Catholic, you say, so there's better chance of your keeping it. Down on your knees here, and swear to me that not a word, whatever you know, whatever you believe, shall escape your lips."

Ashlock started back, looking about him, as though he would find some diversion or excuse. But the blue, sunlit sky was above us, the brown fells about us, and never a living soul beside us two.

"Come!" said I, insisting. "Swear it! Swear it by the Cross; swear it by the Holy Virgin."

"I swear," he began, holding up his hand.

"Nay," I broke in upon him. "On your knees! on your knees!"

Again he looked about him, and then to my face. But I kept my eyes stubbornly upon him. I would have him swear that oath, and I gathered all my strength into the resolution, that I might compel him; for I felt, in some strange way, that we were pitted in a contest for the mastery of Blackladies, and I was minded to settle that contest before I set foot across its door. I looked upon this oath that he would swear before me on his knees chiefly as an emblem of his submission. I might be to him a vicarious master; still, his master I would be, not having that confidence in him that I could allow him to harbour doubts upon the score.

Of a sudden his horse gave a startled plunge and broke away from him. It ran past me, and, leaning over as it passed, I caught it by the bridle and so held it.

"Come!" said I. "There will be many days on which I can see the sunset from Coldbarrow Fell."

There was no escape for Ashlock except by a direct refusal, and that he did not venture. So with a very ill grace he plumped down on his knees upon the heather and grumbled out his oath.

"Now," said I, "we will ride down to Blackladies;" and I descended the track mightily pleased with myself at the high way in which I had carried it. But my elation was short-lived, for so engaged was I in pluming myself, that I took little care of how my horse set his feet, and in a short while he slips on a stone, shies of one side, and I—I was lying with all the breath knocked out of my body on the grass.

I picked myself up on to my knees; I saw Ashlock sitting on his horse in front of me, and he held my horse by the bridle. I remained on my knees for a moment, recovering my breath and my wits. Then of a sudden I realised that here was I kneeling before Ashlock as but a minute since he had knelt before me; and here was Ashlock sitting his horse and holding mine by the bridle, precisely as I had sat and held his. In a word, we had just changed places, by the purest accident, no doubt, but I had set such great store upon bringing about that earlier position and relationship, that this complete reversal of it within the space of a few moments filled me with the keenest humiliation. And mingled with that humiliation was a certain fear that ran through my veins, chilling my blood. I felt that the man mocked at me. I looked into his face, expecting to discover on it a supercilious smile. But there was no trace of such a thing.

"You are hurt, sir?" he asked gravely, and dismounted.

"No," said I, rising to my feet

Ashlock moved a few steps from me, and stooped down, parting the grass with his hands.

"What is it?" I asked, setting a foot in the stirrup.

"Something, sir, that you dropped when you fell. It is too big for a coin."

He was standing with his back to me, turning that something over in his palms. I clapped my hand into my fob.

"It is mine, yes!" I cried, and I ran towards him. "Give it to me at once;" and I made as though I would take it from him.

"You asked me what it was," said Ashlock, and he placed in my hands the medal the King had given me. I looked it over carefully, noticing certain scratches upon the King's face, and seeking to rub them out I saw Ashlock looking at me shrewdly.

"I know," said I in a fluster; "but it has memories for me, and I would not lose it;" and with that we got again to our horses, and so down to the Blackladies.

The rest of that day I spent in examining the many corridors and galleries of the house, and in particular the garden, which had greatly whetted my curiosity. It had been laid out, Ashlock informed me, by Sir John Rookley's father, and with a taste so fantastic as would have gladdened Sir William Temple himself. There were three terraces linked to each other by three stone staircases—one at each of the two ends, and the third in the centre, and at the top of each of these last flights were heavy iron gates. From the bottom of these steps the parterre spread out, and beyond the parterre was a space of meadow-land, fringed by a grove of trees which they called the wilderness. The strangest device of all, however, was a sort of labyrinth beyond the trees at the extreme end of the garden. The labyrinth, in fact, was a number of little gardens, each with a tiny plot of grass, and flowers planted about it, like so many rows of buttons. These gardens were shut in by hedges of quickset ten feet or more in height, and led from one to the other by such a perplexing diversity of paths, that once you had entered deep among them it was as much as you could do to find your way out of them again. Even Ashlock, who guided me amongst them, ended by losing his way, so nearly alike was one to the other; and I, not stopping to consider that where he failed, I, a stranger, was little likely to succeed, must needs separate from him and go a-searching on my own account, with this very natural result—that I got more and more enmeshed in the labyrinth, and was parted from Ashlock into the bargain.

"Ashlock!" I shouted, and again and again, with never a reply, for the space of half an hour or more. At last, by the merest chance, I happened upon the right path, and so came out upon that meadow-like space they called the wilderness.

"Ashlock!" I called again, and again there was no answer. Had he got himself free, I wondered, and gone quietly about his business, leaving me there? I walked up the steps in an ill enough humour at the slight, and passed through the parlour into the hall.

It was of a great size and height, with long, painted windows from the ceiling to the ground; its roof, indeed, was the roof of the house, and somehow it struck upon me as very empty and desolate.

"Ashlock!" I cried, and I heard my voice reverberating and dying away down the corridors. Then came the sound of a man running from the inner part of the house.

"Ashlock!" I repeated, and a servant appeared. He was a tall, spare man, past the middle age, I should say, and was called Jonnage Aron. I sent him to look for the steward, but it was evening before he found him.

"I thought, sir, that you had hit upon the path before I did," Ashlock explained.

"But you heard me shouting?"

"No, sir," said he. "I found the way out a few minutes after you had parted from me, and thought that I was following you."

I bade him show me to his office and give me some account of the estate, which he did, laying considerable stress upon the wad-mines, from which some part of the revenue was derived.

"Sir John's attorney," said I, when he had finished, "lives at Keswick. It will be well that I should see him to-morrow."

"It is but nine miles from here to Keswick," he assented, "and the road is good."

"Then send a servant early in the morning to fetch him here." Ashlock shot a quick glance at me. "We will go over these matters again," I continued, "with his help—the three of us together."

Ashlock bent his head down upon the papers.

"Very well," he said, and seemed diligently to peruse them. Indeed, he held one in his hand so long that I believed he must be learning it by heart. "Very well," he repeated, in a tone of much thought.

But during the night I changed my mind, reasoning in this way. I recognised clearly enough that the advice which King James had given me—I mean that I should not disclose myself as a Jacobite—was due to the promptings of Lord Bolingbroke, and those promptings in their turn took their origin from a regard for my safety, rather than for the King's interest I was, therefore, inclined to look upon the recommendation as a piece of advice to be followed or not, as occasion pointed, rather than as a command. On the whole, I believed that it would be best, considering the ends I had in view, to express myself moderately as favouring the Stuart claims. Moderately, I say, because I could not avow myself an emissary of King James without stating the special business on which I had come, and that I was forbidden to do. At the same time, I had to carry that business to an issue, and with as little delay as might be. Now, it was evident to me that I should get little knowledge of the Jacobite resources, and less of their genuine thoughts, if I were to sit down at Blackladies in this nook of Borrowdale. I must go abroad to do that, and if I was to excite no suspicion, I must have a simple and definite excuse. The attorney at Keswick would, for the outset, at all events, serve my turn very well.

So the next morning I countermanded the order I had given to Ashlock, and rode in past Castle Crag and Rosthwaite to Keswick. And this I did on many a succeeding day, to the great perturbation of the little attorney, who had never been so honoured before by the courtesy of his clients. Also, I made it my business to attend the otter-hunts, coursing matches, fairs, and wrestling-bouts, of which there were many here and there about the country-side; so that in a short while I became acquainted with the principal gentry, and got some insight, moreover, into the dispositions of the ruder country folk.

Now amongst the gentry with whom I fell in, was my Lord Derwentwater and his lady, who were then living in their great house upon Lord's island of that lake, and from them I received great courtesy when they came to know of my religion and yet more after that I had made avowal of my politics; so that often I was rowed across and dined with them.

Upon one such occasion, some three weeks after I had come to Blackladies, that is to say, about midway through August, Lord Derwentwater showed to me a portrait of his wife, newly painted and but that day brought to the house. I was much struck by the delicacy of the craftsmanship, and stooped to examine the signature.

"You will not know the name," said Lord Derwentwater. "The man is young and, as yet, of no repute—Anthony Herbert."

"Anthony Herbert," I repeated. "No, I have never heard the name, though, were he better known, I should doubtless be as ignorant. For this long while I have lived in France."

"It is very careful work," said I, looking closely at the picture.

"Indeed, it errs through excess of care," replied he, "for one's attention is fixed thereby upon the details separately."

"One need have no fear of that," said I, with a bow to Lady Derwentwater, "when such details are so faithfully represented."

The pair smiled at one another, and she laid her hand upon her husband's arm in the prettiest way imaginable.

"The man is staying at Keswick," Lord Derwentwater continued. "That is how I chanced on him. He came hither in the spring for the sake of the landscapes."

"Oh," said I, "at Keswick? Is he, indeed?" and I spoke with something of a start. For a new idea had been brought to me from his words. For, having come clean to the end of my business with the attorney, I had been casting about during the last few days for some fresh cloak and pretext to cover my diurnal journeys from Blackladies, and here, it seemed to me, was as good a solution of the difficulty as a man could wish. It may be that I set too much stress on the need for such a pretext; it may be that I could have ridden hither and thither about the country without any one turning aside to busy himself about my errand. But, in the first place, I was the youngest scholar of conspiracy certainly in experience, if not quite in years, and I was on that account inclined to exaggerate the value of a mysterious secrecy. I took my responsibilities *au plus grand sérieux*, shrouding them from gaze with an elaborate care, when no one suspected so much as their existence. Moreover, it was the habit of the people in those parts to stay much within their native boundaries; they rarely went afield; indeed, I have heard a dalesman of Howray, by Keswick, confidently assert that at Seatoller, a little village not two miles from Blackladies, the sun never shone between the months of September and March owing to the height of the circumjacent mountains. In a word, those fells which these countrymen saw close before their eyes each morning that they rose, enclosed their country; what lay beyond was foreign land, wherein they had no manner of concern. And this same habit of mind was repeated in their betters, though in a less rude degree. Therefore I thought it did behove me to practise some dissimulation lest either my friends or my enemies should get the wind of my business. So again I said—

"The painter stays at Keswick. And where does he lodge?"

"In the High Street," said Lady Derwentwater; and she named the house.

"But, Mr. Clavering," added the husband, with a laugh, "the painter has a wife, very young and not ill-looking; and he is very jealous. I would warn you to pay no such compliments to her as you have paid to Lady Derwentwater." And he clapped me on the back, and so we went in to dinner.

He was silent through the first courses, and his wife rallied him on his reserve.

"I was thinking," said he, and he roused himself suddenly. "I was thinking," and then he stopped with a whimsical glance at me. "But perhaps I am forestalled."

Lady Derwentwater clapped her hands and gave a little laugh of delight.

"I know," she said, and turned to me. "My husband is the most inveterate match-maker in the kingdom, Mr. Clavering. He is like any old maid that sits by the window planning matrimony for every couple that passes in the streets. I should like to dress him up in a gown of linsey-woolsey and lappets of bone-lace."

"That's unfair," he returned "For there is this difference between the old maid and me—she is a match-maker by theory, I through experience."

He spoke lightly, as befitted him in the presence of an acquaintance, but his eyes were upon his wife's face, and her eyes met his. She reddened ever so little, and looked at her plate. Then she sent a shyish glance towards me, another to her husband—and all her heart was pulsing in that—and so again to her plate, with a ripple of happy laughter. I seemed to be trespassing upon the intimacy of a couple but half an hour married—and there were children asleep in their cots upstairs. A pang of genuine envy shot through me, the which Lady Derwentwater remarked, though she misunderstood it For—

"James," she said, turning reproachfully to her husband, "there is Mr. Clavering absolutely disconcerted, and no wonder. Darby and Joan may be well enough by themselves, but with a guest they are the most impertinent people in the world."

"True," said he, "and if Mr. Clavering patronises Herbert, he will have enough of Darby and Joan to sicken him for his lifetime, though it is a Darby and Joan in the April rather than the autumn of their years," he added, with a smile.

"Nay," I interrupted, "to tell the truth, I was thinking of the big, empty galleries of Blackladies."

"There!" he exclaimed, triumphantly, "Mr. Clavering justifies my match-making. Out of his own mouth he justifies me. We must marry him. Now, to whom?" and once or twice he patted the table with the flat of his hand in a weighty deliberation.

His wife broke into a ringing laugh.

"James, you are incorrigible," says she,

"There is Miss Burthwaite," says he.

"Impossible," says I. "I have met her. She says nothing but 'O La!' and 'Well, there!' and shakes her curls, and giggles."

"Her vocabulary is limited," he allowed "But there's the widow at Portinscale."

"She swears," I objected.

"Only when she's coursing," he corrected. "But, no matter, there's——"

"Nay," said I, interrupting his list. "This is no time, I take it, for a man to think of marrying. For who knows but what the country may be ablaze from sea to sea before we are three months older."

With that a sudden silence fell upon as all, and I sat inwardly cursing myself for the heedlessness which had prompted so inopportune a saying. Looking back upon that evening now, it seems to me as though all the disaster with which that year of 1715 was heavy, and near its time, for her, for him—ay, and for me, too, projected its shadow over our heads. I looked into their faces, grown at once grave and predestinate; the shadow was there, a cloud upon their brows, a veil across the brightness of their eyes. And then very solemnly my Lord Derwentwater rose from his chair, and lifted up his glass. The light from candle and lamp flashed upon the goblet, turning the wine to a ruby fire.

"The King!" he said simply, without passion, without heat. But the simplicity had in it something august. We also rose to our feet.

"The King!" he said again, his eyes fixed and steady upon the dark panels over against him, as though there he read the picture of his destiny. And so he drained his glass, pledging his life and his home in that wine he drank, making it sacramental.

We followed his example, and so sat ourselves down again. But, as you may think, there was little talk of any kind between us after that Lord Derwentwater made no effort at all that way, but remained engrossed in silence, with all his thoughts turned inwards. Once or twice his wife sought to break through the spell with some trivial word about the country-side, but ever her eyes turned with concern towards her husband's face, and ever the words flickered out upon her lips. And for my part, being sensible that my indiscretion had brought about this melancholy cloud, I seconded her but ill. At last, and just as I was intending to rise up and take my leave, Lord Derwentwater starts forward in his chair.

"I have it!" he cried triumphantly, bringing his fist smack upon the table.

"Well?" asked his wife, leaning forward.

"I have it!" he repeated, turning to me.

"What?" I asked anxiously.

"There's Dorothy Curwen, of Applegarth," said he, laying a finger on my arm; and at that we all fell to laughing like children, as though the unexpected rejoinder had been the wittiest sally in the world. "It would be very appropriate, too," he continued, with a laugh, "for it was rumoured that Mr. Jervas Rookley was paying his attentions in that quarter at one time, and the girl deserves a better fate."

"Jervas Rookley?" said I, curiously. "You knew him, of course. What sort of a man was he?"

For a moment there was a pause.

"The honestest man in the world," replied Lord Derwentwater—"to look at. But there it ends. His honesty, Mr. Clavering, is all on the outside of him, like the virtues of a cinnamon tree. He should have been a sailor. It was ever his wish, and maybe the hindrance to its fulfilment warped him."

How that evening lives again in my memories! Indeed, enough happened not so long after its event to keep it for ever green within my thoughts. I recalled Lord Derwentwater's solemn toasting of the King, when, no later than the next February, he went, with the King's name upon his tongue, to the block on Tower Hill. I recalled his wife's loving glance and happy laugh—with what pity!—when, dressed as a fishwife, she crept to Temple Bar and bribed the guardians of that gate to drop into her apron his head fixed there on the spikes. And more—that evening was a finger-post to me, pointing the road; but, alas! a finger-post that I passed unheeding, and only remembered after that I had gone astray into a slough.

For that device of a picture was fixed firmly in my mind, and I acted in the consequence of the thought. I rode home to Blackladies that night, and passed at once into the great hall. A fire of logs was burning on the hearth—for even in August I felt at times the nights fall chilly there—and the glow of the flames played upon the portraits of the Rookleys, dancing them into frowns and smiles and glances, as though the faces lived. Father and son, master and heir, they were ranged orderly about the walls in a double row, the father above the heir, who in his turn figured painted anew as the master. I turned to the lackey, a roughish fellow named Luke Blacket who had admitted me.

"Is Mr. Ashlock still up?"

"He is in the office, sir, I think," he answered in some doubt or hesitation. "I will go and see."

"I will go myself." And I crossed the hall.

A man was sitting at the table with his wig off, and his head was bald. His back was towards me, and he did not hear me enter, so engrossed was he about his papers. His pen scratched and scratched as if all time was against him. It was doubtless a fancy, but it seemed to me to run ever quicker and quicker as I stood in the doorway. Behind me the house was very dark and silent; only this pen was scratching across the paper nimble like a live thing. I stepped forward; I heard a startled cry, and Jonnage Aron stood facing me, with his mouth dropping and a look of terror in his eyes.

I waited for him to speak, comprehending neither his fear nor his business in my factor's office. At last in a jerky, trembling voice, resting one hand upon the table to steady him, he asked wherein he could serve me.

"It was Mr. Ashlock I needed," I replied.

"He is not here, sir," faltered Aron, looking about him like a trapped beast.

"I can see that for myself, Where is he?"

"I don't know, sir," and his confusion increased, "in bed, maybe. Shall I send him to you?"

He made a hasty movement as though he would escape from further questioning.

"No," said I, "stay where you are," and I stepped forward to the table. I took up the last paper he had been writing; the ink was still wet upon it, and I saw that it was a letter to one of my tenants in Johnny Wood concerning some improvements of which I had spoken to Ashlock.

"You do the work I pay my steward for," I said. "And how comes that about?"

"Very seldom, sir," he babbled out; "once or twice only, when Mr. Ashlock has been busy. It is not well done," and he made as though he would take the paper from my hands, "for I am no clerk, but he told me the letter was not of the first importance."

I looked at the sharp, precise characters of the letter.

"I'll tell you what is not well done, Aron," I cried in some heat, "and that is your excuse. The handwriting here tells of practice, and I see that you thrust your pen behind your ear."

Aron's yellow face flushed a dull red. He gave a start and plucked the pen from behind his ear; and the impulsive movement ludicrously betrayed his sense of detection.

"Ah!" said I with a sneer. "You had best ask Mr. Ashlock in the future to provide you with the excuse at the same time that he provides you with the work."

I bent over the table to examine the other papers which were littered upon it I had just time to remark that they were all in Aron's handwriting when a sharp click sounded through the silent house, not loud, but very clear, like the cocking of a trigger. The door was open; I stepped into the passage and peered along it. Aron moved uneasily in the room at my side, and his movement brought him betwixt me and the lamp, so that a shadow fell across my face and on the passage wall. I realized that I had been standing visible and distinct in a panel of light that was thrown from the open doorway. Aron moved again out of the light. I took a couple of paces into the dark, and again stretched forward, peering in front of me. I could see well nigh the length of the house. The corridor in which I stood ran straight to the hall. On the far side of the hall, opposite to me, there opened a wide gallery, which was closed at the end by a parlour, and this parlour lay at the east end of the house, and gave on to the topmost terrace of the garden. The door of the parlour stood open, so that I saw right through it to the moonlight shining white upon the window-panes. But I saw more than this. I saw the window opening—it was the catch of the window which I had heard—and a man, with his hat pulled down upon his brows and a heavy cloak about him, stealing in. I was the more astonished at the sight because Ashlock had informed me that there was no outlet from the garden at all; and that I had considered to be true, since on one side a cliff rose sheer above it, while on the other side and at the end it was enclosed with a sunk fence of stone. The intruder closed the window and came a-tiptoe down the passage. I drew close against the wall and held my breath. He passed by me insensible of my presence and walked into the room, and as he came into the light I saw that he was holding the ends of his peruke in his mouth. I did not, however, on that account fail to recognise that the new-comer was my steward. I followed very softly close upon his heels.

"Ashlock!" he began, and would have said more, but Aron held up a finger to his lips and grimaced at him.

I closed the door behind me with a bang and leaned against its panels. The steward swung round abruptly.

"And what stress of business keeps Mr. Ashlock so late from his bed?" I asked; and added pleasantly, "By the way, which of you is Mr. Ashlock?"

Seldom have I seen a man so completely taken aback, as my steward was then, and I was in the mind to profit by his confusion.

"And which of you is Mr.——" I continued, and came all at once to a dead stop. For the strangest suspicion flashed into my mind.

"I rode over to the farmer of Johnny Wood," explained the steward, and Aron's brows went up into his forehead, as well they might, "thinking that a word with him would expedite the business."

"It was a pity then," I returned, "that you kept Aron up so late writing a letter on that very subject."

I picked up the paper from the table and placed it in his hands. His face puckered for a second and then smoothed again. He read it through from beginning to end with the completest nonchalance.

"It will do very well," he said easily to Aron, and then turned to me with a smile. "The letter, of course, is a usual formality."

"Surely an unnecessary one," I insisted.

"Men of business," he returned suavely, "will hold it the reverse. I presume, sir, that you have some urgent need of me."

I recovered myself with a laugh.

"Not urgent," I replied, "but since you are here — —" I took up the lamp from the table and went into the passage. The steward followed me, and after him, though at some distance, Aron stumbled in the dark. So we came into the hall. I held up the lamp above my head. At one point, in the lower row of pictures, there was a gap; the oak panels made as it were a black hollow amongst the bright colours of the figures, and the hollow was just beneath the portrait of Sir John.

I pointed an arm to it.

"It is the one vacant space left in the hall."

Ashlock glanced sharply at me.

"Mr. Jervas Rookley's picture should have hung there," he replied in a rising tone, which claimed the prerogative of that space still for Mr. Jervas Rookley.

"But it did not," I replied. "The space is vacant, and since it is the fashion of the house that the master's portrait should hang in the hall, why, I will take my predecessors for my example."

Ashlock took a quick step forward as though pushed by some instinct to get between me and the wall, and turned upon me such a look of perplexity and distrust, that for a moment I was well-nigh dissuaded from the project.

I heard a step behind me. It was Jonnage Aron drawing nearer. I turned and gave the lamp to him to hold, bidding him stand further off, and I said with a careless laugh, though I fixed my eyes significantly upon Ashlock—

"My successor has full licence from me to displace it when his time comes to inherit, but for the present my picture will hang there."

Ashlock looked me steadily In the eyes. The distrust faded out of his face, but the perplexity remained and deepened.

"Your picture, sir?" he asked in a wondering tone, as though he would be asking what in the devil's name I needed with a picture at all.

"Yes, Mr. Ashlock," said I with a swaggering air, which I doubt not was vilely overdone, "my picture. And why not, if you please?"

"It must needs be painted first," he said.

"That is very true," I replied. "I had even thought of that myself, and so apt an occasion has presented itself, that it would be folly to disregard it. For a painter has but lately come to Keswick. My Lord Derwentwater spoke of him to me, and indeed showed me some signal evidence of his skill."

"Lord Derwentwater?" exclaimed Ashlock, In a curious change of tone. The perplexity in its turn began to die off his face, and it was succeeded by an eager curiosity. It seemed as though the name gave to him a glimmering of comprehension. Though what it was that he comprehended I could not tell.

"Yes, Lord Derwentwater told me of the man," I repeated, anxious to colour my pretext with all the plausibility of which it was capable. "Mr. Anthony Herbert— —"

"Mr. Anthony Herbert?" questioned Ashlock, slowly.

"It is the painter's name," said I, and he seemed to be, as it were, savouring it in his mind. "You will not have heard it before. Mr. Herbert has painted a portrait of Lady Derwentwater," and I turned away and got me to my room, with Aron to light the way. I left Ashlock standing in the hall, and as I mounted the lower steps of the staircase, I heard him murmur to himself in a tone of reflection—

"Mr. Anthony Herbert!"—and he shook his head and moved away.

Now, some half an hour afterwards, as I was lying in bed, a thought occurred to me. I got me to the door and opened it. The house was still as a pool. I took my candle in my hand and crept to the stairhead. The moonlight pouring through the tall windows, lay in great silver stripes upon the floor. I stood for a little and listened. Once or twice a board of the staircase cracked; once or twice an ember spurted into flame and chattered on the hearth, but that was all. I stole downstairs, not without a queer shame that I should be creeping about my own house. At the bottom I lighted my candle, and shading it with my hand, crossed swiftly to the vacant space among the portraits. I held the light close against the panels. Yes, there were the splintered holes where the nails had been driven in.

I lowered the candle till it was level with the lowest rim of the picture-frames on either side of the space. Yes, there was a dimming of the oak, like breath upon a window-pane, where the edge of a picture had rubbed and rested against it. I rose upright, blew the candle out, and stood in the dark, thinking. "Mr. Jervas Rookley's portrait should have hung there," he had said. It *had* hung there—not a doubt of it. Was it destroyed, I wondered? Was it in some lumber-room, hidden away? And I remembered a room in the upper part of the house which I had found locked, and was told the key was lost. Why had the picture been removed? Was it so that I might not recognize it? Well, it did not matter so long as I never stumbled across it. I groped my way up the staircase, repeating to myself one sentence from the will, "I must not knowingly support Mr. Jervas Rookley." I did not *know*, I said to myself. I might suspect, I might believe, but I had no proof; I did not know. I clutched the phrase to my very heart. I could keep my trust—the estate need not enrich the Hanoverian—Jervas Rookley should come to his own, if God willed it, in his own time. For I did not know. My steward was my steward—no more. What if he was ever out of sight when a visitor reined in his horse at the door? He might be busy in his office. What if another wrote his letters? There was work enough for the steward, and who should blame him for that he lightened his labours, so long as his work was done? I did not know.

Yet how the man must hate me, I thought, as I recalled that hour on the ridge of Coldbarrow Fell.

CHAPTER VI
MR. HERBERT

It was eleven of the forenoon when I stopped at Mr. Herbert's door, and the long incline of the street was empty. At the bottom of the hill, beyond the little bridge, there was a shimmer of green trees, and beyond the trees a flashing corner of the lake. Through a gap in the houses on my left, I caught a glimpse of the woods of Brandelaw, and the brown slope of Catbells rising from the midst of them. A shadowless August morning bent over the country, cradling it to sleep with all its drowsy murmurings, so that contentment was like a perfume in the air. And it was with a contentment untroubled by any presage that I tied up my horse and knocked at the door.

Mr. Herbert's lodging was on the first floor, and as I mounted the stairs the noise of an altercation came to me from behind the closed door. The woman who led me up shrugged her shoulders and stopped.

"One of the April showers," I thought, recalling Lord Derwentwater's words.

"Will you go up?" she asked doubtfully.

"Yes," said I. "For I take it that if I deferred the visit till to-morrow, to-morrow might be own brother of to-day."

She knocked at the door twice and got no answer. I heard a man's voice exclaim acrimoniously:

"It was the worst mistake man ever made," and a woman cry in a passion—

"Or woman either. Deary me, I wish I were dead!"

And "Deary me, I wish it too," said my attendant, and impatiently she turned the handle and opened the door. A man sprang forwards. He was young, I noticed, of a delicate face, with a dark, bilious complexion.

"Mr. Anthony Herbert, I suppose," I said, taking off my hat, and I stepped into the room. The next moment I regretted nothing so much as that I had not taken the landlady's advice, for a woman sat at the table, with her face couched upon her arms, crying.

"Your business?" asked Mr. Herbert, abruptly, getting between myself and the table.

I turned my back to the room and looked out of the window, making as though I had not seen his wife.

"Lord Derwentwater showed me yesterday a picture of his wife painted by you," I said; and I unfolded the purport of my visit slowly. In the midst of my speech I heard the rustle of a dress and a door cautiously open and shut. A second or two later I turned back into the room; it was empty. The artist accepted the commission, and I arranged with him that he should set to work next day.

"I am afraid," he said awkwardly, as he bowed me from the room, "that you caught me at an inopportune moment."

"Did I?" I returned, playing surprise. "Ah yes, you are not dressed," for he was wearing a dressing-gown. "But it is my fault in that I came too early."

And he closed the door.

"Thank you!"

The words were breathed in a whisper from the landing above that on which I stood. I looked up; the staircase was ill-lighted and panelled with a dark mahogany, so that I saw nothing but the outline of a head bent over the balustrade; and even as I looked that outline was withdrawn.

"Not at all," I replied to the empty air.

The door behind me was thrown open.

"What is it, Mr. Clavering?" asked Herbert, and he glanced suspiciously up the stairs.

I, on the contrary, stared down them.

"It is," I answered, "that your staircase is cursedly dark."

"True," says he, and steps to my side. "One cannot see an inch further than is needful;" and he looked down them too.

"One cannot even see so far," says I, and I peered upwards.

"One might break one's neck if one were careless," he continued in a musing tone.

"Oh, I did not stretch it out enough for that," I replied, thinking of something totally different.

Herbert looked at me with a puzzled expression.

"It occurs to me, Mr. Clavering," he resumed, "that if it would please you better I could fetch my easel over to Blackladies."

"There is no manner of occasion for that," I replied hastily, and I got me into the street with as little difficulty as if there had been a window to every step of the stairs.

Thus, then, I had my excuse. I rode back to Blackladies that afternoon, and bade Luke Blacket carry such clothes as I required to Mr. Herbert's lodging.

"Very well, sir," he said, but did not go. For just as it was getting dusk I saw from the library window Ashlock—for so I still called him, even or perhaps more particularly to myself—ride down the drive with the package upon his saddle-bow. I was as much surprised now at this voluntary exposure of himself as I had been previously at his sedulous concealments. But I bethought me in time that it would be dark long before Ashlock reached the village of Keswick, and as to his doings—well, I deemed it wisest to busy myself as little as possible on that head. For I was never certain from one minute to the next but what I might stumble upon some proof which I could not disregard. Consequently neither then, nor when he returned, did I utter a single word.

But on the next morning I followed my clothes to Mr. Herbert's lodging, sat to him for an hour or so, and then went about my business. And this I did day after day, visiting the gentry about, and attending the fairs and markets until I had acquired as complete a knowledge of what the district intended as would have satisfied my Lord Bolingbroke in person. That there were a great many, not merely of the gentry, but of the smallest statesmen and even peasants who favoured King James, I was rejoiced to perceive. But against this disposition I had to set a deplorable lack of arms and all munitions of war. Here and there, indeed, one came across a gentleman, like Mr. Richard Salkeld, of Whitehall, in Cumberland, who had carefully collected and stored away any weapon that he could lay his hands on, and I remember that in Patterdale, one Mr. John Burtham, a man very advanced in years, led me with tottering steps down to his cellar and showed me with the greatest glee a pile of antique musketoons and a couple of barrels of gunpowder, which his grandfather had hidden there for the service of King Charles I., but had discovered no use for after Marstoon Moor. For the most part, however, such as took the field I saw would take it with no more effectual armament than scythes and sickles and beaten-out ploughshares; and, indeed, I am not sure but what I would rather have so armed myself than with the musketoons and gunpowder of Mr. Burtham. One necessary condition, however, or rather I should say, one necessary preliminary of a rising, all with whom I had speech required and in a unanimous voice—I mean that his Most Christian Majesty should land twenty thousand troops in England and with them money for their subsistence. On the other hand, I knew that the French King, howbeit disposed to the utmost friendliness, was yet anxious, before he violated the peace of Utrecht, to ascertain which way the wind blew in England, and whether it was a steady breeze or no more than a flickering gust. It was about this time, too, that news was brought to me of the Duke of Ormond's flight to Paris, and I did not need the letter of Lord Bolingbroke which conveyed the news, to assure me how great a discouragement that flight must be to our friends in France. This, then, was the posture of affairs: France waited upon the Jacobites in England, and they in their turn waited upon France.

"There is but one hope," said Lord Derwentwater, when we were discussing the uncertainty wherein we lived—"there is but one hope of precipitating the matter to an issue, and that hope lies in the activity of the English Government. The Commons have suspended the Act of Habeas Corpus until next January, in the case of all persons suspected of conspiracy; Papists and Non-jurors are banished from the cities of Westminster and London and for ten miles round; the laws against them are to be put into the strictest execution. I do not know but what the rigour of these proceedings may goad the Jacobites to an extremity. But therein lies the one hope. And how goes it with Darby and Joan?" he broke off in a laugh. "I saw the portrait but yesterday, and it will do no discredit to the young Master of Blackladies."

But the young Master of Blackladies turned his face awkwardly to the window, and felt the blood rush to his cheeks, but never a word of answer to his lips. For, alas! what before had been the pretext and excuse was now become the real object of my journeyings. I had garnered my information— and the picture was still a-painting and little more than halfway to completion. I cannot even after this long interval of years think of that period without a lurking sense of shame—though I paid for the wrong— yes, to the uttermost farthing, and thank God in all humility that it was given me to repair it. For this, indeed, is true: the wrong went not beyond the possibility of reparation.

It was on the third occasion of my coming to the artist's apartment that I first met Mrs. Herbert face to face. She entered the room by chance, as it seemed, in the search for some embroidery. Mr. Herbert, for a wonder, was in a great good-humour that morning and presented me to her.

"This is Mr. Clavering, of Blackladies," he said with a wave of the hand, and so went on with his work. I rose from my chair and bowed to her. But with a quick impulsive movement she came forward and held out her hand to me, reddening, I must think, with some remembrance of the occasion whereon I had first seen her. And then—

"Tony," she cried reproachfully, with a glance about the room. Indeed, it had something of a slatternly appearance, which seemed to me to accord very ill with the woman who dwelled in it. The poor remains of breakfast—a dish of clammy fish, a crumbled oatmeal cake, and a plate of butter soft and oily—were spread upon a stained table-cloth. But the stains were only upon one side, and I chose to think it was there the man had sat.

"Well," says he, looking up in a flash of irritation, "what is it? What is it?" And then following the direction of her gaze, "We can afford nothing better," he snapped out.

"That is no reason," she replied, "why it should drag here till midday;" and she rang a little bell upon a side-table. He shrugged his shoulders and returned to his picture. She stood looking at him for a second, as though she expected him to speak, but he did not.

"Then, Mr. Clavering," she said, turning to me with a flush of anger upon her face, "I must needs undertake my husband's duty and make you his apologies."

Herbert started up from his seat, throwing the brush which he held petulantly on to the floor.

"Nay," I answered in some distress, for this apology was the last thing I expected or desired, "madam, there is no manner of need that such consideration should be shown me. Mr. Herbert honours me sufficiently by painting my portrait."

"That is very courteous of you," she answered with a little bow, "and I expected nothing less. *But*," and she drew herself up again and faced her husband, "it is not fitting we should receive our patrons with so little regard."

"Madam," I blurted out in the greatest confusion, "I beseech you. It would cause me the greatest distress to think that I had proved a trouble betwixt your husband and yourself."

It was not the discreetest phrase I could have chosen, but it served its turn, for it brought them both to a stop, and in a little Mrs. Herbert left us alone. Thereupon I put my hand in my pocket and drew out the medal of which I have spoken.

"Mr. Herbert," I said, "I have an ornament here, which I would fain have you add to the portrait;" and I held it out to him.

"Very well," said he, taking it "If you will leave it here, I will paint it in at my leisure."

"But," said I, "it would not be wise to let it lie open to the gaze of any chance-comer."

He turned it over in his hands and glanced at it

"For myself," said he, "I do not meddle in politics one way or the other. I will keep it locked. See!" And he placed it in a little iron box, and locking it put the key in his pocket.

On the next day that I came, the room was all tidied and newly swept, though the improvement brought no more peace than did its previous disorder. For, this time Mr. Herbert could find nothing that he wanted— even his brushes and colours had been tidied out of sight; so that he was forced to call in his wife to help him in the search for them, and seeing her thus engaged somehow fell ungratefully to rating her. The which she listened to with a patience which I could not but greatly admire; and after all it was she who discovered the brushes. Then very quietly she said:

"I will be no party to a quarrel before Mr. Clavering. It might perchance savour of ill-breeding;" and so she departed with the pleasantest smile, leaving Herbert in a speechless exasperation. For my part I wished intensely that she had not dragged my name into the business.

Herbert turned from the door to me, and from me again to the door; his mouth opened and shut; he spread out his hands in despair, as though the whole world was a riddle to be given up. Then he looked at the brushes in his hand.

"She hid them," he cried. "Damme but she hid them."

I felt inclined to rise from my chair and determine my visits there and then. I changed my mind, however, bethinking me that the couple were poor, and that if I acted on the inclination, I should be punishing not merely the husband but the wife as well.

To drive the notion finally from my head I needed nothing more than that by accident I should chance upon Mrs. Herbert on the stairs. For she spoke to that very point as I wished her good day.

"It will be good-bye you mean, Mr. Clavering," she answered, with something of a sigh for the loss which would befall them, since the defection of a client thus prematurely could not but damage his reputation in those parts.

"It will be good-bye if you wish it," I returned with a laugh, "but not otherwise."

Mrs. Herbert gave a start and looked across my shoulder. I turned sharply and saw Mr. Herbert himself standing in the doorway above me. He must have heard the words, I knew, but he stood quite still, his face passionless as stone, and for that reason, maybe, I did not at the time consider the construction he would be likely to put on them.

"Speaking for myself," I continued, "I shall not easily part from Mr. Herbert until the picture is finished and in my safe keeping."

So I spake with a polite bow to the painter, little thinking in how strange and hazardous a fashion I was destined to fulfil my words.

It must not, however, be thought that the pair were ever a-seething in this pot of quarrels. The sun shone betwixt the thunderclaps and with no dubious rays. At times, for instance, Mrs. Herbert would bring a book of plays into the room and read them aloud whilst her husband worked, and I—I, alas! watched the changes of her face. Once I remember she read in this way Mr. Congreve's "Love for Love," with a decent slurring of some passages and a romantical declaiming of others, at which Mr. Herbert would break into languishments and sighs, and Mr. Lawrence Clavering would feel himself the most awkward intruder in the world.

It was in the midst of this particular reading that Anthony Herbert was called downstairs upon some business, and she and I were left for a little to our devices. Mrs. Herbert continued to read with her eyes glued upon the pages, but gradually I could not but notice that a certain constraint and awkwardness crept into her voice. At last she stumbled over a passage and stopped. I rose from my chair, and, sensible that a like awkwardness was stealing over me, went and gazed at the picture. I made the mistake, however, of praising it, and of praising it, perhaps, with some extravagance, for the encomium naturally enough being couched in that vein, brought the artist's wife across the room to consider of it too.

"In truth," says she, looking from the portrait to myself, "he has caught your features, Mr. Clavering, even to the eyes and the curve of the chin."

"Yes!" I replied. "It needs no connoisseur to foretell how much Mr. Herbert will achieve."

She did not answer, but kept looking at me curiously, and I continued, in an unaccountable flurry:

"Sir Godfrey Kneller ages; one hears of no one who can fitly claim his place. The honour of it should fall to Mr. Herbert—nay, must fall to him, I think—and it is no barren honour. He has an estate at Witton, Lord Derwentwater tells me. He sits as Justice of the Peace there, and he is even now painting his tenth monarch. It is no barren honour."

I spoke with all the earnestness I could command, but of a sudden, from the corner of my eye, I saw her lips part in a queer smile. I felt my voice shake, and covered the shaking with a feeble laugh.

"So an obscure country gentleman," I continued, "has reason to count himself lucky in getting his picture done by Mr. Herbert before the sovereigns of Europe engross his art;" and at that, for sheer want of assistance, I faltered to a stop. The silence crept about us, insidious, laden with danger, and every second that passed made it yet more dangerous to speak. The woman at my side stood motionless as a statue. I did not dare to glance at her; I stared at the portrait and saw nothing of it. It was as though my face had faded from the canvas in a mist I was conscious only of the tall figure at my side. I tried to speak, but no thoughts came to me—nothing but a tumult of unconsidered words—words which I had never spoken before, and of which even now I did not apprehend the meaning. They whirled up within me and beat against my teeth for passage, I locked my mouth to keep them in, and then I began to be afraid; I began to tremble, too, lest the woman should move. At last I conned over a sentence in my mind, and repeated it and repeated it, silently, until I was sure that I could utter it without a trip.

"It must be a noble thing to be the wife of so great an artist," and as I spoke the words I was able to move away.

She gave a little quiet laugh, and answered—

"With, besides, the prospect of being wife to a Justice of the Peace at Witton."

For speaking that word I almost felt that I hated her.

"Oh, why won't you help?" I cried in a veritable despair, stretching out my arms to her.

She turned on me suddenly with her face aflame and a cry half uttered on her lips. What would have been the upshot I cannot tell, but the door opened or ever she could articulate a word, and Mr. Herbert returned to put an end to our talk. For a week after that I mounted the stairs with uncertain steps, each footfall accusing me for that I came. However, during that week I saw her no more, and was beginning to acquire some confidence in my powers of self-mastery. Indeed, I went further, and became even vaingloriously anxious that I might chance upon her in order to put those powers to the test.

The opportunity came, and this is what I made of it. There had been some dispute that morning over a trivial domestic matter, and Mr. Herbert sat glooming before his easel, when his wife entered the room with a certain air of defiance and took her customary seat. She held a book in her hand, bound in old leather, with gold lettering upon the back, so that I was able to read the title. It was Sir Thomas Malory's Book of the Morte d'Arthur, and in a very deliberate voice she read out of the story of Lancelot and Guinevere, and much emphasis she laid on the temperate gentleness of King Arthur and his unreadiness to believe in any misdoings either of his wife or his companions. But her words fell vainly upon deaf ears, for Herbert took no heed of any word she read or any accent of her voice; the which she came to see, and losing all her defiant dignity in a little, shut the book with a bang and ran out of the room.

For my part I had listened to the story in the greatest disorder of spirit, and was very glad to be quit of it, and of Mr. Herbert too, for that day at all events, in spite of the supremacy of his genius.

But the staircase, as I have said, was very dark, and particularly so at one corner where it turned sharply two flights below the doorway and made an angle in the wall. Now as I passed this angle, something moved in it I stopped, wondering what it was, and then a voice came to me in a whisper—

"Lancelot!"

Instinctively I drew back and threw out my hands. They touched—they held another pair of hands—for the fraction of a second.

"No," said I with an attempt at a laugh, hollow as the clatter of an empty mug, "the name does not fit me, for at all events Lancelot could fight, and I have not learnt even so much skill as that."

Unconsciously I raised my voice as I spoke, and a second after the door creaked gently above us. She drew back into the corner all a-tremble, like a chided dog, and the movement touched me with a pity that made my heart sicken. The angle I knew could not be seen from the stair-head. I slipped purposely on a step, and swore a little not over-quietly.

"What is it?" asked Mr. Herbert.

"An ill-lighted staircase is the devil," said I; and I grumbled my way to the street-door. But I heard Mr. Herbert's door shut before I left the house.

Whither I went after leaving the house I was in that perturbation of mind I cannot tell. It was my habit to stable my horse at the Lamb and Flag, opposite, and subsequently I was told that I entered the courtyard and wandered out of it again like one blind. A fire burned in my blood, and the aspect of the world was fiery to my vision. I went whither my footsteps guided me, and all places they led me to were alike. Afterwards it came upon me like the memory of a dream, that I had stood for some while with the sheen of water beneath my eyes, and the lapping of water in my ears, and that hereafter I had climbed for long hours up a wearisome green slope; and indeed my insteps and knees ached for days to come, so it may be that I went down to Derwentwater and thence toiled up some part of Skiddaw. But of all this I knew nothing at the time; I only knew that I came again to the possession of my wits in Keswick Street about ten o'clock of the night, very hungry and very tired. I entered the inn and bade the landlord get me some supper before I started homewards. And this he did, laying a table for me in the best parlour of the house—a long room on the first floor, with window-seats, from which one commanded the street. The landlord prepared the table for me at the inner end of the apartment and set the lamp there; so that as the light was but dim, and I rested myself in the window until such time as supper should be brought, I was well-nigh in the actual dark.

Now while I was seated there, a man came down the street towards me. I should not, I think, have noticed him at all but for the caution of his movements. For he kept very close to the houses and stepped lightly upon his toes; and when for all his care his spurs clinked or his foot rolled on a loose stone, he paused and looked behind and about him. So he walked until he came in front of Mr. Herbert's house. Then he stopped, and it came upon me that there was something familiar in his appearance.

I drew back into the curtains. He gazed up and down the street and then to the windows of the Lamb and Flag. A heavy tramp sounded on the cobbles some yards away, very loud and unexpected, so that it startled me little less than it did the man I watched. I drew yet farther into the curtains; he slunk into a cavity between two of the houses, and that action of his flashed of a sudden a plan into my mind; I remembered that dark angle on the staircase. The footfalls grew louder, a dalesman passed along the centre of the roadway, his steps died away up the hill. My man crept from his hiding-place, and whistled softly under Mr. Herbert's windows. The blind was pushed aside from the window an inch or so, and I saw a head against the light pressed upon the window-pane. Then the window creaked and opened. The head was thrust out and a few words were interchanged, but in so low a tone that I could catch nothing of their purport. Then the window was shut and the man advanced to the door. One thing was clear to me from these proceedings, that whosoever he might be, and I had little doubts upon that score, this was by no means his first visit to Mr. Anthony Herbert.

I set that piece of knowledge aside, however, for the present. There was a further point which concerned me more particularly just then. Was the street-door on the latch? Or must Mr. Herbert descend to give his visitor entrance?

The visitor turned the handle, opened the door, and closed it again behind him. I waited until I saw his shadow on the blind. He had taken off his hat and his cloak, and his profile was figured upon it in a silhouette.

I ran down the stairs and across the street without so much as picking up my hat. I opened Mr. Herbert's door, and crept up the staircase until I came to the angle which I had reason to know so well. There I hid myself and waited in the dark. And how dark it was and how intolerably still! Very rarely a burst of laughter, or a voice louder than the usual, would filter up to me from the back part of the house. But from the studio above, nothing— not the tread of a foot, not the whisper of a voice, not the shuffle of a chair.

What were they debating in such secrecy? I asked myself and then, "Perhaps I had been mistaken after all?" I clung to the possibility, though I had little faith in it. At all events, this night I should make sure—one way or another I should make sure.

After the weariest span, the door was opened. I could not see it because of the turn of the staircase. I stood, in fact, just under the door; but I could see on the wall facing me, at the point where the stairs turned a bright disk of light suddenly appear, such as a lamp will throw. The visitor would pass by that disk; he would intercept the rays of the lamp; those rays would burn upon his face. I leaned forward, holding my breath; the steps above me cracked as a man descended them. I heard a short "good night," but it was Mr. Herbert who spoke; and then the door was closed again and the disk vanished from the wall I could have cursed aloud, so bent was I upon discovering this visitor; but the footsteps descended towards me in the dark, and I drew myself back into my corner.

As they passed me I felt a sudden flap of wind across my face, as though the man was moving his hands in the air to guide him, and I reckoned that the hand was waved within an inch of my nose. A few seconds later and the street-door opened. The sound brought home to me all the folly of my mistake. If I had only waited outside, in that alley, say, where he himself had crept, I should have seen him—I should have known him! Now I must needs wait where I stood until he was clean out of reach, I counted a hundred, a hundred and fifty, two hundred and then in my turn I slipped down the stairs and out of the house. The night was not over-clear, and I could perceive no one in the street. I strained my ears until they ached, and it seemed to me that I heard a light tip-toe tread very faint, diminishing up the hill. I ran in its direction with as little noise as I might. But I heard my spurs clink-clinking even as his had done, only ten times louder.

I stooped and loosed them from my feet. Then I ran on again; it seemed to me that the footsteps grew louder. I turned the corner at the head of the street. In front of me there was a blur of light; the blur defined itself into four moving points of flame as I approached, and, or ever I was aware of it, I had plumped full into my Lord Derwentwater, who was walking homewards behind his torch-bearers to the lake.

"Come, my man," said he, "what manners are these?"

"The manners of a man in a desperate hurry," says I, "and so good night to you, my lord;" and I moved on one side.

"Lawrence Clavering!" he cried out and caught me by the arm. "The very man I would be speaking with."

"But to-morrow, my lord—to-morrow."

"Nay, to-night. You come so pat upon my wish that I must needs believe God sent you;" and the deep gravity of his tone was the very counterpart of his words. I stopped, undecided, and listened. But I could no longer hear the faintest echo of those stealthy footsteps.

"Then there is something new afoot," said I.

"Something new, indeed," says he, "though I take it, it concerns no one but you." And he bade his footmen go forward. "A minute ago a man passed me on this road, his cloak was drawn about his face, his hat thrust down upon his ears, but the light of my torches flickered into his eyes, and I knew the man."

"It was doubtless my steward," I blurted out. "He was in Keswick to-day."

"Your steward?" he asked in wonderment "Your steward? No, I should not pester you with news about your steward. It was young Jervas Rookley."

"Well," said I, "what of him, my lord? I have nothing to fear from Jervas Rookley."

"You think that?"

"I know it," I answered, a trifle unsteadily. "At all events, there is solid reason why I should have no grounds for fear." For I bethought me that I had loyally kept faith with him.

Lord Derwentwater stood for a moment silent.

"Walk a step with me," he said, and holding my arm he continued, "I would not meddle in your private concerns, Mr. Clavering, but I know Jervas Rookley, and it will be a very ill day for you when you hear his step across the threshold of Blackladies."

I felt a chill slip into my veins, for if he spoke truth and his words fitted so aptly with my suspicions that I could not disbelieve them—why, that day was long become irrevocable. However, I sought to laugh the matter off.

"A very ill day indeed, for on that day I lose Blackladies to the Crown."

"The danger will come from Jervas Rookley himself."

"Then it will be man to man."

We were now come within a few paces of the footmen, so that the flare of their torches lighted up our faces fitfully. My companion stopped.

"I have known men, Lawrence," he said, "who went down to their graves in the winter of their years—children—all the more lovable for that, maybe," for an instant his grip tightened about my arm, "but none the less children, and I have known others who were greybeards in their teens."

He paused and looked at me doubtfully, as though he would say more.

"You will be wary of this man. He can have little friendliness for you and it will be no common motive that can bring him back to these parts. You will be wary of him, Lawrence?"

So much I readily promised, and again he stood shifting from one foot to the other, balanced, uneasily, betwixt speech and silence. But all he said was, again—

"You will be wary of him, Lawrence," and so with a grasp of the hand moved off.

I watched him going, and as the torches dwindled to candle-flames and, from candle-flames to sparks, a great desire grew in me to run after him and disclose all that I knew of Jervas Rookley. The desire grew almost to a passion. Had I spoken then, doubtless he would have spoken then, and so, much would have been saved me. But I had given my word to hold this estate in trust, and ignorance or the assumption of ignorance was the condition of my keeping it. The torches vanished in the darkness. I walked back to the inn and mounted my horse. As I rode out of the courtyard, I saw, far away down the street and close to the lake's edge, four stars, as it were, burning. There was still time. I turned my horse; but I had given my word, and I spurred him to a gallop up the Castle Hill and rode down Borrowdale to Blackladies.

CHAPTER VII
A DISPUTE AND ITS CONSEQUENCES

But as I rode, this warning I had received swelled in importance; it became magnified to a menace, and my desire to speak changed into an overmastering regret that I had not spoken. I had kept my word loyally to—well, to Ashlock, since so I still must term him, even in my thoughts—nay, was still keeping it the while he played false with me. That he trusted me to keep it I was assured by the memory of his words and looks on that night when he had talked of my picture in the hall. Why, then, should he play false? There was but one man who might be able to enlighten me upon the point—Lord Derwentwater—and to that one man my lips were closed, I was, moreover, disturbed too by the knowledge that I had planned to travel to Grasmere on the following day, and be absent there until the night, thus leaving Rookley a free hand. It was late when I turned out of Borrowdale, but I noticed that there was a light still burning in the steward's office. I rode into the courtyard of the stables, and, leaving my horse there, walked to the front of the house. One or two of the attic windows still showed bright, and the ground floor was dimly lit. But somehow the house smote on me as strangely desolate and dark.

Luke Blacket was waiting to let me in, and whether it was that my strained fancies tricked me into discovering a mute hostility upon his face, but it broke in upon me with a full significance that all the servants, down to the lowest scullion, must be in the secret, and were leagued against me. I saw myself entering a trap, and so piercing a sense of loneliness invaded me, that I plumbed to the very bottom of despondency. I stood in the doorway gazing across the valley. The hills stood sentinel leaguering me about, the voices of innumerable freshets sounded chilly in my ears, as though their laughter had something of a heedless cruelty; my whole nature cried out for a companion, and with so urgent a demand that I bethought me of the light shining in the steward's office. It would be Aron without a doubt, sitting late over the books. I went down the passage and opened the door.

Aron rose hastily to his feet, and began some apology.

"Mr. Ashlock," he said, "requested me——" But I cut him short, weary for one honest word of truth.

"That will do, Aron. I have no wish to disturb you;" and I threw myself on to a couch which was ranged against the wall. "I am very tired," said I, and lay with my eyes closed.

Aron's pen stopped scratching. He sat for a second without moving. Then he came over to the couch, and, or ever I was aware of it, began pulling off my boots.

I opened my eyes and started up. In his old, worn face there was a look of friendliness which at that moment cheered me inexpressibly.

"Nay," said I, "you are too old a servant, Aron, to offer help of that kind, and I too young a master to accept it. Let it be!"

He straightened his back, and the friendliness increased upon his face. He glanced quickly about the room, and stepped softly to my side.

"Master Lawrence," he began, in much the tone a nurse may use to a child, and then, "sir, I mean, I beg your pardon." In a trice he was the formal, precise servant again.

"Nay," said I, "I know not but what I like the first title the better."

"It was a liberty," said he, with his face grown rigid.

"And the privilege of an old servant," I replied. "But that is just the point. You are not my servant, except in name," and I turned my head petulantly away.

The next moment his mouth was at my ear.

"Master Lawrence," he said, in a voice which was very low, "Master Lawrence, were I you, I would not ride again to Keswick."

I started up. Aron flushed so that the bald top of his head grew red, hopped back to his table, bit his pen, and set to writing at an indescribable rate, as though he was sensible he had said too much.

I leaned upon my elbow and looked at him. So I had a friend in the household, after all! I hugged the thought close to me. Had he any precise knowledge which prompted the advice? I wondered. But I could not ask him, and for this reason amongst others—I was too grateful for this proof of his goodwill to provoke him to a further indiscretion. But as I looked at him, I recalled something which I had noticed whilst riding about the estate. I suppose it was his scribbling at the papers put it into my head, but once it had come there, I thought vaguely that it might be of relevance.

"Aron," I said, "this plumbago? It is a valuable product?"

He looked at me startled.

"Yes," said he.

"The mine is opened once in five years?"

"Yes."

"And on that side of the mountain which faces Borrowdale?"

"Yes."

And with each assent his uneasiness increased.

"But there's a ravine runs back by the flank of the mountain, and on the mountain-side there I saw a small lateral shaft."

"It is closed now, and has been for long," he interrupted eagerly.

"But it was open once," I persisted. "The place is secret. Who opened it?"

"It was opened during Sir John Rookley's life," he answered, evading the question.

"No doubt; but by whom?"

He shuffled his feet beneath the table.

I repeated the question.

"By whom?"

"By Mr. Jervas," he answered reluctantly.

"With Sir John's knowledge and consent?"

Aron glanced at me with an almost piteous expression.

"Sir John knew of it."

"But before it was opened, or afterwards?"

The answer was slow in coming, but it came at last.

"Afterwards."

"Then I take it," I resumed, "that Mr. Jervas Rookley robbed his father?"

I spoke in a loud tone, and Aron started from his seat, his eyes drawn towards the door. I rose from the sofa and opened it; there was no one in the passage, but I left the door open. When I turned back again I saw that Aron was looking at me in some perplexity, as if he wondered whether I *knew*.

"But his father forgave him," he said gently.

"Very true," said I, fixing my eyes steadily upon him; "and besides, it is hardly fair to rake up the misdeeds of a man who is so very far away."

I spoke the words very slowly one by one. Aron's mouth dropped; a paper which he had been holding in his hand fluttered to the floor. The perplexity in his eyes changed into a blank bewilderment, and from bewilderment to fear.

"You know, sir?" he whispered, nodding his head once or twice in a way that was grotesque. "Then you know?"

"I know this, Aron," I interrupted hastily. "I hold the estate of Blackladies upon this condition: that I do not knowingly part with a farthing of its revenue to Mr. Jervas Rookley. You know that? You know that if I fail to fulfil that condition the estate goes to the Crown?"

Aron nodded.

"But this you do not know," I continued. "When Ashlock came to me in Paris, and told me that Mr. Jervas was disinherited because he was a Jacobite, I refused to supplant him, being a Jacobite myself. It was my steward who persuaded me, and by this argument: that when King James came to his throne, the will might easily be set aside. I accepted Blackladies upon those terms—as a trust for Mr. Jervas. But to keep that trust I must fulfil the conditions of the will. I must not knowingly do aught for Mr. Rookley. The condition should be easy, for I have never been presented to Mr. Jervas. I have not so much as seen a portrait of him"—and at this Aron started a little; "he might be living in my house as one of my servants. I might even suspect which was he; but I should have no proof. I should not know."

Aron gazed at me with wondering eyes.

"You hold Blackladies in trust for Mr. Jervas?" he asked, and I gathered from the tone of the question that my steward had thought fit to keep that knowledge to himself.

"And hope to do so until it can be restored to him. But," I urged, "I am in no great favour with the Whigs in these parts, and if they could prove I knowingly supported Mr. Jervas, they would not, I fancy, miss the occasion. My attorney, for instance, is a Whig and the attorney of Whigs, and they tell me strangely enough that Mr. Jervas Rookley has been seen in Keswick."

Aron, however, seemed to be thinking of something totally apart. He said again, and with the same wonderment—

"You hold Blackladies in trust for Mr. Jervas?"

"That is so," said I, "but it need not keep us out of bed." And I walked into the passage.

Aron lifted up the lamp and very politely led the way to my door. There he stopped and came into the room with me.

"Sir," said he, setting down the lamp, "you will pardon me one more question?"

"It is another privilege of the old servant," I answered with a yawn.

"You were poor when Mr. Ashlock came to you in Paris?"

"Penniless," said I, and I began kicking off my boots lazily.

"Then God knows," he cried, "I would you were Sir John Rookley's son;" and with that he plumped down on his knees and drew off my boots. And this time I suffered him to do it.

I had not done with him, however, even for that night. For an hour or so later, when I was asleep in bed, some one shook me by the shoulder. I looked with blinking eyes at the flame of a candle held an inch from my nose. Behind the candle was Aron, with a coat buttoned up to his chin as though he had thrown it over his nightgear.

"Aron," I said plaintively, "the question will keep till to-morrow."

"It is no question, sir, and to-morrow I shall be in Newlands," he said gravely. "I know nothing—only, were I you, I would not ride again to Keswick."

"Well, I shall not ride there to-morrow, at all events," I said, "since to-morrow I leave for Grasmere."

But on the morrow I did ride thither after all. For I woke up the next morning with one thought fixed in my mind, as though it had taken definite shape there the while I lay asleep. I must discover Rookley's business with Anthony Herbert. The matter was too urgent for delay. My resolve to sit no more for my portrait, my journey to Grasmere I set on one side; and while I was yet at breakfast I ordered a horse to be saddled. The fellow hurried off upon the errand, and I seemed to detect, not merely in his bearing but in the bearing of all who had attended me that morning, a new deference and alertness in their service; and I wondered whether Aron had shared with them his recent knowledge of my purpose.

As I rode down the drive I chanced to look back to the house, and I saw Aron on the steps, shaking his head dolefully, but I kept on my way.

Mr. Herbert received me with the air of a man that seeks to master an excitement. He worked fitfully, with fitful intervals of talk, and I remarked a deep-seated fire in his eyes, and a tremulous wavering of the lips. His manner kept me watchful, but never a hint did he drop of any design between my steward and himself. On the contrary, his conversation was all in praise of his wife, and the great store and reliance he set on her. I listened to it for some while, deeming it not altogether extravagant; but after a little I began again to fall back upon my old question, "What end could my steward serve by playing me false?" and again, "In what respect could Herbert help him?"

In the midst of these speculations, an incident occurred which struck them clean out of my mind. I was attracted first of all by something which Herbert was saying.

"It is out of the fashion," he said, with a sneer, "for a man to care for his wife, and ludicrous to own to it. But it is one of the few privileges of an artist, however poor he be, that he need take no stock of fashions; and for my part, Mr. Clavering, I love my wife."

I replied carelessly enough that the profession was very creditable to him, for in truth I had seen him behave towards her with so cruel an inconsistency of temper that I was disinclined to rate his protestations very high.

"And so greatly, Mr. Clavering," he went on—"so greatly do I love her, that"—and here he threw down his pencils and took a step or two until he reached the window—"that if aught happened amiss to her I do not think I should live long after it, If she deceived me, I do not think that I should care to live. I do not think I should even hold it worth while to exact a retribution from the man who helped in the deceit."

And I saw his wife in the open doorway. She must have caught every word. I saw a flush as of anger overspread her face, and the flush give place to pallor.

"Mr. Ashlock, my steward, was with you last night, Mr. Herbert. Was it upon this subject that you talked?"

Herbert flung round upon his heel

"You take a tone I do not understand," he said, after a pause. "You may have a right to pry into the conversations of your servants, Mr. Clavering, but I am not one of them"—and of a sudden he caught sight of his wife in the doorway. "You here?" he asked with a start.

"It is only fair," she answered, "that I should be present when you discuss my frailties with your patrons. But it seems," and her voice hardened audibly, "you do me the kindness to discuss them with your patrons' servants too."

She stood before him superb in pride; every line of her body seemed to demand an answer.

"It is because I love you," he answered feebly; and at that her quietude gave way.

She flung up her arms above her head.

"Because you love me!" she cried "Was ever woman so insulted, and on so mean a plea?" And she sank down at the table in a passion of tears.

Herbert stepped over to her, and laid a hand upon her shoulder.

She shook his hand off, and rising of a sudden, confronted me with a blazing face.

"And you!" she cried bitterly—"you could listen to such talk—ay, like your servant!" And she swept out of the room before either her husband or myself could find a word to say.

Indeed, though I had not thought of the matter in that light before, I considered her accusation of the justest, and the sound of her sobbing remained in my ears, tingling me to pity of the woman and a sore indignation against the husband. It was for myself I should have felt that indignation I knew well, but I am relating what occurred, and—well, maybe I paid for the offence heavily enough.

"Mr. Herbert," said I, rising, with as much calmness as I could command, "I will not trouble you to continue the work."

"But the portrait!" he exclaimed, almost in alarm. "It is my best work!" And he stood a little aloof gazing at it.

"The portrait!" I cried, in a fury at his insensibility—"the portrait may go hang!"

"On the walls of Blackladies?" he asked, with a quick sneer.

"Oh," said I slowly, "you gossiped to some purpose with my steward, it appears."

He stood confused and silent I went into the room where it was my habit to change my dress, and left him. But when I came out I found him standing in the passage with a lighted candle in his hand, though it was broad noonday. Doubtless I looked my surprise at him.

"An ill-lighted staircase, Mr. Clavering, is the devil," he remarked; and with a sardonic deference he preceded me to the street.

"It will rain, I think," he said, looking op at the sky.

"The air is very heavy," said I.

He stretched out the candlestick to the full length of his arm, and the flame barely wavered.

"Yes, no doubt it will rain," he repeated.

I noticed that one or two people who were passing up the street stopped, as well they might, and stared at us. I bent forward and blew out the candle.

"You will pardon me," I said.

"It has served its purpose," said he, and he kicked the door to behind me.

I mounted, and walked my horse slowly homewards. About two miles from the town I dismounted, and tethering my horse to a tree, paced about the lake shores, resolved to unpick his sentences word by word until I had disentangled from amongst them some reference which would give me an inkling into the steward's designs. He had told Herbert of that talk we had had together in the hall concerning the hanging of the picture. Of so much I was assured, and so much I still found myself abstractedly repeating an hour later. For alas! in spite of my resolve, my thoughts had flown along a very different path. I had a vision of the woman, and her alternations from pride to tears, ever fixed before my eyes. It was myself who had caused them. One moment I accused myself for not undertaking her defence, the next for that I had ever entered her lodging; and whatever outcry I made sprang from the single conviction that I was responsible to her for the distress which she had shown. Just for that moment there seemed but two people upon God's earth—myself and a woman wronged by me.

"Mr. Clavering."

The name was uttered behind me with an involuntary cry, and I knew the voice. I turned me about, and there was Mrs. Herbert standing in a gap of the trees.

She was dressed as I had seen her an hour ago, with the addition of a hood thrown loosely over her head.

"What can I do?" I cried. "I can think of nothing. It is my fault, all this. God knows I am sensible of the remorse; I feel it at the very core of my heart; but that does not help me to the remedy. What can I do?"

"It is not your fault," she replied gently. "This would have happened sooner or later. Jealousy is never at a loss to invent an opportunity. No, it is not your fault."

"But it is," I cried. "You know it; you know that the excuse you make for me is no more than a kindly sophistry. It is my fault. What can I do?"

She gave me no answer; indeed, it almost seemed as though there was something of impatience in her attitude.

I moved a few steps away and sat down upon a boulder by the water's edge, with my head between my hands.

"There is but one thing that I can do," I said, and I heard her move a step or two nearer. "But it is so small, so poor a thing;" and at that I think she stopped. "I shall not go back again to Mr. Herbert's lodging."

"Neither shall I."

The words dulled and stupefied me like a blow. I sat staring out across the lake, and I noticed a ripple that broke and broke in a tiny wave, ever at the same spot, some thirty yards from the shore. I fell to counting the waves, I remember, and lost my reckoning and began afresh; and in a while I commenced to laugh, though it did not sound like laughter.

"Neither shall I," she repeated, and struck the laugh dead. I started from my seat. She stood patiently before me with folded hands, and to argue against that patience seemed the merest waste of words. Before, however, I could make the effort, her spirit changed. Passion leapt out of her like a flame. "I hate him," she cried, beating her hands one upon the other. "Oh, to be made a common talk for his acquaintances! The humiliation of it! Servants too, he will debate of me with them, for them to mock at."

"No!" I answered vehemently. "You do not know that. It was I that spoke of my steward and I knew nothing. I did but guess idly, heedlessly. It was not he, it was I who spoke of Ashlock." But there was no sign of assent in her demeanour. "It was I spoke of him," I repeated, "and before you. Ah, God, it is my doing this, from the beginning to the end!"

"Think!" she went on, taking no more notice of my interruption. "They are making merry over me in your servants' hall. Think, Lancelot!"

She tried to check the name, but it was carried beyond her lips on the stream of her passion. A great silence fell upon us both; I saw the colour come and go fitfully upon her face, and her bosom rise and fall with her fitful breath. Then she covered her face with her hands and sank down upon the boulder.

Yes, I thought, it was my fault. They had quarrelled before, but never for such a reason; and that reason I had provided. I had gone there of my own free will to serve my own objects. But, somehow, as I looked at her seated by my side, the thought of the slatternly room she had been compelled to live in shot into my mind. I remembered how unfitted to her I had thought it on my first going thither. Of a sudden, while I was thus watching her, she lifted her eyes to mine. What babbling incoherencies I spoke, I do not know; I do not think she caught more than their drift. If they are known at all, it is because they stand ranged against my name in the Judgment Book. I became like one drunk, his senses reeling, his words the froth of his vilest passions. I think that I cried.

"Be it so, then! Since the harm is done, let the name be Lancelot;" but I know that she rode before me on my horse to the gates of Blackladies, that we dismounted there and walked up to the house; and that I found the hall-door open, and the house to all seeming deserted.

Now, this day was the 23rd of August.

CHAPTER VIII
THE AFTERNOON OF THE 23RD OF AUGUST

I led her into the little parlour which gives on to the terraces at the south end of the house. The wall upon one side was broken by a great open fireplace faced with bricks, and all too big for the room, into which a man could walk and wherein he could sit too, were he so disposed, upon a chilly night, and smoke his pipe with a crony over against him; for there were cushioned seats on either side of the hearth and a curtain hung to keep your head from the bricks.

The room seemed very silent as we entered it, and the silence deepened. She crossed over to this fireplace and stood with a foot raised towards the hearth, though there was no fire to warm it by. I tossed my hat and whip on to the table with more noise than was necessary and made a step as if to join her. She drew back instinctively. I stopped as though the step had been a liberty; and neither of us had a word to say. Once she untied the ribands of her hood, for she must be doing something; but the moment she was aware of what it was she did, she tied them again with hasty uncertain fingers, and then reddened and paled, of a sudden becoming, it seemed to me, sensible of the hastiness of her action. I sent my eyes wandering to every corner of the room, so that they should not rest upon her face; but none the less, after a little our glances crossed, and with one movement we averted our heads. After that one of us had to speak.

"You will be hungry," I said lamely. "You have eaten nothing since the morning;" and I walked to a little sideboard on which a bell was standing.

"No, no!" she cried, but I had struck the bell or ever the words were past her lips. "Oh, what have you done?" she said with a shiver; "one of your servants will come;" and then she checked herself and added, with her fingers plucking at her gown in a pitiful helpless way, "Well, what does it matter? They had the story before it happened. This will but confirm and seal it."

I went out into the hall to stop whosoever should be answering the summons. But no one came to answer it I crossed the hall and opened the door which led to the kitchens. As a rule, the noise of women's voices was incessant in that quarter of the house, but to-day not a sound, not so much as the clatter of a dish-cover! I went back to the hall and listened. The house was as still as on that night when I crept down the stairs and discovered the marks of a picture-frame upon the wall.

Was the house empty? I wondered, and shouted to solve the doubt. My voice went echoing and diminishing along corridor and gallery, but that was all. I moved down the passage to the office, half thinking that I might find Aron there, but remembered that he would be away, and so returned reluctantly. Thereupon I mounted the stairs and walked from room to room, and maybe lingered over-long in each. I was not, indeed, concerned with their silence and vacancy so much as with the knowledge that each step brought me actually a step nearer to the parlour-door. But I came to the end of my search, and there was nothing for it but to descend again. The hall-door, however, stood open, and I saw my horse at the bottom of the steps tethered by the rein to a knob of the stone balustrade. I walked down the steps, loosed it, and led it round to the stables. There was a boy or two in the stable-yard, and I remember putting to them a number of aimless questions which I was at great pains to think of, but did not listen to the answers; until their fidgeting made me sensible of the cowardice of my delay and drove me back to the house. Then I remembered why I had left the parlour, and going to the pantry, I got together some food upon a tray and brought it with a decanter of Burgundy into the parlour. Mrs. Herbert was standing where I had last seen her. I set out the table saying, "My servants seem all to have taken holiday;" and more for something to do, you may be sure, than from any sense of hunger, she sat herself at the table and began to play with the food. I had brought but one plate and set a chair for but one person; and neither of us noticed that. The truth is, there was a shadow in the room; the shadow cast by sin, and we watched it as children in a fitful firelight will watch a strange shadow on the wall—neither drawing near to it nor fleeing from it, but crouched watching it. Once she said, "I have brought nothing with me;" and after a little, some thought seemed to strike her. For she lifted her head suddenly and said:

"There is no one in the house but you and I?"

"No one," I said.

"That is strange," she said absently.

Strange! The word was an arrow of light piercing through the mist of my senses. Strange! It was indeed strange! Aron had warned me not to ride to Keswick; that was strange too. For the first time I set this desertion of my servants together in my mind with my suspicions of Ashlock's treachery. I started to my feet, invaded by a sudden fear; but I saw Mrs. Herbert at the table running her fingers along the hem of my fine tablecloth and her throat working as though she was swallowing her tears. I knew by some instinct of what she was thinking. She was thinking of her poor furniture in her lodging at Keswick. It was hers, you see, won by her husband's toil, and maybe she had a passing thought, too, of Sir Godfrey Kneller's estate at Witton—earned, too, by a painter's art. And such a pity for her, such a loathing of myself, flooded my mind as drove out all thought of Mr. Ashlock's machinations. I recalled how I had deemed that slatternly apartment unfit for her. It needed that we two should be here with the shadow about us, for me to realize how contemptible was the thought.

Again she said:

"No one is in the house except yourself and me," and in the same thoughtful tone. Then she rose from her chair with the air of one that has come upon an outlet when all outlets seemed barred. "It was kind of you," she said, "to show me your house, I would gladly have seen the gardens too, but the day is clouding, and it will rain, I think, ere long."

She dropped me a formal curtsey as she spoke. I did not want the urgent appeal of her eyes to take her meaning. My heart rose to it with a spring.

"I will have a carriage made ready for you," I replied; and I turned me to the window. "Yes, I am afraid that it will rain."

"Thank you!" she said.

And I, like the blundering fool I was, must needs, in my great joy, add:

"It is no long journey into Keswick, after all"

"Keswick!" says she with a start, and drops her eyes. "I had not thought of that. I had not thought where I should go to."

I stood before her dumb. I knew—yes, I knew that the only place for her was that little apartment in Keswick. Grant her but the sight of it, and the sight of her husband in it—for he loved her—and, well, it needed no magician to forecast the result. But there was one person in the world who could not use that argument—myself. However, she helped me out.

"I cannot go back," she said, "without he knows. It would not be just No! it is not possible;" and at that the tears came at last. The sound of her weeping pierced me like a sword.

"He shall know, then," I cried. "He shall know. I myself will ride to Keswick and tell him."

"You will?" she asked, suddenly lifting her head.

"Maybe, too, I may find means to bring him back."

"If that might be!" she whispered in a fervour of hope, her whole face lightening and a timorous smile dawning through her tears. "But no!" and the hope died out of her face. "Payment will have to be made for this. You'll see, payment will be made."

She spoke in a low tone of such perfect certainty, that it seemed to me it was not so much the woman who spoke, but that Providence chose her voice that moment for its mouthpiece.

"Heaven send the payment fall to me," I said.

She glanced at me quickly.

"Oh," she said, in a complete change of voice, "what will you tell him?"

"Why, the truth," I answered. "That I found you by the lake, and brought you here."

"No!" she exclaimed, "I will not have you say that. It must be the truth—that I came to you."

She drew a note from her pocket as she spoke, and tossed it on to the table. I picked it up, wondering what she meant. It was a line scribbled in a hand which was familiar to me, and there was a word curiously misspelled—"wateing" for "waiting." Somewhere I had seen that word misspelled precisely in that way before, and surely in this handwriting too. Then the truth flashed upon me. It was in the inn at Commercy, and the handwriting was Jervas Rookley's. The line was this:

"I shall be wateing for you by the lake, on the road to Blackladies."

But Jervas Rookley knew that I was journeying to Grasmere, that I was not returning to Blackladies until night The letter was a snare, then, to draw Mrs. Herbert from the house.

If so, all the more need for haste.

I opened the door and stepped into the hall. But the hall was no longer empty. The hall-door was still open; I had left it open, and a man stood in the centre of the hall. It was Anthony Herbert. His back was towards me, and from his manner I gathered that he was considering which of the passages giving upon the hall he should choose. It was for no more than a second that he stood thus, but that second gave me time enough to do the stupidest thing that ever a man out of his wits conceived; and yet in a way it was natural. For I slammed the door to behind my back, and stood barring it, with my hand upon the knob. Mr. Herbert twisted round upon his heel.

"Caught!" he cried, spitting the word at me.

I realized the folly of my action, and let go of the handle.

"I was this instant setting out to find you."

The words sounded false to me, though I knew them to be true, and my voice took a trembling indecision from the foreknowledge that he would disbelieve them.

"No doubt," said he. "Otherwise you would not be guarding the door."

He spoke with a great effort to be calm, but his eyes were aflame, his limbs quivered with his wrath, and now and again his voice lost its steadiness and ran up and down in a fitful scale.

"I thought to find you in the garden," he continued.

"In the garden?" I asked.

"But doubtless you point me out the way;" and he took a step towards me. With the movement his cloak slipped from his left shoulder, and I noticed that he was carrying a sword and a pistol in his belt. My hand went back to the handle.

"The few words I have to say to you," said I, "had better be spoken here."

"But it would be best of all," he returned, "to defer them altogether. I have some business with you, it is true, but that business comes second, and I think we shall need no words for its discussion." He took yet another step.

"Your business with me, Mr. Herbert, may come when it will," said I, "but these words cannot be deferred. They are few."

"However few, they are still too many," he broke in. "Out of my way!"

"You must hear them before you pass this door." I gripped the handle tighter.

"I'll not listen to you," he cried. "You overrate my credulity, Mr. Clavering. Out of the way!"

"I will not. This is my house."

"But it shelters my wife."

"It was she sent me to fetch you."

I gathered all my strength into the utterance of the words, that I might enforce their truth upon him. But they only served to whet his fury and confirm him in disbelief.

"That's a lie," he shouted, and in a flash his sword was out of the scabbard and the point of it pricking my breast. "If she sent you to fetch me, why do you guard the door? Stand aside!"

But since I had made that mistake, I must go through with it.

"I will not," I answered doggedly, and I set a hand upon each side of the doorway. "There is more to tell. I will not."

"Will not," says he grimly, "gives the wall to must," and he leaned a little very gently on the sword.

I did not move, but behind me the handle of the door rattled. I tried to seize it, but the door was pulled open from within; I staggered back into the room. Herbert sprang through the opening after me, and stood, drawing in his breath, his eyes fixed upon his wife. She recoiled towards the hearth.

"It is the bare truth I told you," I exclaimed passionately. "Oh, believe that! When I caught sight of you, I had taken the first step in pursuit of you; and it was Mrs. Herbert who set me on the task. Oh, believe that too! It was no doing of mine; it was she sent me. For myself, I gave little thought to you, I own it. It was she declared she could not return without you knew. I but obeyed her."

For a moment it seemed to me that his anger lulled. I watched his eyes. They were fixed upon his wife, and I saw the conviction in them fade to doubt, the doubt waver and melt into—was it forgiveness? I do not know, for Mrs. Herbert shifted her position; his eyes wandered from her face and fell upon the table. The note which she had shown me was lying open beneath his gaze. He stooped his head towards it. I made a movement to hinder him. He remarked the movement, and on the instant snatched the paper up.

"You persuade me to read it," said he, which accordingly he did. As he read, an idea occurred to me. For let him believe I wrote that note, and he would be the more likely to attribute the blame where it was due and exhaust his anger in the same quarter. So that when he asked, rapping the note with his knuckles—

"This is your hand?" I kept silence.

He repeated the question, and I positively relished the growing menace of his voice, and still kept silence. But he gave me credit for more subtlety than I possessed.

"Oh, I understand," he burst out "You were going to fetch me, no doubt. This letter bears you out so well. And my wife sent you to fetch me—a cunning afterthought when the first excuse had missed its mark. A very likely story, to be sure, but enough to hoodwink a dull-witted fool of a husband, eh? Reconcile husband and wife, and Mr. Lawrence Clavering may laugh in his sleeve—damn him!"

"It is the truth," I exclaimed in despair. "Believe it! Believe it!"

"The truth," he retorted with bitterest sneer, "the truth, and you are speaking it God, I believe truth itself would become a lie if you had the uttering of it! Believe you! Why, every trickster keeps his excuses ready on his tongue against the time he's caught. I would not believe you kneeling before the judgment-seat."

He poured his abuse upon me with an indescribable fury and in a voice gusty with passion.

"But you shall answer for it," he continued.

"When you will," I answered quietly.

He was still carrying his sword in his hand, and he suddenly thrust it out at arm's length before him, and turned it to and fro with his wrist, so that the light flashed on it and streaked up the blade to the hilt.

"Then I will now," he replied "now—now!" and at each word he flashed the sword, and with each word his voice rose exultingly. "In your garden, now!"

He moved towards the window. His wife stepped forward with a cry, and laid a hand upon his arm. He stopped and looked at her, with eyes that told her nothing. It must have been a full minute, I should think, that he stood thus. He had as yet spoken no word to her, and he spoke no word now. I saw her head decline, her whole frame relapse and droop, and she slipped on to her knees. Herbert shook her hand from his arm, kicked open the window, and crossed the terrace. I went into the hall to fetch my sword. As I crossed the threshold of the room, I heard the iron gates clang at the top of the terrace steps as though he had flung them to behind him. While I picked up my sword I heard the sound repeated but more faintly from the second terrace. And as I entered the room again and drew the sword from its scabbard I heard it yet a third time. Through the open window I could see him descending the steps of the third terrace. But between myself and the window, the wife was kneeling on the floor. Said she:

"You will not harm him;" and she clasped her hands in her entreaty. "Say you will not! The payment must not fall to him."

I almost laughed, so strange and needless did the entreaty sound.

"Madam," I said, "this is the pommel of the sword and this the point. One holds the sword too by the pommel, I believe. In fact, I know so much, but there my knowledge ends."

She spoke a little more, but I gave scant heed to what she said. For a sentence which she had spoken somewhile since, drummed in my ears to the exclusion of her present speech, and the import of it shone in my mind like a clear light. "Payment will have to be made for this," she had said.

Over her shoulder I saw Mr. Herbert move further and further from the house. It was about six o'clock of the afternoon and very windless and still. A great strip of cloud, hung from Green Comb to High Knott, gloomed across the garden, thick as wool and bulging like a sail, so that even the scarlet flowers of the parterre took from it a tint of grey. And underneath this cloud, from end to end, from side to side, the garden seemed to me to be waiting—waiting consciously in a sinister quietude for this payment to be made. The fantastic figures into which the box-trees were shaped, bears, leopards, and I know not what strange mammoths, appeared patient and alert in the fixity of a sure expectation, while the oaks and larches in the Wilderness beyond seemed purposely to restrain the flutter of their leaves. I felt the garden beckon me by its immobility and call me by its silence.

Mr. Herbert had stripped his cloak from his shoulders, and dropped it upon the third flight of steps; so that he now moved, a brown figure, here showing plain against the grotto, or the grass, there confounded with the flowers. He held his sword in his hand—at that distance, and in that dull light it looked no more dangerous than a strip of lead, and ever and again he would cut at a bush as he passed.

"No harm can come to him," I said, seeking to disengage myself, for the wife still clung to me in her misplaced fear. "I could not harm him if I would. For they do not teach one swordsmanship at the Jesuit Colleges."

The words rose to my lips by chance and by chance were spoken. But I know that the moment after I heard them, I staggered forward with a groan, and stood leaning my forehead against the framework of the window. Mrs. Herbert rose to her feet.

I was looking down the terraces across the parterres to the brown figure moving away, but I did not see that. It was as though a black curtain had swung down between the garden and myself. What I saw was a very different scene—a little twilight room far away in Paris and a stern face that warned me. I heard a voice telling me of a supreme hour wherein God would put me to His touchstone, an hour for which I must stand sentinel. Well, the hour had passed me and I had not challenged it; and I might have foreseen its

coming had I watched. I lifted my head; the garden again floated into vie
Anthony Herbert was marching through the long grass of the Wildernes
with never a look backwards. In a moment he reached the fringe of tree
The trees were sparse at the border, and I knew that he would not sto
there, but would rather advance until he arrived at some little dingle close
wooded about from view of the house. In and out amongst the boles of th
trees I saw him wind. Then for a second he disappeared and came to sigh
again upon a little patch of unshadowed grass. I remember that the sun
gleamed of a sudden through an interstice of the cloud as he stepped into
the open. The patch of grass shone like an emerald and the dull strip of lead
in his hand turned gold; and a larch upon the far rim where the trees grew
dense, taking some stray breath of wind, rippled and shook the sunlight
from its leaves. In some unaccountable way my spirits rose at the sight. I
still was sensible of that saying, "Payment must be made for this," but it
took a colour from the sunlight. It became rather, "Payment can be made
for this."

I slipped out of the window. Mrs. Herbert started forward to detain me.

"A duel," she exclaimed, in a tone as though the idea became yet more
inconceivable to her. "Oh no! Not a duel."

"No, not a duel," I replied across my shoulder, "only the pretence
of one;" and while my head was thus turned a pistol-shot rang from the
Wilderness.

It sounded like the crack of a whip, and I might have counted it no more
than that but I saw a wisp of blue smoke float upwards above a shrubbery
and hang curling this way and that in the sunlight.

"God save us," I cried, "but he carried a pistol!" and I made as though I
would run across the terrace towards him. But or ever I could move, I felt a
hand tighten and tighten upon my arm. I tried to shake it off.

"You do not understand," I exclaimed. "He carried a pistol. It was
pistol that we heard. Maybe he was looking to the priming. Maybe he
wounded I must go to him;" and I seized Mrs. Herbert's hand at the wri
and sought to drag it away from my sleeve. I felt her fingers only grip mo
closely. I dropped her wrist and began to unclasp them, one by one.

"It is you who do not understand," she said, "and he is not wounded

She spoke in a dry, passionless voice, which daunted me more than
words she uttered. I turned and looked at her in perplexity. Her face v
like paper, even her lips were white—and her eyes shone from it sun
and black; I was reminded of them afterwards by the sight of a black
set in a moor of snow, which I was destined to look upon one sad Noven

afternoon in this same year. They seemed to have grown bigger, the better to express the horror which she felt.

"He is not wounded. Be sure—be very sure of that!" she continued, nodding her head at me in a queer, matter-of-fact way, which, joined with the contrast of her face, had something, to my thinking, awsomely grotesque.

"What do you mean?" I gasped, and in a momentary weakness staggered back against the framework of the window. I felt her clasp strengthen upon my arm, drawing me within the parlour.

"He carried a pistol—yes, but why should he look to the priming since you were to fight with swords?" she whispered, shaking my arm with a little impatient movement. "Did you not see? His walk grew slow, his head drooped—drooped. He was tired, you see, so tired;" and she uttered a low, mirthless laugh while her eyes burned into me. It was a sound which, I thank God, I have never heard but the once. It was as though a preternatural horror claimed a preternatural expression. "It was not worth while," she resumed.

"Ah, no," I cried, as her meaning broke in upon me. "I'll not believe that. I'll not believe it;" and once or twice I thrust out with my hands as if that way I could keep belief aloof.

"But you do," she returned, and the whisper of her voice took on a certain eagerness. It seemed that she must have a partner in her thought. "You do believe it. Look, am I pale? Then I am your mirror. Do I tremble? It is an ague caught from you. You do believe it. We know, you and I—guilt binds us in knowledge. We heard this morning. He told us, he warned us. If his wife proved false, he would not count it worth his while to punish the betrayer. But he has—he has punished us, so perfectly that he himself would pity us, were he alive to do it. Would God we both were dead!" And again she laughed, and letting drop my arm she moved away into the room.

I had no doubt her words were true, and from the bottom of my heart I echoed her vain prayer. I remembered the conviction with which he had spoken—all the more assured for the very quietude of his voice. Yes, those trees, motionless under a leaden sky, in a leaden silence, were the watchers about his bed. I braced myself to descend, but as my first step crunched the gravel of the terrace, Mrs. Herbert was again as my side.

"No," she cried. "Not yet, not without me, and I dare not go."

"Nay, madam," I replied, "do you stay here. There is no need for you to come."

"But there is—there is," she insisted, looking at me wildly, like one distraught "Step by step we must go together. And so it will be always. You will see, you and I are fettered each to each by sin, and there's no breaking the locks." She shook her hands piteously.

"Nay," I said, "I will go alone."

"I dare not be left alone," she replied. "For what if he passed you while you searched for him!" and she gave a shuddering cry and recoiled into the room. "What if he came striding from the thicket across the grass to where I waited here! No! No! Wait, wait until it's dark. I will go down with you. But now, in the daylight! His eyes will be open; I dare not."

She stood with her hands clasped before her, toppling towards madness. I dared not leave her. There was no choice for me; between the dead man and the living woman there was no choice. I returned to the room.

"You will wait?" she asked.

"Until it is dark."

She moved into the alcove of the fireplace and crouched down upon the seat, with her back against the wall nearest to the garden. I remained by the window, looking down the garden with the valley on my right. I saw the strip of cloud unfold across the valley and lower upon the hilltops like a solid roof, The hillsides darkened, the bed of the valley grew black—it seemed to me with the shadow of the wings of death. Here a tree shivered; from another there, the birds of a sudden chattered noisily. I turned and gazed across to Eagle Crag. The dale of Langstrath sloped upwards, facing me between the mountains; and as I gazed I saw the rain drive down from the Stake Pass to the mouth in a great slanting column. It deployed along the hillsides;—the mountains became unsubstantial behind it—it swept across the valley, lashing the house, bending the trees in the garden.

"And his eyes will be open," said Mrs. Herbert behind my shoulder.

I started round. Her white face was like a wax mask in the gloom of the chamber. But as I turned she moved back again to the fireplace. "It is cold," she said with a shiver. I set fire to the wood upon the hearth, and as the logs crackled and blazed, she bent forward and spread out her hands to the flame.

I dropped into the seat opposite to her, and so we sat for a long while in silence. Once, it seemed to me, that I heard the hoofs of a horse upon the gravel of the drive—galloping up to the house, and in a little galloping away from it. But what with the beating of the rain and the turmoil of the wind I could not make sure—nor, indeed, did I feel any concern to know.

Once Mrs. Herbert raised her head to me and said, as if answering some objection which I had urged:

"It *was* because he loved me that he told the steward. That was his way. God made him so;" and her voice as she spoke was very soft. Her face, too, softened, as I could see from the glow of the fire, and I knew that her husband in his death was drawing her more surely towards him than he had ever done in life.

"He was very good to me," she said to herself. "It was I that plagued him. He was very good to me, and I—I love him."

It was as though she had forgotten he was dead, and more than one remark of the kind she made while the room darkened behind as and the night fell upon the world without, and the raindrops hissed down the chimney into the fire. I dared not rouse her, though the forgetfulness struck me as horrible, but once, I know, I shifted restively upon my seat, and she looked at me suddenly as though she had forgotten that I was there, as though, indeed, she did not know me. But in a little, recognition gleamed in her eyes, and they hardened slowly to hatred. However, she said nothing, but turned her face again to the fire, and so stared into it with eyes like pebbles.

After a while the wind lulled, the rain-drops hissed less often down the chimney and finally ceased altogether. A line of moonlight shot into the room and lay upon the carpet like a silver rod. The room became mistily luminous and then pitilessly bright. Meanwhile no one seemed as yet to be astir within the house.

I rose unsteadily from my seat; she followed my example,

"Yes, let us go," she said, and we went out on to the terrace.

CHAPTER IX
THE NIGHT OF THE 23RD: IN THE GARDEN

As we descended the terrace-steps, the horror of this task on which we were set broke in upon me in its full significance. Above our heads, it is true, the moon sailed through a clear sky; upon the trees in the Wilderness the rain-drops glistened with a sprightly brilliancy like the silver lamps of fairies; but beneath us, on the floor of the garden, a white mist smoked and writhed, and somewhere—somewhere under that mist lay the dead body slain by me.

We met the mist at the line where the parterre borders on the Wilderness, and walked through it knee-deep until the trees grew dense. At that point, however, we separated and moved forwards thenceforth with an interval between us that we might the sooner end our search, and so doing we quickly lost sight of one another. I made directly so far as I could guess for the bushes above which I had seen the smoke of the pistol float, but, being come near to the spot, what with the delusive light and the many shrubs crowding thereabouts, I could by no means determine which was the particular one I sought.

Moreover, since I walked, as I say, knee-deep in mist, it was a very easy and possible thing for me to pass within an inch of the body and be never a jot the wiser unless my foot chanced to knock on it. I walked, therefore, very slowly and in a great agony and desolation of remorse. It seemed to me that his wraith was a presence in the garden, and the garden its most fitting habitation. For now that I had left the open, and was circled about with the boskage, I moved through a world shadowy and fantastic. The shadows of the branches laced the floor of mist in a grotesque pattern, and amongst them my shadow moved and moved alone, swelling and dwindling as I turned this way and that in the moonlight; and now and again invisible beneath the mist a creeping plant would twine of a sudden about my ankle, and I would stop with a cry half-checked upon my lips, fancying for a moment that it was the dead man's fingers clutching me.

Moreover, as I brushed against the boughs, the raindrops would patter from the leaves with the most melancholy sound that ever a man heard. To me I know they sounded like the pattering feet of little children. I remember that when the thought first struck me I groaned aloud in the anguish of my spirit. The pattering of little children's feet, and here was the young husband dead through me as surely as though my hand had pulled the trigger and the young wife as surely widowed! And when I rose and continued my search, that sound pursued me. It was as though the children ran after me, with many steps to my one stride. I was like the Dutch piper they tell of in story-books, who led the little children in a long train from Hamlin town; only those children laughed and sang and played as they went, merriment in their voices, rosy expectation in their looks; but those who followed me that night, followed in the saddest silence. The only noise they made was the pattering of their feet, unborn children mutely accusing me for that they would never see the day. Indeed, I drank my fill of punishment that night.

How long it was that I wandered thus I do not know, but all at once a cry rang out through the quiet. It came from some distance upon my right and was the cry of a woman. I hurried in that direction as quickly as the long wet grass allowed, and in a little I came to an open space. Mrs. Herbert was kneeling in the centre with her arms in front of her, buried in the mist. I ran towards her, but she did not perceive me until I was within a few yards of her.

"No!" she cried suddenly, and she lifted up her arms and held them towards me to keep me off. "Not you! Not you!" and with that she dipped her arms again into the mist and began to croon over to herself a little tender lullaby such as mothers will sing about a cradle. I noticed that she moved her hands, and I fancied that I understood the significance of the movements. For now they seemed to caress a face, now to repose upon a breast.

"Madam," I said gently, "I know that my help must be the most unwelcome thing to you in all the world. Yet I must offer it and you must accept it. There is no other way;" and I bent down towards the ground.

"No," she cried, and with all her strength she thrust my arms aside, repulsing me. The moonlight shone in her eyes, and they glared at me wild with hatred.

"No!"—she leaned forwards over the spot protecting it—"your touch would stain;" and with a sudden movement she caught hold of a hand, of mine, and peered at it as though she thought to see blood there. "No, you must not — —"

"But I must," I interrupted her, for her wits seemed all distraught, and I could endure this evidence of her suffering no longer. "I must," I repeated, and in my turn I dipped my hands into the curling mist. She gave a shrill scream, as though I had laid violent hands on her, sprang to her feet, and made in a stumbling run beneath the trees towards the house. I kneeled down where she had kneeled and plunged my hands in the mist as she had done.

What they touched was a fallen tree-trunk.

I started to my feet and ran back to the house. There was no one in the parlour. I hurried into the hall. There was no one there. I ran down the road. At the gates I saw ahead of me in the darkness the flutter of a dress. I raced after it; I heard a cry, which the sound of my running provoked, and Mrs. Herbert began to run from me.

I called to her, but she only quickened her pace, and accordingly I relaxed mine. In a little her run became a walk, and so keeping behind her I followed her to the outskirts of Keswick and then returned to Blackladies.

The house, however, was now lighted up, and the door closed. I knocked, and one of the servants opened it to me. I did not speak to him, but ran through the hall to the garden and resumed the search, I continued it until the sky in the east grew white, and after that when the sun had risen and the birds were singing. The mist cleared from the ground, and at last in the clear daylight I came again to the shrubs whither I had marched at the outset, and I saw something which made the hope spring again in my breast. The grass for some yards was trampled and crushed as though from a struggle. I picked up a shred of lace; it might have been torn in a struggle from a ruffle or cravat. I dropped upon my knees and searched in the grass; in a little I came upon a pistol—it was the pistol which I had noticed in Mr. Herbert's lodging, and, moreover, it was discharged. It was he, then, who had fired, but—but it was plain he had not fired it at himself. In a feverish haste I crawled on my knees within this trampled circle. If he had been attacked, who attacked him? I needed a clue to answer me that question, and I found the clue. After a long while, it is true, but nevertheless I found it. It was no more than a metal button, but I had seen the like upon the uniforms of King George's officers.

I held it in my hands, turning it over and over. For, to my thinking, the mines of Golconda held no jewel half so precious. It was a sign to me that Anthony Herbert was not dead. The one pistol which had been discharged was his own. He had been captured, and capture seemed to me so small a thing in the revulsion of my feelings. Of the reason for his capture I did not conjecture at all; I stood with an intense feeling of gratefulness softening at my heart and dimming my eyes. Then I remembered that there was one whose right to share my knowledge and my gratitude I had already too long deferred. I started with all speed for the house; the garden laughed in the sunshine as I ran, and the flowers took on a richer beauty and sprinkled the air with a sweeter perfume.

But as I neared the open space, I saw through an opening of the trees Aron run from the parlour and down the steps in a great haste. I shouted to him, and he lifted his head and seemed to look for the spot whence the shout came. But he did not in any measure slacken his pace. I shouted again, and he caught sight of me and waved his hands. I ran on, and again he waved his hands, but with a more violent gesture. I met him halfway across the open space of meadow.

"Quick, sir," said he, panting in a great disorder, "back—back to the trees;" and he caught me by the flap of the coat.

I tugged the coat away.

"For God's sake, Master Lawrence, stop!"

But I was already running past him; the which he saw, and putting out a foot tripped me up without ceremony. I sprawled full length on the grass.

"How dare you?" I spluttered out in a rage.

"I would do as much again, sir, and more, were there the same need. Quick, sir, to the trees;" and he stooped to help me to my feet. Then, "It's too late," he whispered, and pressing me down by the shoulder dropped at my side.

"Look, Master Lawrence. Look!" and he nodded towards the house.

I saw the flash of a red-coat in the little parlour, then another and another. The room filled with soldiers.

"Keep your head low, sir! God send they do not look this way. If only we had reached the trees!" And he stretched himself flat in the grass and began to wriggle and crawl towards the shelter.

"They come for me?" I whispered, imitating his example.

"Yes!" he returned. "I must needs think so."

"Why?"

"I saw them marching up the drive, and Mr."—he paused over the name—"Mr. Ashlock was with them."

"Ashlock?" I exclaimed with a start, for in the press of trouble which these last twelve hours had brought, I had clean forgotten the man.

"Hush!" replied Aron.

"Oh, why keep up the lie?" I answered savagely. "Call him Jervas Rookley and have done with it. He came with King George's soldiers, did he? Aron, or Ashlock, I take it, I should call you, when next Mr. Jervas Rookley makes up his accounts for me, he shall make them up with his own hand, I promise you that."

The old man shook his head very sadly.

"I fear me," he agreed, "that Mr. Jervas is for something in all this."

"For more than you know," I replied, "and indeed for more than I know too as yet."

Of a sudden I remembered that evening when I had seen Jervas Rookley enter through the parlour window.

"There is a secret way into the garden," I said, and then a new thought flashed in upon me. "It was doubtless by that way the soldiers came."

"No, sir," said Ashlock, "they came by the highroad. Else I should not have seen them."

"True," said I, "those soldiers did, but they are not all the soldiers in Cumberland. And this secret way—you know it?"

"I know it," he answered. "But we must reach the thicket first."

I looked backwards across my shoulder. The soldiers were spreading over the terrace. I turned my face and strained every muscle to help me forward. Each moment I expected to hear the clink of a sabre against a spur, and a voice cry "Halt," or to see a shadow fall from behind my shoulder across the grass in front. "I must not be taken," I said to myself, yet knew full well that I might, "I must not be taken." It was not so much the thought of my own peril that plagued me, but rather the desire to inform Mrs. Herbert that her husband was not dead. It pressed upon me like a sheer necessity. I must escape.

Ashlock at my side uttered a groan.

"I can go no further, Master Lawrence," he said, and lay prone in an extremity of exhaustion, his face purple, and the veins pulsing upon it "Were I ten years younger—but I cannot."

For answer I twined my arm about his body and dragged him forward. Every muscle in his body was a-quiver, the sweat poured from his forehead, and his chest heaved upon my arm as though it would crack; and all the while the screen of grass was close about our eyes and the sun burning upon our backs and heads. At last a shadow fell between the sun and us. I stopped with a groan and let my forehead fall forward on the ground. In a trice I saw myself captured, tried, executed, and meanwhile Mrs. Herbert would sit a-weeping in Keswick for a husband who was not dead.

"Thank God!" said Ashlock. "It is the shadow of the first tree."

I raised my head, just checking the cry of joy which sprang to my lips. A little to the left of us a great leafy branch stretched out towards us. We crawled forward again, past a tree-trunk, then another, then another, and in a minute I was standing up behind a shrub, and Ashlock was lying at my feet, his breath coming in hoarse gasps from between his parched lips, his eyes closed, and his whole body limp and broken.

I peered round the shrub. The soldiers were scattered over the parterre, and then of a sudden I saw something which doubled my fears. For right across the meadow a furrow was drawn in a wavering line as though by the clumsiest scytheman. And it led straight to this bush. In a very short while the soldiers must see it. I sprang to Ashlock. It was no less than a necessity that Ashlock should escape from that garden without incurring a suspicion. I needed a friend in the house for one thing. For another I needed a messenger who could safely show himself in Keswick.

Accordingly I raised Ashlock to his feet and supported him through the thicket until we came to the labyrinth. The secret entrance to the garden lay in the last square of the labyrinth at the corner against the hillside, and had been constructed by Jervas Rookley during the lifetime of his father. It consisted of no more than a number of iron pegs driven into the interstices of the stone wall and hidden beneath a drapery of ivy. I descended first, and Ashlock followed me closely, so that if by any chance he slipped I might be able to lend him a hand. As soon as we were safely at the bottom, I said—

"Now, Ashlock, your way lies down the valley, mine up the hillside. You will get back into the house unnoticed, make sure of that! And to-day you will ride into Keswick and take this message from me to Mrs. Herbert."

I tore a page from the note-book which I carried in my pocket, and hurriedly scribbled on it, "He is not dead," and added thereto my initials. "Now good-bye. Be instant with the message! I doubt me but it is the last order you will ever take from me," and so I turned from him and began running up the hillside.

Ashlock called out to me—

"Sir," he cried, "I know not where I can have news of you. It will be well that I should know."

"You can have news of me," I replied, "at my Lord Derwentwater's, but be careful how you come there lest you imperil him;" and of a sudden he snatched up my hand and kissed it.

"Master Lawrence," he said in a broken voice of apology, "my father served Sir John Rookley's father."

"Therefore," I interrupted, "you must serve Sir John Rookley's son. It is very right," and I patted him gently on the shoulder. "It is just for that reason a man serves his King. It is the house one serves, not the man who heads it."

"But I would you were Sir John Rookley's son."

The tenderness with which he spoke cut me like a knife.

"Nay," said I, "if there were a choice to be made, you would not be right in choosing me."

I had barely ended the sentence before a cry rang out from the garden. It came, however, faintly to our ears.

"Quick!" I said. "They have come upon our tracks in the grass. Quick! That note must reach Keswick to-day, and your hand must deliver it."

With that we parted. I mounted the hillside until I came to a large boulder, and threw myself on the ground beneath its shelter. In a fever of impatience I watched Ashlock descend along the wall, and yet the moment he had turned the corner and was clean out of my sight, I wished him back again. I was, in truth, sunk to such a depth of shame and self-contempt as made this old servant's goodwill an extraordinary consolation. For now that I had had time to grow used to the knowledge that Anthony Herbert was not dead, I began to see more clearly the wickedness of my preceding conduct.

It was, then, with a very lonely feeling that I climbed to the ridge of Green Comb. Beneath me I could see Blackladies and its garden much as on that morning when I first rode thither over Coldbarrow Fell. But I saw it with very different eyes. Then, proud of my entrusted mission, I had looked upon it as an instrument of loyalty, a prop, however fragile, of the cause I served and my father had served before me. Now it was to me a monument of failure. Here I had failed through and through. I had proved false to Mr. Herbert; I had been juggled like the merest fool in my service to the King. I had but to turn, and over against me I could see the very spot where I had forced Jervas Rookley to make his vow of concealment upon his knees, and a little lower down the winding path, where I had come to my knees and Jervas Rookley had sat his horse over me. Well, I had kept faith with him, at all events, and how had he kept faith with me? The red-coats sprinkled in the garden below gave me the answer. Yes, I had kept faith with him. It seemed to me a wonderful and astonishing thing, so deep was my humiliation, but it was true. I had kept faith with him, and I hugged the thought to my very breast. In the wreck of my hopes and pride, it stood erect as you may see a single column standing amidst a pile of ruins; and perhaps, I thought, since that one column stands, if he could but bring perseverance to the work, a man might in time rebuild the whole.

To effect anything of this sort, however, I must needs first of all escape, and to that end I kept all the day along the hilltops, and at the fall of the dark came down Bleaberry Fell, to the great wood that fringes Derwentwater over against Rampsholme Island. About a mile to the east of the wood was a fisherman's cottage with which I was sufficiently familiar, since the fisherman had ferried me over often enough to Lord's Island, and many another visitor to my Lord Derwentwater besides, who came in a great hurry when the night was fallen dark. To this cottage I crept, and tapping at the window-pane presently the man came out and joined me.

He asked no questions, being well practised in the habit of secrecy, but put me across to the steps and so pushed off again without a word. I thought it best not to openly knock at the door, but crept round to a room wherein I knew Lord Derwentwater was used to sit of an evening. To my inexpressible relief I saw that the windows were lighted. I knocked on the pane; the sash was thrown up.

"Who is it?" asked Lord Derwentwater.

I set my hand on the sill and climbed into the room.

CHAPTER X
A TALK WITH LORD DERWENTWATER. I ESCAPE

"Lawrence!" he exclaimed, starting back at the sight of me, and with a cry Lady Derwentwater came forward and took my hand. In truth, I must have cut a sufficiently pitiable figure, for my dress was all fouled from head to foot, and my face, I have no doubt, the complement of my dress.

"The soldiers are after me," I gasped out.

"Ah! Jervas Rookley!" cried Lord Derwentwater, with a bang of his fist upon the table, the while his wife got me some brandy from a sideboard. "But I warned you, Lawrence! I warned you, when I caught sight of him in Keswick."

"I know," I answered. "But you did not warn me he was a traitor. All this while Jervas Rookley has been my steward at Blackladies."

"Your steward!" exclaimed Lord Derwentwater; "and you did not know."

"Nay," I replied, "it was not so much that. But I would not know. I pledged my word to him." With that I drank off the brandy.

"Oh, if you had only told me this!" he cried.

"I could not," I answered "I had but conjectures, and they were not enough to warrant me. There was but one fact in all the business which was clearly known to me: I had pledged my word to him."

"Nay," said Lady Derwentwater, and she laid a pitying hand upon my shoulder, "he was right, since he had given his word;" and I—why, I groaned aloud and let my face fall forward on my arms. "Ah, poor boy!" she exclaimed. "All this day he has been out upon the hills, and here we stand plaguing him with questions, when we should be ransacking the pantry. We deserve to be whipped."

She cautiously slipped out of the room.

But it was not any bodily want that troubled me so much as the unmerited kindliness of her tone and gesture. It wrought on me, indeed, with such a melting compulsion that had she remained within the room, I verily believe I should have blurted out that other story, with a "Withold your pity until it is deserved."

Lord Derwentwater locked the door behind his wife and began to walk about the room.

"Lawrence," said he, "I am in some way to blame for this. But I did not know the fellow was masquerading at Blackladies as your steward. He was disinherited, you know. But do you know why?"

"Because he was a Jacobite," I replied.

"Because he was a spy," cried Lord Derwentwater. "A spy—do you understand?—paid by the Government to worm himself into the Jacobite councils. I know, for his father told me, and told me on his death-bed. Sir John was a Whig, you know, but an honest one and a gentleman, and the shock the knowledge caused him, caused his death."

"A spy!" I exclaimed. "And I might have known! I might have known it at Commercy."

"At Commercy?" said he with a start

"I might have known it in mid-channel. It was the letter his hands were searching for;" and noticing Lord Derwentwater's perplexity, I related to him the whole story of Rookley's coming to Paris, the promise I made to him there, the journey to Lorraine.

"You had speech with the King!" he exclaimed, "and Jervas Rookley knew. You carried a letter——"

"In the King's hand, to the Duke of Ormond."

"And Jervas Rookley knew!"

"Ay, for he tried to steal it," and a great silence fell upon us both. We looked into each other's eyes; I know I held my breath. With a swift, stealthy movement, more significant to me than even the silence was, he unlocked the door again and peered into the passage.

"We were speaking over-loud, Lawrence," he said, in a hushed whisper.

He was on the point of locking the door again, when Lady Derwentwater returned, bearing a loaded tray.

"It is a bad case you are in," said Lord Derwentwater. "You had best fall to. It must not be known you were here to-night. I would gladly hide you."

"Nay," said I, "I have brought you near enough to danger as it is."

He waved the remark aside.

"There is no sense in such talk between friends. But Lord's Island is no safe place for you. I am suspected; you are known for my friend. Here will they come first to search for you."

"But to-morrow," interrupted his wife, "not to-night"

"It were best he leave to-night," replied Lord Derwentwater.

"Ah, no, James," she returned, "it would be ill-usage in any case to dismiss so easily a friend so hard put to it, and the worst usage in the world towards Mr. Clavering. For look, what the boy most needs is a bed."

"And what if he were taken in it! That would be worse usage still. Anna, we cannot risk his life for the sake of our manners."

I seconded him in his advice, for though I was dropping with fatigue, and Lady Derwentwater's words called up I know not what sweet visions of lavender sheets, I knew that at any moment the sheriff's messenger might come rapping at the doors. Lady Derwentwater accordingly said no more, but betook herself to filling my glass and heaping up my plate with an air of such maternal tenderness as pierced me to the heart. If she only knew, I thought—if she only knew what manner of man she tended on! And again I was very near to blurting out my story.

"There is one thing," said I, "which I do not understand. For if Rookley meant my ruin, why should he wait so long to accomplish it? He had the means to hand, the day that I set foot in England."

Lord Derwentwater stopped suddenly in his walk.

"You received my letter yesterday?"

"A letter?" said I. "No! What time of the day was it sent?"

"In the afternoon."

I remembered that I had seemed to hear the hoofs of a horse upon the drive when I was in the parlour. Lord Derwentwater slipped out of the room. In a little he came back with a scared face.

"The letter was handed to your steward," he said. "The man I sent was a new servant, else he would have known who the steward was."

"But what was in the letter?"

"It was a message from Harry St John, enclosed in a letter which came to me. It said the French King was dying, and no help was to be expected from the Regent, who would follow him. It said the rising was to be deferred."

"Then I understand!" I exclaimed, starting to my feet "I had promised Rookley to restore the estate when the King came to his own. So long as there was a chance of that, he would let me go free. But when that chance failed, he might buy back Blackladies by selling me."

"Ay," said Derwentwater, "that is Jervas Rookley from top to toe. He would have one foot marking time with King George, and the other stepping forward with King James."

And again he paced musingly about the room whilst I betook myself to my supper. At last—

"I know," he said; and then turning to me, "I was thinking whither I should send you. There is old Ralph Curwen. You will be safe with him at Applegarth."

It seemed to me that I had heard the name before, but on what occasion I could not at the moment remember.

"He lives in Ennerdale," continued he; "an honest Jack, but he is old, and since his son died, has known little company beyond his books. You will be safe with him."

"Ay, but will he be safe with me?" I objected.

"No doubt of that He has taken no part in these quarrels of ours for many a day, and they will not look for you in Ennerdale."

He sat down and wrote a letter.

"I will send you thither," he said, "with a servant I can trust, and as soon as may be we'll get you out of England;" and he rose, he crossed over to a table, and unlocking a drawer took out a little diary.

"Let me see!" he said. "To-day is St. Bartholomew's Day. It may be that I can send you across to France. Why, what ails you?"

"It is nothing," I replied hastily.

It was, indeed, the mere mention of the date which made me sway like a man falling and grasp at the table. To-day was St Bartholomew's Day. Then yesterday was the Eve, the Eve of St. Bartholomew. My thoughts went back to the preacher I had heard in Paris and to the picture of the dead man speaking, who had seemed in my imagination to thunder out at me, "The Eve of St. Bartholomew."

Lord Derwentwater went from the room to give his orders, and ten minutes later I was being rowed across the lake towards Silver Hill and watching two heads at the lighted window diminish into specks.

There was but the one man in the boat besides myself—Lord Derwentwater's servant Tash. Accordingly, on disembarking in a little wood on the west shores of Derwentwater, we drew the boat on to dry ground, and striking up the hillside walked southwards along the slopes of Catbells and Maiden Moor. But for my part I took little note of our direction. My head nodded on my shoulders, my feet stumbled behind my guide's in a mechanic progression. Had he led me back into Keswick town I should have followed him. I walked in a daze of weariness, sensible of but two things in the world: one that the fresh smell of the grass and parsley-fern was every way as sweet as lavender to lie in; the other that I must still walk on, since there was something to be done that I and I alone could do.

In the morning we moved yet higher up the slopes, and so walking ever southwards past Dale Head Tarn and Honister, came to a lofty ridge between Grey Knotts and Brandreth about nine o'clock of the morning. There my guide called a halt, and pulling my hat over my eyes I plumped down on the grass and slept without more ado.

CHAPTER XI
APPLEGARTH

When I fell asleep the sun was just climbing above the shoulder of Skiddaw; when I waked again, it was down very close above the Isle of Man, so that I could see the surf flash in a line of gold as it broke against the rocks. Tash had brought with him some cheese and a loaf of bread; and being hard set with my long fast, I spent no great while over grace, but fell to and moistened the food with the sweetest water that ever I drank, fetching it from a little stream which bubbled by through the grass a few yards away. Tash pointed me out a valley which cleft the mountains westwards a little to our left and made a right angle with the ridge on which we lay. At the end of the valley I saw the corner of a lake. The valley, he told me, was called Gillerthwaite and the lake Ennerdale Water. Mr. Curwen's house was built upon the banks of the Water, but was invisible to us, since it lay in a kind of bay to the north behind some projecting cliffs of a reddish stone.

"But we will wait here till nightfall," he said; and nothing loth I turned over on my back and fell to resolving, so well as I could, the perplexities in which I was coiled. I now saw very clearly that Rookley's plot had not, as I had imagined, been aimed against myself, but rather against Anthony Herbert; and my new knowledge that my worthy cousin was a Government spy gave me some light to conjecture of a cause. For I reflected that Herbert had come suddenly to Keswick at the very time when rebellion was a-brewing in these parts; that he had made Lord Derwentwater's acquaintance and had painted his lady's portrait; that upon my coming to Blackladies, Lord Derwentwater had put me into relations with the man; and that I too had commissioned a portrait of him. Now Lord Derwentwater was suspected of favouring the Stuart claims, and certainly Rookley knew that I not merely favoured them but was working to further them. It would be, then, a natural suspicion for Rookley to draw that we were all three implicated in the same business, and that Herbert was merely using his skill as a concealment of his genuine purpose. Moreover, I thought of a sudden, there was that medal in Mr. Herbert's apartment. True, I had seen him lock it up. But he must bring it out again to copy it, and he was not of that orderliness which would ensure his replacing it. What if Rookley had seen the medal in Herbert's lodging? Joined to his suspicions, that one certain fact would change those suspicions to convictions. Rookley would believe, and would have reason to believe, that Herbert was a Jacobite agent. Granted that presumption, and Rookley's conduct became clear. He was marking time with King George and stepping forward with King James. He would lay Herbert by the heels in the one interest and leave me untouched in the other, so long as it was doubtful which way the wind was setting. I found an additional reason to credit this hypothesis in this, that it was plainly Rookley's intention to bring about Herbert's arrest secretly, or at all events without my knowledge.

"I had thought to find you in the garden," Herbert had said; the words came back to me in a flash. I sprang to my feet in some excitement. Tash in a flurry asked me what it was I saw; but I moved away without answering him, certain that I had a hold upon the key of the plot, fearful lest I should lose it.

"I had thought to find you in the garden" — and the soldiers were in the garden. Moreover, there was but one man who could have led Mr. Herbert to believe that he would find us in the garden — Jervas Rookley. And Jervas Rookley had every reason in the world to feel assured that neither Mrs. Herbert nor myself would be discovered there.

I had no longer a shadow of doubt. Anthony Herbert had been beguiled to Blackladies that his arrest might be brought about with secrecy. Only Jervas Rookley had made one mistake: he had presumed in his victim the same cunning and concealment of which he was master himself. Mr. Herbert had defeated the secrecy of the plan by his outburst in his lodging; but for that outburst, the arrest would have been effected with all the secrecy which Rookley desired.

From that point in my speculations I went forward to a resolve. I knew Herbert to be in no way concerned with our plans and hopes. Indeed, I doubted whether he cared a straw which King occupied the throne, so long as he could continue in the exercise of his art. But, on the other hand, there was the medal in his possession, and I distrusted the impartiality of justice in a matter where passions were so inflamed. My resolve, then, was no more than this: that if by any means a man could, I would secure Mr. Herbert's enlargement, if only as an act of reparation, and if it cost me my life. But to tell the truth, my life at this moment had not the least savour of sweetness, and to let it go seemed the easiest thing in the world.

The question, however, which weighed on me was how I should accomplish his enlargement; for I did not know and had no means of knowing whither he had been taken. They might have carried him to London, there to be examined. Suppose that was true and I went down into the valley and gave myself up? Why, I had not sufficient trust in the authorities to be certain that Herbert would get the benefit of my evidence. I could prove that the medal belonged to me; but should I be allowed to tender that proof on Herbert's behalf? I might lie in prison the while he was brought to his trial. No, before I gave myself up I must know whither Anthony Herbert had been taken. And as far as I could tell, there was but one man who could give me the information. Could I force it from Jervas Rookley? I asked myself, and even in the asking laughed. For here was the darkness coming up out of the sea and wrapping the mountains about, and here was I hiding in the midst of them, a hunted outlaw. Tash called to me that it was time for us to set out, and we started down the hillside into Gillerthwaite, he leading as before, I as before following him, but no longer in the daze and stupor of yesternight. Rather, on the contrary, I walked with eyes needlessly alert and with feet over-timorous and careful. For if I got no other profit from my reflections, I had drawn from them this one conviction, and I was sensible of it as of a sheer necessity: I must be ready, I thought—since I knew so little, I must be ready to seize any occasion of Mr. Herbert's enlargement, at the instant of its discovery. So that as we scrambled down the slope with the mist gathering around us, I came to fear a slip with an extraordinary apprehension; where the grass steepened, I straightway imagined a fatal precipice; and when a stone slid beneath my heel, I felt all the blood drain from my heart and leave me shaking in a panic. The night in consequence had completely fallen by the time we came to a pony-track in the bed of the valley. I remember that I asked carelessly whither it led from Ennerdale, and Tash told me that it passed into the valley called Newlands, which runs parallel with Derwentwater, and is only separated from the lake by that line of hills along which we had walked during the night.

"Then," said I carelessly, "it is a path by which one may travel to Keswick."

"Ay," he replied; and for the moment I thought no more of the matter.

Before we had come to the head of Ennerdale Water, the moon was up and shining fitfully through a wrack of clouds. The valley, however, was clear of mist, so that I was able to distinguish the house of Applegarth, while I was as yet at some distance from its doors. It was a long, plain building, which promised comfort within by its very lack of ornamentation without, built in a single story and painted a white colour. But it seemed to me, even in that uncertain light, to bear the marks of neglect and decay. There was a little garden in front of the house separated from the lake-shores by an unkempt hedge, and planted only with a few fuchsia bushes; the walls of the house were here and there discoloured, and once or twice as I passed up the garden-path I stepped upon a broken tile.

A woman-servant opened the door and I asked for Mr. Curwen. She looked me over for a second.

"And what may be your business with Mr. Curwen?"

"That I can hardly tell you," said I with a laugh.

"Ah, but you must," said she. She was a woman of some bulk, and she stood with her arms akimbo, filling the doorway. "Is it his last few guineas you might be wanting?" she asked with a slow sarcasm.

"Why, goodwife," I answered impatiently, "do you look for gentlemen of the road in Ennerdale?"

"Goodwife!" she said with a toss of the head. "Goodwife to a ninny-hammer!" and she looked me over again. Indeed, I doubt not but we cut sufficiently disreputable figures. "Not I! And you'll just tell me your business. There are others besides gentlemen of the road who put their fingers into pockets which don't belong to them."

"Hold your noise, Mary Tyson!" said Tash, behind my shoulder. "Do you know me?"

"Oh," said she with a start, "it's William Tash from——"

"That'll do," he broke in; "no need to speak names. Show the gentleman to Mr. Curwen."

Mary Tyson stood aside from the door. I stepped into the hall.

"You'll find him in the room," she said with a curt nod towards a door facing me.

I crossed to it and rapped on the panels, but got no answer whatsoever. It is true I could hear a voice within, but the voice seemed to be declaiming a speech. I rapped again.

"Oh, the dainty knuckles!" cried Mary; and pushing roughly past me she banged upon the door with a great fist like a ham and threw it open without further ceremony. The voice ceased from its declamation. I entered the room. It was very dark, being panelled all about with book-cases and the ceiling very low. A single lamp glimmered on a table in the centre of the carpet An old gentleman rose from before a great folio spread out upon the table.

"What is it, Mary?" he asked in a tone of gentle annoyance. "You interrupt me."

"A visitor, he says," replied Mary, "though——"

The hostility of her eyes and a great heave of her shoulders filled up the gap.

"A visitor!" said the old gentleman, his voice changing on the instant to an eager politeness. "A visitor is always welcome at Applegarth at whatever hour he comes."

I heard not so much a sigh as a snort behind me, and the door was slammed. The old gentleman advanced a few steps towards me and then came to a sudden stop. I was neither hurt nor surprised at his evident disappointment and perplexity, for Mary's behaviour had shown me pretty clearly what sort of a picture I made.

"It is not a visitor, Mr. Curwen," said I, "but a fugitive;" and I handed to him Lord Derwentwater's letter.

"Indeed?" said he, all his suavity rekindling. "A fugitive!" and he spoke as though to be a fugitive was a very fine and enviable thing. "You will take a chair, Mr.——"

"Clavering," I added.

"Of Blackladies?" he inquired

"Of Blackladies," said I.

"You are very welcome, Mr. Clavering," said he, and he broke open the seal and read the letter through, with many interruptions of "Shield us!" and "To be sure!" and with many a glance over his spectacles at me. He was a tall man, though his shoulders stooped as if he spent many an evening over his folio, and I should say of sixty years and more. He wore his own white hair, which was very long and fine, making a silver frame to as beautiful a face, except one, as it has ever been my lot to see. The features, it may be, were over-delicately chiselled, the cheeks too bloodless, the eyes too large, if you looked for a man of dominating activity. It was the face of a dreamer, no doubt, but there would be nothing ignoble in the dreams.

"You are yet more welcome, Mr. Clavering," said he as he folded up the letter; "shelter indeed you shall have, and such comfort as we can add thereto, for so long as you will be pleased to stay with us. Nay," said he, checking me, "I know what you would say, but we are solitary people here and the debt will be with us."

"That can hardly be," said I, "since I bring danger to you by my presence."

"Some while ago," he replied, "I would not have denied it, though I should have welcomed you no less. But since my fortunes have declined and I have grown into years, I have taken little part in politics and keep much within my doors. They will not come here, I think, to look for you. It is a consolation for my poverty," said he with the simplest dignity, "that I can therefore offer you a safer harbourage. But indeed it is with you that the times have gone hard. We are not so solitary but that now and again a scrap of news will float to us, and we have heard of you. You were much at one time in Paris?" And his voice of a sudden took on a pleasant eagerness.

"Yes," I replied, "though I saw little of the town."

"Ah," said he with a nod of the head, "to gain and lose Blackladies in so short a space—it is a hard case, Mr. Clavering."

In the hurry and stress of these last two days I had given no thought to what the loss Blackladies meant, but the meaning rushed in upon me winged with his words.

"Ay," I answered, and my voice trembled as I spoke, so that the old man came over to me and laid a hand upon my shoulder, "for it is the King who loses it, and through my folly, for I might have known."

I felt his hand patting me with a helpless consolation. "So we all say, after the event. It is a hard thing to bear, but philosophy will help us. You must study philosophy while you are here, Mr. Clavering. I have books"—and he glanced round the room and then came to an abrupt pause—"I have books," he repeated in a lame fashion, "which you may find profit in studying;" and as he spoke, the music of a song quivered up from the next room like a bird on the wing. I understood that "we," which had much perplexed me in his talk; I remembered where and when I had heard of Applegarth before. You may talk, if you will, of Cuzzoni and Faustina and the rest of the Italian women who have filled Heidegger's pockets; doubtless they made more noise, but not one of them, I'll be sworn, had a tenth of the sweetness and purity of the voice which sang this song. Give to a lark a human soul and then maybe you will hear it. For it was more than a voice that sang; it was as though the wings of a soul beat and throbbed in the singer's throat. I lack words to describe the effect it wrought on me. All the shame I had been sensible of during the long hours since that pistol rang out in the garden of Blackladies, came back to me massed within the compass of a second, and on that shame, more and ever more. I know that I buried my face in my hands to hide the anguish of my spirit from Mr. Curwen; and sitting there with my fingers pressed upon my eyes I listened. The words came clearly to my ears through the doorway behind my chair; the voice carried my thoughts back to Paris, was the crystal wherein I saw pitilessly plain all the dreams I had fashioned of what I would do, had I but liberty and the power to do it; then carried me again to England, and showed me the miserable contrast between those airy dreams and the solid truth. I saw myself now riding to Lorraine; now lingering in Mr. Herbert's apartment. And the words of that song pointed my remorse—how bitterly! Even now, after this interval of thirty-five years, the humiliation and pain I endured return to me with so poignant a force that I can hardly bring myself to write of them. I could not indeed at all, but for this faded yellow sheet of paper which I take up in my hands. It was given to me upon an occasion notable within my memory, and the words of this very song are inscribed upon it, blurred and well-nigh indecipherable, but I do not need the writing to help me to remember them. The song was called "The Honest Lover," and I set it down here since here it was that I first heard it.

"THE HONEST LOVER" [1]

"Would any doubting maid discover
What's he that is a worthy lover:
His is no fine fantastic breath,
But lowly mien and steadfast faith.

For he that so would move her,

By simple art,
And humble heart,

Why, he's the honest lover.

"His is a heart that never played
The light-o'-love to wife or maid,
But reverenced all womankind
Before he found one to his mind.

For he that so would move her

By simple art,
And humble heart,

Why, he's the honest lover.

"And if he quake to meet her eyes,
Stammer and blush whene'er he tries
His worship'd lady to address,
Be sure she'll love him none the less,

For he that so would move her
By simple art,
And humble heart,

Why, he's the honest lover."

Footnote 1: The song is written by Harold Child, Esq., to whom the author is indebted for it.

This was the song to which I listened as I sat—the dishonest outlaw in the dark library of Applegarth.

"It is my daughter Dorothy," said Mr. Curwen, with a smile. "In talking of our youngest martyr I had forgotten her;" and he took a step towards the door. But at his first movement the youngest martyr—Heaven save the mark!—had risen from his chair with a foolish abruptness.

"Nay, Mr. Curwen," he cried in disorder; and then he stopped, for the truth is, he shrank in very shame from standing face to face with the singer of that song.

"But," and I seized the first excuse, "I have this long while been wandering on the fells, and am in no way fitted for the company of ladies. Your servant even would have no truck with me, and I think you too were taken aback." I looked down at my garments as I spoke.

"My servant," he began, and he looked towards the other door through which I had entered with a timorous air, as though he would fain see whether or no she was listening on the far side of it, "Mary Tyson," he said, lowering his voice, "is a strange and unaccountable person. A good servant, but— —" and very wisely he tapped his forehead. "For myself," he continued, his voice softening with a great wistfulness, "it was something very different from the stains of your journey that gave me pause. Lord Derwentwater may have told you that I had once a son. He was much of your height and figure, and the room is dim, and old men are fanciful."

I bowed my head, for whenever he made mention of his misfortunes, he spoke with so brave and simple a dignity that any word of sympathy became the merest impertinence. For a moment he stood looking down at me and revolving some question in his mind.

"Yes," said he, and more to himself than to me, "I will speak to her and give her the order. Why should I not?" He walked slowly halfway to the bell and stopped, "Yes," he repeated, "I will speak to her;" and with a word of excuse to me and a certain bracing of the shoulders, he went out of the room.

I had no doubt that it was with Mary Tyson that he wished to speak. I remained, half-hoping, half-afraid that the chords of the spinet would wake to the touch again, and the voice again ring out, sprinkling its melody through the room like so much perfume from a philtre. But there was no recurrence of the music. I walked idly to the table, and my eyes fell upon that great tome in which Mr. Curwen had been so absorbed at the moment of my interruption. In wonderment I bent more closely over it. I had expected to see some laborious monument of philosophy gemmed with unintelligible terms. Unintelligible terms there were, in truth, but not of the philosopher's kind. They were curious old terms of chivalry.

I remembered how Mr. Curwen had hesitated over the mention of his books, and I took the lamp from the table, and glanced about the book-shelves. The books were all of a-piece with that great folio on the table—romaunts, and histories of crusades, and suchlike matters.

I wondered whether "Don Quixote de la Mancha" had found a place amongst them, and with an impertinent smile I began to glance along the letterings in search of it, but very soon I stopped, and stood staring at a couple of volumes which faced me, and bore upon their backs the title of the "Morte D'Arthur."

I set the lamp again upon the table. The old man was right, I thought sadly. There was in that room philosophy which it would indeed profit me to study.

Mr. Curwen returned, rubbing his long, delicate hands one against the other in a flush of triumph.

"I have given orders," he said, and with a gentle accent of conscious pride he repeated the phrase—"I have given orders, Mr. Clavering. You will sleep in my boy's room, and since you are, as I say, very like to him in size——" But his voice trembled, and he turned away and lifted the lamp from the table.

"I will show you the room," he said.

I followed him into the hall, up the staircase, and down a long passage to the very end of the house.

A door stood open. Mr. Curwen led me through it. The room was warmly furnished, and hung with curtains of a dark green, while a newly-lit fire was crackling in the hearth. A couple of candles were burning on the mantelpiece, and Mary Tyson was arranging the bed. She took no notice of me whatever as I entered, being busy with the bed, as I thought.

"You can go, Mary," said Mr. Curwen, with a timid friendliness plainly intended to appease.

Mary sniffed for an answer, and as she turned to go I saw that she had been crying.

"She was Harry's nurse, poor woman," explained Mr. Curwen. "You must forgive her, Mr. Clavering." And then, "He died at Malplaquet."

He crossed over to the bed, and stood looking down at it silently in a very fixed attitude. Then he took up from it a white silk stocking. I approached him, and saw that a suit of white satin was neatly folded upon the white counterpane.

"It is a fortunate thing," he said, with a smile all the more sad for its effort at cheerfulness, "that you and he are alike;" and he drew the stocking slowly through his fingers. "He died at Malplaquet, and Marlborough—the Marlborough of Malplaquet—spoke to him as he died." His voice broke on the words, and laying the stocking down, he turned towards a japan toilette with a "Even a father has no right to ask for more than that." But Harry's shoe-buckles were laid upon the chintz-coverlid, and he took them in his hands one after the other, repeating, "He died at Malplaquet. I have given you this room," he said, "for a reason. See! These two windows point down the valley, and are set high above the ground. But this"—and he crossed over to a smaller window set in the wall near the fireplace—"this looks on to the hillside, and since the ground rises against the house, a man may drop from it and come to no harm. To the left are the stables, or what serves us for stables. We lock no doors at Applegarth, Mr. Clavering, fearing no robbers. You will find a horse in the stables, should there be need for you to flee."

It was some while after Mr. Curwen had left me, before I could make up my mind to don these clothes. I might be like to what Harry Curwen was in size and figure, but there the likeness ended, and the sharpest contrast in the world set in. I unfolded the suit, and spread it out upon the bed. The coat was of white velvet, the waistcoat and breeches of white satin, and all richly laced with an embroidery of silver. A fragrant scent of lavender, which breathed from the dress, coupled with its freshness as of a suit worn but once or twice and so laid aside, lent an added sadness to the thought of young Harry Curwen. I imagined him stripping off these fine clothes in a fumbling excitement one night, in this very room, kicking from his feet those lacquered shoes—these with their soles and red-heels upturned now to the fire for the guest who was so like him! I imagined him pulling on his boots, and riding off from Applegarth with, I know not what, martial visions in his eyes, and hardly a glance, maybe, for the old man and the sister standing in the light of the porch, to join his troop and perish on the plains of Flanders. Well, he had died at Malplaquet, and the great Marlborough—not the huckstering time-server whom we knew—the Marlborough of Malplaquet had spoken to him as he lay a-dying, and no father had a right to look for more than that. I picked up the stockings, and drew them through my fingers as the father had done.

At that, however, I bethought me that the father and his daughter were awaiting me downstairs, and so dressed in a hurry, and combing out my peruke to such neatness as I could, I got me down into the hall.

Supper was already laid out in the dining-room, and Mr. Curwen waiting. In a little I heard a light step upon the stair and the rustle of a dress. Instinctively I turned my face towards the window-curtains, my back to the door. I heard the door open, but I did not hear it shut again.

"Mr. Clavering," said the old man.

I was forced to turn. His daughter stood in the doorway, her lips parted, her eyes startled.

"Mr. Clavering—my daughter Dorothy."

I bowed to her. She drew in her breath, then advanced to me frankly, and held out her hand.

"My father told me you were like," she said, "but since your back was turned, I almost thought I saw him."

I took the hand by the finger-tips.

"He was very dear to you?"

"Very."

"Miss Curwen," said I, gravely, "I would, with all my heart, that you had seen him, and that I had died in his place at Malplaquet."

Her face clouded for an instant, and she drew her hand quickly away, taking my speech, no doubt, for nothing more than an awkward and ill-timed compliment. But compliment it was not, being, indeed, the truth and summary of my recent thoughts quickened into speech against my will. She was of a slender figure, with a rosebud face, delicate as her father's. Her hair was drawn simply back from a broad, white forehead, and in colour was nut-brown, gleaming where it took the light as though powdered with gold-dust. She was dressed in the simplest gown of white, set off here and there with a warm ribbon. But I took little note of her dress, beyond remarking that no other could so well become her. From the pure oval of her face, her eyes big and grey looked out at me, each like a quiet pool with a lanthorn lighted somewhere in its depths, and she seemed to me her voice incarnate. She was unlike to her father in the proportion of her height, for she was not tall—and like to him again in a certain wilfulness which the set of her lips betokened, and again unlike in the masterful firmness of her rounded chin; so that she could put off and on, with the quickest change of humours, the gravity of a woman and the sunny petulance of a child.

"It is our homely fashion," said Mr. Curwen, "to wait upon ourselves." And we sat down to the table.

It was a fashion, however, which the guest, much to his discomfort, was not that night allowed to follow. For father and daughter alike joined to show him courtesy. The daughter would have waited on me, even as Lady Derwentwater had done, and began, like her, to fill my glass. But this time I could not permit it.

"Madam," I cried hoarsely, "you must not Your kindness hurts me."

"Hurts you?" she asked, and from her tone I knew it was she who was hurt.

"You do not know. If you did, your kindness would turn to the bitterest contempt."

I spoke without thought and barely with knowledge of what I said, but in a passion of self-reproach.

"Mr. Clavering," she replied very gently, "you are overwrought, and I do not wonder. Else would you know that it must honour any woman to serve any man who has so served his King."

I dropped my head into my hands. My very soul rose against this praise.

"If I had served my King," I exclaimed in a despairing remorse, "I should have been in France this many a week back."

"France!" repeated Mr. Curwen, suddenly looking up. "You take the delay too much to heart. For it need be nothing more than a delay, and a brief one besides." He spoke with some significance in his tone. "Lord Derwentwater mentioned in his letter that he would discover a means to set you across in France, but perhaps"—and his voice became almost sly—"perhaps we may find a more expeditious way." He checked himself abruptly, like one that has said too much, and shot a timid glance towards his daughter. I noticed that her face grew a trifle grave, but she did not explain or comment on his words, and Mr. Curwen diverted his talk to indifferent topics. I fear me that I must have proved the dullest auditor, for I gave little heed to what he said, my thoughts being occupied in a quite other fashion. For since his daughter sat over against me at the table, since each time that I lifted my eyes, they must needs encounter hers; since each time that she spoke, the mere sound of her voice was as a stern rebuke; I fell from depth to depth of shame and humiliation. I was sheltering there under the same roof with her, to all seeming an honourable refugee, in very truth an impostor, and bound, moreover, to continue in his imposition. The very clothes which I was wearing forced the truth upon me. I had, indeed, but one thought wherewith to comfort me, and though the comfort was of the coldest, I yet clung to it as my only solace. The thought was this: that I had already determined, at whatsoever cost to me, whether of liberty or life, to repair, so far as a man could, the consequence of my misdoing. It was not that I took any credit from the resolve—I was not, thank God, so far fallen as that—but what comforted me was that I had come to the resolve up there on the hillside between Brandreth and Grey Knotts before I had descended into Ennerdale, before I had set foot within Applegarth; before, in a word, I had heard Dorothy Curwen sing or looked into her eyes. I did not explain to myself the comfort which the thought gave me; I was merely sensible of it. "It was before," I said to myself; and over and over again I gladly repeated the thought.

However, a word which Mr. Curwen spoke, finally aroused my attention, for he made mention of the garden of Blackladies. I suppose that I must by some movement have shown my distaste for the subject, and—

"You do not admire it," he said.

"It is very quaint and ingenious, no doubt," I replied, "but the ingenuity seems misplaced there."

Miss Curwen nodded.

"It is like a fine French ribbon on a homespun gown," said she.

I remembered on the instant something which Lord Derwentwater had said to me concerning Dorothy Curwen.

"You know Blackladies?" I inquired, and perhaps with some anxiety.

"Very well," said she, with a smile of amusement.

"So I thought," said I.

"Yes," she continued, "my father was very familiar with Sir John Rookley;" and her eyes rested quietly upon mine.

"A hard man, people said, Mr. Clavering," interrupted Mr. Curwen, "but a just man and to my liking. If he was hard, God knows he had enough in Jervas to make him so."

I glanced at the daughter. She was regarding the beams which roofed the room, with supreme unconsciousness, but the very moment that I looked at her she dropped her eyes to the level of mine.

"You lack something, Mr. Clavering," said she with great politeness.

"Indeed!" said my host, rising from his chair in the excess of his hospitality.

"Indeed, sir, no; I beg of you!" I replied in confusion. And Dorothy Curwen laughed.

"A strange man was Jervas Rookley," continued Mr. Curwen, and there could be no doubt whatever about the sincerity of his unconsciousness. "He came warped from his cradle. But you will have heard of him, I doubt not, more than we know, though at one time he honoured us not infrequently with his company. But that was before I knew of his transgression in the matter of the wad-mines."

"Oh," said I, "I thought that that was not generally known."

"Nor is it," replied Mr. Curwen. "I had the story from Sir John's lips. He was a very just man, and since Jervas came to visit me frequently, he thought that I ought to know."

Again my eyes went to the daughter's face. But this time she was already looking at me.

"I am sure, Mr. Clavering, that you need something," said she very anxiously.

"Indeed, no!" I replied in confusion.

And she smiled with the pleasantest air of contentment in the world.

Mr. Curwen did not on this occasion rise to satisfy my imaginary needs, but remained absorbed in thought.

"I suppose," he said dreamily, "that Jervas Rookley was a fairy's changeling."

I started at the words; they were not spoken in jest. I looked at him; he was seriously revolving the question in his mind.

"What do you think?" he asked of me.

His daughter bent forwards across the table with something of appeal in her eyes.

"The theory," said I, "would most easily explain him;" and the appeal in her eyes changed to gratitude.

This was not the only strange remark he made to me that night, for he accompanied me up to my bedroom and closed the door carefully behind him.

"By this time you should have been in France?" he asked, lowering his voice.

"Yes," said I, doubtfully. For since his Most Christian Majesty was at death's door, and all thought of a rising abandoned for the moment, there was no longer any call for me to hurry to Lorraine with the information I had gathered; while, on the other hand, there was the greatest need that I should remain in England, since once out of England I was powerless even to attempt anything towards Anthony Herbert's liberation.

"I spoke at supper," he continued in a yet more secret voice, "of a more expeditious way than Lord Derwentwater's." He glanced around him and came nearer to me. "It was no idle boast," he said with a little chuckle, "but I have a ship," and he nodded in a sort of childish guilefulness. "I have a ship." He went tip-toeing to the door as though already he had stayed too long. "Snug's the word," he whispered with a finger on his lip; and in the sweetest tone of encouragement, again, "I have a ship." And so he went gently from the room and descended the stairs.

His manner no less than his words somewhat bewildered me. I thought it, in truth, a very unlikely thing that he should possess a ship, seeing that he had made no concealment of his poverty, and that if indeed he did, his ship would be a very unlikely thing for a man to put to sea in. But in this I made a great mistake, since his ship not merely existed, but had a very considerable share in the issue from those misfortunes which were so soon to befall us. At the time, however, I was not greatly troubled with the matter one way or the other, for while Mr. Curwen had been speaking, I had been standing at the open window. The slope of the hillside was in front of me, a corner of the stable-roof was just visible to my left; but most clearly of all I saw as in a vision the picture of a woman seated in a lonely lodging at Keswick with a crumpled paper spread before her, whereon was scribbled one single line: "He is not dead." I shall not be particular to account for the reason why that vision should now of a sudden stand fixed within my sight, though I could give a very definite opinion concerning it I will only state that it was there, so vivid and distinct that I could read the paper she so sadly fingered; and reading it, the one line written thereon called on me for a supplement and explanation.

I opened the door and hurried quietly along the passage. I heard Mr. Curwen's step in the hall below, and holding my candle in my hand leaned over the balusters.

"Mr. Curwen," I said in a breathless whisper, "you told me of a horse which stood ready in your stables, should my safety call for it."

"Yes," said he looking up at me.

"There is the greatest need in the world that I should make use of your kindness this night. It is a need that imperils my safety, but my honour is concerned, or rather, that poor remnant of my honour which I have left to me. When I fled from Blackladies, there remained something to be done and to be done by me, and it remains undone. Some small part of the omission I may haply repair to-night."

He answered me, as I knew he would, with the strangeness gone from his manner and replaced with a kindly gravity. He was the truest of gentlemen, with all a gentleman's simple code of faith.

"Mr. Clavering," he said, "so long as you are my guest I am the trustee of your safety. But there are things of greater value than a man's safety, of which you have mentioned one. I shall look to seeing you in the morning."

He asked no questions; that word "honour" was enough for him; it stamped my purpose in his eyes with a holy seal. He came up the stairs towards me and shook me by the hand, and so passed on to his own chamber.

CHAPTER XII
I RETURN TO KESWICK

I went back to my own room, changed my dress, and carrying my boots in one hand and my candle in the other, went softly down the stairs. By the clock in the hall I could see that it was five minutes after ten o'clock. I drew on my boots in the porch, saddled the horse by the candle-light, led it past the house along a strip of grass, and when I thought the sound of its hoofs would be no longer heard, I mounted and rode up the pathway. The sky was cloudy but the valleys clear of mist I could have wished for no better night for my purpose except in one respect: I mean that now and again a silver brilliancy would be diffused through the air, making the night vaguely luminous. And looking up I would see a patch of cloud very thin and very bright, and behind that cloud I knew the moon was sailing. I chose that road of which Tash had spoken. Towards the head of Gillerthwaite the track turned northwards over a pass they call the Scarf Gap, and thence westwards again past Buttermere lake to Buttermere village. At the point where the hill descends steeply from the lake, I dismounted. I could see the scattered village beneath me. It slept without a sound, nor was there a light to be seen in any window. But none the less I dreaded to ride through it; its very quietude frightened me. I feared the lively echoes which the beat of my horse's shoes would send ringing about the silent cottages. I descended, therefore, on foot, leading my horse cautiously by the bridle, and in a little I came to a gateway upon the right which gave on to a field. I crossed the field and several others which adjoined it, and finally came out again upon the track beyond the village, where it climbs upwards to Buttermere Hause. From the farther side of the Hause I had a clear road of six miles down Newlands valley to Portinscale, and I spurred my horse to a gallop. Once or twice the clouds rifted and the moon shone out full, so that I rode in a tremor of alarm, twisting every shadow that fell across my path from rock or tree into the shadow of a sentinel. But the clouds closed up again and canopied me in a gracious obscurity as I drew near to Keswick.

I tied up my horse in a thicket of trees half a mile from the town, and slunk from house to house in the shadow. Never before or since have

I known such fear as I knew that night in Keswick, so urgent had the necessity that I must keep free, become with me during these last hours since I had climbed from Brandreth down to Applegarth. If the wind drove the leaves of the trees fluttering up the roadway, I cowered against the wall and trembled. If a dog barked from a farmhouse in the distance, I stood with my heart fainting in my breast, listening—listening for the rhythmic tread of soldiers; and when I saw on the opposite side of the street, some yards above me, a light glimmering in a window, I stopped altogether, in two minds whether or no to turn back. I looked irresolutely up and down the street It was so dark, so still; only that one steady light burned in a window. The melancholy voice of a watchman, a couple of streets away, chanted out, "Half-past twelve, and a dull, cloudy morning." The phrase was repeated and repeated in a dwindling tone. I waited until it had died away, and afterwards. But the light burned wakeful, persistent, a little heart of fire in a body of darkness. I felt that I dared not pass it. Some one watched beside that lamp, with eyes fixed on the yellow path it traced across the road. My fears fed upon themselves and swelled into a panic. I turned and took a step or two down the hill, and it was precisely that movement which brought me to my senses and revealed to me the cowardice of the action. For if I dared not pass that lamp, still less dared I return to Applegarth with the night's work undone. I retraced my steps very slowly until I came opposite to the window, and then, so great was the revulsion of my feeling that I reeled back against the wall, my heart jerking, my whole strength gone from me. For there at the window, beside the lamp, her face buried in her hands, was the woman I had come to seek. I might have known, I thought! For who else should be watching at this lone hour in Keswick if not this woman? I might have guessed from the position of the house in the street. It was a beacon which I had seen, this glimmering lamp, and I had taken it for no more than a wrecker's light.

I looked about me. The street was deserted from end to end I crossed it, and picking up a pebble flung it lightly at the window. The pebble cracked against the pane—how loudly, to my impatient ears! Mrs. Herbert raised her head from her hands. I sent a second pebble to follow the first. She opened the sash, but so noisily I thought!

"Who is it?" she asked.

"Hush!" said I.

She leaned forward over the side of the window and peered into the darkness.

"You!" she whispered in a tone of wonderment, and again with a shiver of repulsion; "you!"

"Let me in!" said I.

She made a movement as if to close the window.

"You close the window on your hopes," I said. "Let me in!"

"You bring news of—of Anthony?" she asked, with a catch in her voice.

"The smallest budget," said I, "but a promise of more;" and as she, undecided, still leaned on the sill, "If I am captured here to-night, there will be no news at all."

"Captured?" she began, and breaking off hurriedly came down the stairs and opened the door.

I followed her up into the room and drew the curtains across the window. She stood by the table in the full light of the lamp, her eyelids red, her eyes lustreless, her face worn; the very gloss seemed to have faded off her hair.

"How you have suffered!" I said, and again faltered the words, "How you have suffered!"

"And you?" she asked with a glance towards me, and nodded her head as though answering the question. "I said that payment would be made," she remarked simply. "It is beginning."

"My servant brought a note to you?"

"Yes. Was it true? I did not believe that it was true." She spoke in a dull voice. "He came yesterday night after the soldiers had been here."

"The soldiers," I cried, lifting my voice. The sound of it warned me; I realized that I was standing between the lamp and the window, and that if any one should pass down the street, it was my figure which would be seen. I crossed over to get behind the chair.

"Do you sit there!" said I, pointing to her former seat.

She obeyed me like a child.

"So the soldiers came here?"

"Twice."

"When?"

"The first time, that evening—I was not here—we were in the garden of Blackladies. They searched the house and took his papers away."

"His papers!" said I. I looked over to that box in which the medal had been locked. The lid was shut I crossed to it and tried it The lid lifted, the lock was broken and the medal gone.

"The second time they came," said Mrs. Herbert, "was the afternoon of the next day."

"That would be a few hours after I had escaped. They searched the house again?"

"Yes. For you."

"For me?" I exclaimed; and her eyes flashed out at me.

"For whom else should they come to search, here in my lodging?"

My eyes fell from her face.

"But did they question you?" I continued. "What did they ask? For perchance I may find help in that."

But Mrs. Herbert had relapsed into her dull insensibility.

"They questioned me without end," she answered wearily, "but I forget the questions. It was all concerning you, not a word about Anthony, and I forget."

"Oh, but think!" I exclaimed, and I heard the watchman crying the hour in the distance. I stopped, listening. The cry grew louder. The man was coming down the street. This window alone was lighted up, and once already the soldiers had been here to search for me. I heard the watchman's footsteps grow separate and distinct. I heard the rattle of his lantern as it swung in his hand, and beneath the window he stopped. I counted the seconds. In a little I found myself choking, and realized that in the greatness of my anxiety I was holding my breath. Then the man moved, but it seemed to me, not down the road, but nearer to the wall of the house. A new fear burst in on me.

"You left the door below unlocked?" I whispered to Mrs. Herbert.

She nodded a reply.

What if he opened that door and came stumbling up the stairs? What if he found the door not merely unlocked but open, and roused the house? To be sure he would have no warrant in his pocket. But for her sake—for the sake of that tiny chance I clung to with so despairing a grip, that perhaps—perhaps I might restore to her her husband, no rumour must go out that I or any man had been there this night I crept to the door of the room and laid my hand upon the handle. What I should do I did not think. I was trying to remember whether I had closed the door behind me, and all my faculties were engrossed in the effort I was still busy upon that profitless task, when I heard—with what relief!—the watchman's footsteps sound again upon the stones, his voice again take up its melancholy cry.

"Quick!" said I, turning again to Mrs. Herbert "Madam, help me in this matter, if you can. Think! The officer put to you questions concerning me?"

"Oh!" she cried, waking from her lethargy, "I cannot help you. You must save yourself, as best you may. I do not remember what they said. It was of you they spoke and not at all of Anthony."

"It is just for your husband's sake," I said, "that I implore you to remember."

And she looked at me blankly.

"God!" I exclaimed, taking the thought "You believe that I journeyed hither to you in your loneliness at this hour, to plague you with questions for my safety's sake!" And I paused, staring at her.

"Well," she replied, in an even voice, "is the belief so strange?"

There was no sarcasm in the question, and hardly any curiosity. It was the mere natural utterance of a natural thought. My eyes, I know, fell from her face to the floor.

"Madam," I replied slowly, "when I set out to-night, I thought that the cup of my humiliation was already full. You prove to me that my thought was wrong. It remained for you very fitly to fill it to the brim;" and again I lifted my eyes to her. "I had no purposes of my own to serve in riding hither. I know the charge against myself to its last letter. It is the charge against your husband brings me here. Neither do I know whither he has been taken. Yet these two things I must know, and I came to you on the chance that you might help me."

I saw her face change as she listened. She leaned forward on her elbows, her chin propped upon her hands, her eyes losing their indifference. A spark of hope kindled in the depths of them, and when I had ended, she remained silent for a little, as though fearing to quench that spark by the utterance of any words. At last she asked, in almost a timid voice:

"But why—why would you know?" And she bent still further forward with parted lips, breathless for the answer.

"Why?" I answered. "Forgive me! I should have told you that before, but, like a fool, I put the questions first. They are foremost in my thoughts, you see, being the means, and as yet unsolved. The end is so clear to me, that I forgot it in looking for the road which leads to it. I believe that Mr. Herbert has been seized, on the ground that he shares my—treason, let us call it, for so our judges will. Of that charge I know him innocent, and maybe can prove him so. And if I can, be sure of this—I will."

"But how can you?" she interrupted.

"If I know the charge, if I know whither he has been taken, the place of his trial, then it may be that I can serve him. But until I know, I am like one striking at random in the dark. Suppose I go to meet the sheriff and give myself up, not knowing these things, I shall be laid by the heels and no good done. They may have taken him to London. He may be in prison for months. Meanwhile I should be tried—and they would not need Mr. Herbert's evidence to secure a verdict against me."

"You would give yourself up?" she asked.

"But I must know the place, I must know the charge. It would avail your husband little without that knowledge. They would keep me in prison cozening me with excuses, however urgently I might plead for him. It is enough that a man should be suspected of favouring King James. To such they dispense convictions; they make no pother about justice."

"But," said she, "it would mean your life."

"Have you not said yourself that payment must be made?"

"Yes, but by us," she said, stretching out a hand eagerly. "Not by you alone."

"Madam," said I, "you will have your share in it, for you will have to wait—to wait here with such patience as you can command, ignorant of the issue until the issue is reached. God knows but I think you have the harder part of it."

We stood for a little looking into each other's eyes sealing our compact.

"Now," I continued, "think! Was any word said which we could shape into a clue? Was any name mentioned? Was your husband's name linked with mine? Oh, think, and quickly!"

She sat with her face covered by her hands while I stood anxiously before her.

"I do not remember," she said, drawing her hands apart and shaking them in a helpless gesture. "It all happened so long ago."

"It happened only yesterday," I urged.

"I know, I know," she said with the utmost weariness. All that light of hope had died from her eyes as quickly as it had brightened them. "But I measure by a calendar of pain. It is so long ago, I do not remember. I do not even remember how I returned here."

There was no hint plainly to be gained from her, and I had stayed too long, as it was. I took up my hat.

"You will stay here?" I asked. "I do not say that you will hear from me soon, but I must needs know where you are."

"I will stay here," she replied. She almost stretched out her hand and drew it in again. "Goodbye."

I went to the door. She followed me with the lamp and held it over the balusters of the landing.

"Nay," said I, "there is no need for that."

"The staircase," said she, "is very dark." As I came out from the houses at the bottom of the hill I heard again the watchman's voice behind me bawling out the hour. It was half-past one, and a cloudy morning, it may be, but the clouds were lighter in the north, as I remarked with some anxiety. I was still riding along Newlands valley when the morning began to break. As I reached the summit of Buttermere Hause I looked backwards over my shoulder. The sky in the north-east was a fiery glow, saffron, orange, and red were mingled there, and right across the medley of colours lay black, angry strips of cloud. The blaze of a fire, it seemed to me, seen through prison bars. It was daylight when I passed by Buttermere, sunlight as I rode down Gillerthwaite. The sweet stillness of the morning renewed my blood. The bracken bloomed upon the hillsides, here a rusty brown, there in the shadow a blackish purple, and then again gold where the sunlight kissed it Below me, by the water's side, I could see the blue tiles of Applegarth. And as I looked about me the fever of my thoughts died, they took a new and unfamiliar quietude from the stable quietude of the hills. I felt as if something of their patience, something of their strength was entering into me. My memories went back again to the Superior's study in the College at Paris; and in my heart of hearts I knew that the Superior was wrong. The mountains have their message, I think, for whoso will lend an ear to them, and that morning they seemed to speak to me with an unanimous voice. I can repair, I thought, this wrong. It was then more to me than a thought. It seemed, indeed, an assured and simple truth, assured and simple like those peaks in the clear air, and, like them, pointing skywards, and the Superior's theory no more substantial than a cloud which may gather upon the peaks and hide them for a little from the eyes.

I rode down, therefore, in a calmer spirit than I had known for some long time. The difficulties which beset my path did not for the moment trouble me. That my journey that night had in no way lightened them I did not consider. I felt that the occasion of which I was in search would of a surety come, only I must be ready to grasp it.

I had passed no one on the road. I had seen, indeed, no sign of life at all beyond the sudden rush of a flock of sheep, as though in an unaccountable panic, up the hillside of the Pillar mountain, while I was as yet in the narrow path of Gillerthwaite. I had reason, therefore, to think that I had escaped all notice, and leading the horse back to the stable with the same precautions I had used on setting out, I let myself in at the door and got quietly to bed.

CHAPTER XIII
DOROTHY CURWEN

I was at the breakfast-table, you may be sure, that morning no later than my host and his daughter. Mr. Curwen greeted me with an evident relief, but neither then nor afterwards did he ever refer to the journey I had taken during the night. On the contrary, his talk was all of Paris and France, plying me with many questions concerning the French generals, the Duc de Vendôme, Maréchal Villars, the Duc de Noailles, and the rest which I was at some loss to answer. Often and often would he return to that subject with something of a boyish zest and enthusiasm. He had never been in France, he informed me, yet would tell me many stories concerning the Court and the magnificence of Versailles and the great hunting-parties at Meudon when Monsieur was alive, with so much detail that but for a certain extravagance, as of one whose curiosity, through much feeding upon itself, has grown fantastic, I could not but have believed that he had himself been present at their enactment. And then he would light his pipe and look across this quiet Ennerdale water to the rugged slopes beyond, with a sigh, and so get him back to his romances. He was no less curious concerning Lorraine and the little Court at Bar-le-Duc; and when I told him that I had myself had speech with the King, his enthusiasm rose to excitement.

"Oh!" he cried, starting up, "you have seen him? you have heard his voice speaking to you, as you hear mine now?" and all at once I acquired a new honour in his eyes. "Mr. Clavering, you have something to compensate you for your outlawry."

"Yes," I replied, "he spoke to me and with the sweetest kindliness."

"And the King was hopeful—was positive in his hopes?"

"Very."

"That is right," he continued, walking about the room and smiling to himself. "That is right So a strong man should be."

"And so weak men are," said I rather sadly, for I recalled all that Lord Bolingbroke had told me.

"Mr. Clavering," said the old gentleman, suddenly pausing in his walk, "you are the last man who should say that. You have lost all that a man holds dear, and are you not hopeful?"

I bowed my head to the rebuke. It was, indeed, well-timed and just, though for a very different reason than that which had inspired Mr. Curwen to utter it.

"I was so," said I humbly, "so lately as this morning. Nay," and I rose to my feet, "I am so still. Besides," I continued, reverting to the King, "he has Lord Bolingbroke to help him, and I set great store on that."

"Bolingbroke!" cried Mr. Curwen, and seldom have I seen a man's face change so suddenly. A flame of anger kindled in his eyes and blazed across his face, shrivelling all the gentleness which made its home there. "Bolingbroke!" he cried wildly—"a knave! a debauched, villainous knave! God help the man, be he king or serf, that takes his counsel! Look you, Mr. Clavering, a very dishonest, treacherous knave;" and he wagged his head at me. I was astonished at the outburst, since the Jacobites were wont to look with some deference towards Lord Bolingbroke.

"He is my kinsman," I said meekly, "and a very good friend to me;" and while Mr. Curwen was still humming and hawing in some confusion, his daughter came into the room, and gazing at his troubled face with some anxiety, put an end to the talk.

This was by no means, however, the last I was to hear of the matter, and in truth Lord Bolingbroke, through merely arousing Mr. Curwen's indignation, was to prove a much better friend to me than ever I had looked for. For when we were again alone together:

"I regret the words I spoke to you," he said a little stiffly and with considerable effort in the apology. "I did not know Lord Bolingbroke was your kinsman;" and then in a rush of sincerity: "But far more than the words, I regret your relationship with the man."

I began to make such defence of my kinsman as I could, pointing to his industry, and declaring how his services had always been thwarted by his colleagues while he was in power.

"And what of the Catalans?" he asked.

Now, I knew very little about the Catalans.

"Well, what of the Catalans?" I asked doubtfully.

"Why, this," he returned. "We instigated them to war; we made them our allies against Philip of Spain by the promise of restoring them their ancient liberties. They fought with us, spilled their blood on the strength of that promise, and then Lord Bolingbroke patches up his peace of Utrecht, and not a word in it from end to end about their liberties. They continue the war alone, and he finds nothing better to do than to sneer at their obstinacy. They still continue, and he is ready to send an English fleet to help in their destruction."

His voice increased in vehemence with every word he spoke, so that I feared each moment another outburst against my kinsman. It may be that he feared it too, for he checked himself with some abruptness, and it was his daughter who revived the subject later on during that same day.

It was after dinner. I had taken a book with me, and climbed up to the orchard behind the house. But little I read in the book. The sun had set behind the hills, but the brightness of that morning lingered on my thoughts. I was, as Mr. Curwen had said, hopeful, though with no great reason, and being besides weary with the fatigue I had undergone, fell into a restful state between sleep and waking. With half-closed eyes I saw Dorothy Curwen come from the back of the house, and talk for a little with Mary Tyson. Then she mounted towards the orchard. I watched her, marked the lightness of her step, the supple carriage of her figure, the delicate poise of her head, and then rose from the grass and went forward to meet her.

"Mr. Clavering," she began very decidedly, and paused in some difficulty. Then she stamped her foot with a little imperious movement. "You talk too much of France and Paris and the great world to my father. You will not do so any more."

She spoke with the prettiest air of command imaginable the while she looked up at me, and it was the air I smiled at, not the command.

"No!" she said, "I mean it. You will not do so any more;" and she coloured a little and spoke with a yet stronger emphasis.

"Madam," said I with a bow, "since you wish it— —"

"I do wish it, Mr. Clavering," she interrupted me.

"I did not think— —" I began.

"No," says she, "you are young and imprudent. I have noticed that already." And with great stateliness and dignity she walked for ten yards down the hillside. Then she began to hum a tune, and laughed as though mightily pleased with herself and her stately walk changed to a dance. A few yards further on, she sat down in the bracken with her back towards me and began plucking at the grasses. I remained where she had left me, quite content to watch from that distance the coils of hair nestling about her head, and to hearken to the rippling music of her song. But after a little she turned her head with a glance across her shoulder towards me, and so back again very quickly. I went down to her.

"The lecture is not ended?" said I, gravely.

She gave a start and looked at me, as though my presence there was the last thing she expected, or indeed wished for. Then in an instant her whole manner changed.

"I will tell you the truth of it," she said. "Something you will perhaps have guessed already, the rest you would discover did not I tell you."

I sat down by her side, and she continued, choosing her words.

"My father is not altogether—strong, and these stories do no good." Then she stopped. "It is more difficult to tell you than I thought."

"There is no need," said I, "that you should say another word."

"Thank you," said she very gratefully; and for a little we were silent.

"Has he spoken to you of a ship?" she asked slowly; and I started. "Ah! he thinks it is a secret from us. But we know, for he sold the land not so long ago wherewith to buy it He is the noblest man in the world," she continued hurriedly. "The thought of any one suffering touches him to the quick; the thought of oppression kindles him to anger, and he will do his part, and more than his part, in relieving the one and fighting against the other. So that unless Mary and I did what we could, he would not possess to-day so much as a farthing."

"I understand," said I, "Mary's welcome to me yesterday."

She looked at me with a smile.

"Yes," said she, "but your looks warranted her. The ship was to be fitted out to help the Catalans. It lies at Whitehaven now. He was there but a few days ago."

"He spoke of it to me," said I, "with some hint that he might put me across to France."

"But you will not go?" she said, turning to me quickly. "Any day the country may rise and every arm will be needed—I mean every young arm."

I shook my head.

"The French King is dying, maybe is dead, and without his help will the country rise? Besides, so long as I stay here, I endanger you."

I spoke reluctantly enough, for though I had no intention whatever to seek a refuge in France, I felt that if once Mr. Curwen definitely promised to send me thither, I could not remain at Applegarth at however small a risk to him and his. I must needs accept the offer and—betake me again to the hillside, in which case there was little probability that I should be able to effect anything towards Anthony Herbert's enlargement before I was captured myself.

"There is no danger to us," she said. "For, some while since, we persuaded my father to take no active share in the plans. There will be no danger," and she stopped for a second, "if you will put out your candle when next you leave it in the stables."

"My candle?" I stammered, taken aback by her words. "I left it burning?"

"Last night," said she.

"I beg your pardon."

"There is very great reason that you should," she said with a laugh. "For I must needs hurry on my clothes and put it out. As I said, you are very imprudent, Mr. Clavering;" and with that she tripped down to the house, leaving me not so much concerned with what she had hinted about her father, as with my own immediate need to secure the knowledge I was after quickly, and avert by my departure the smallest risk from Applegarth.

I was on that account the more relieved when, late upon the third night afterwards, Tash knocked at the door, and brought me a letter from Lord Derwentwater. I opened it eagerly, and read it through. It told me much which is common knowledge now, as that the Earl of Mar had summoned his friends in Scotland to meet him at Aboyne on the 27th, upon the pretext of a great hunting-party; that the mug-house riots in London were daily increasing in number and violence; but that with the French King, so near to his dissolution, and the precautions of the English Government in bringing over Dutch troops, and thronging the Channel with its ships, Lord Bolingbroke was all for delay. "But God knows," he added, "whether delay is any possible, and I fear for the event. We have many of the nobles on our side—but the body of our countrymen? It will be like a game of chess in which one side plays without pawns. We have Bishops and Knights and Castles, but no pawns."

There was more of the same kind, and I glanced through it hurriedly, until I came to that of which I was more particularly in search.

"The sheriff came with his posse to Lord's Island in the morning, so that it was well you left during the night. He is still after you. I passed his messenger yesterday near Braithwaite, so it behoves you to be wary. I do not think, however, he has winded you as yet, and as soon as I can discover an occasion I will have you sent over the water. But being myself under the cloud of their suspicions, I have to step very deliberately. Your cousin, Jervas Rookley, lives openly under his own name at Blackladies, and receives visits from the Whig attorney; and since he can only be staying there with the sufferance of the Government, you may be certain what I told you is true. By the way, Mr. Anthony Herbert, the painter, disappeared on the same day or thereabouts that you did. It is rumoured that he has been arrested, but nothing certain is known. But if the rumour is true I greatly fear that he owes his arrest to his acquaintanceship with you and myself. I suspect Mr. Rookley's finger in the pie. Since he was playing false with the Government concerning you, he would most likely be anxious to give them an earnest of loyalty in some other matter. But I do not know."

So far I read and clapped the letter down with a bang. For here was the fellow to my own suspicion.

I sat down and finished the letter. There was but another line to it.

"I got my information about Rookley from an oldish man who came secretly here from Blackladies. He seemed in some doubt as to which of yourself or your cousin he should call master, but he was very insistent that I should let you know of his coming. I had, indeed, some difficulty in comprehending him, for now he wished me to style him 'Aron' to you and now 'Ashlock.' Altogether I thought it wiser to give him no news as to your whereabouts. This, however, is certain, from what he said to me—there is a watch set about Blackladies on the chance that you might return."

This last sentence troubled me exceedingly. For it had been growing in my mind that there was but one person who could tell me fully what I needed to know, and that person Mr. Jervas Rookley; and a vague purpose was gradually taking shape within me that I would once more make use of Mr. Curwen's stables, and riding one night round by Newlands valley and Keswick, seek to take Mr. Rookley by surprise, and wrest the truth from him. That project the letter seemed to strike dead. Accordingly I took the occasion to write to Lord Derwentwater, and implored him, if by any means he could, to inform himself more particularly of Anthony Herbert's arrest, and whither he had been taken. "For upon these two points," said I, "hangs not my safety, but my soul's salvation;" and so hurried Tash off before the poor man was halfway through his supper, and waited impatiently for an answer.

Now, during this period of waiting, since each time that I found myself alone with Mr. Curwen, his talk would wander back inquisitively to the French Court, discovering there a lustre which no doubt it had, and a chivalry which it no less certainly lacked, I began of a set purpose to avoid him; and avoiding him, was thrown the more into the company of Miss Dorothy. Moreover, the frankness with which she had hinted to me the weakness of her father, brought about a closer intimacy between us as of friend and friend rather than as of hostess and guest. It was as though Mary Tyson and she were continually building up out of their love a fence around the father, and she had joined me in the work.

Many a time, when I was on the hillside behind the house I would be startled by the sight of a horse and the flash of a red-coat upon the horse's back, only to find my heart drumming yet the faster when I perceived that it was Miss Dorothy Curwen in her red cramoisie riding-habit. Maybe I would be standing no great distance from the house, and she would see me and come up the grass while I went down towards her, her hair straying about her ears and forehead in the sweetest disorder, and her cheeks wind-whipped to the rosiest pink. On the wet days, which were by no means infrequent, she would sit at her spinet and sing such old songs as that I had listened to on the first night of my coming. If the evenings were fine, we would sometimes row out upon Ennerdale water, in a crazy battered boat, so that I was more often baling out the leakage in a tin pannikin than pulling at the oars. And on afternoons, when the sunlight fell through the leaves like great spots of a gold rain we would climb up to the orchard, and I would spread an old cloak for her upon the grass, and we would sit amongst the crabbed trunks of trees. But at all times—in the dusk, when she sang and the rain whipped the panes; at night, when we rowed across the moonlit lake as across a silver mirror, in the hush of a world asleep—at all times a feverish impatience would seize on me for an answer to my letter, and a shadow would darken across our talk, so that thereafter I sat mum and glooming and heard little that was said to me. It was not, indeed, the shadow of the gallows, but rather of the fear lest while I lingered here at Applegarth, chance might thwart me of the gallows. For the girl's presence was to me as a perpetual accusation.

Upon one such occasion, when we were together in the orchard, she looked at me once or twice curiously.

"For one so imprudent," said she, a trifle petulantly, "you are extraordinary solemn."

"There are creatures," said I, with a wearified shake of the head, "who are by nature solemn."

"True," says she, placidly, "but even they hoot at night;" and she looked across the valley with extreme unconsciousness. But I noticed that her mouth dimpled at the corners as if she was very pleased.

"I know," said I, remorsefully, "that I make the dullest of companions."

She nodded her head in cordial agreement

"Perhaps you cannot help it," says she, with great sympathy.

"The truth is," I exclaimed sharply, "I have overmuch to make me solemn."

"No doubt," and the sympathy deepened in her voice, "and I am sure every one must pity you. There was a king once who never smiled again. I am sure every one pitied him too."

"He only lost a son," I replied foolishly, meaning thereby that honour was a thing of more worth.

"And you an estate," says she. "It is indeed very true," and she clasped her hands and shook her head.

"Madam," I returned with some dignity, "you put words into my mouth that I had no thought of using. It was not of a mere estate that I was speaking."

"No?" says she reflectively. "Could it be a heart, then? Dear! dear! this is very tragical."

"No," I said very quickly; and on the instant fell to stammering "No, no."

"The word gains little force from repetition. In fact, I have heard that two noes make a yes."

"Madam," said I stiffly, getting to my feet, "you persist in misunderstanding me;" and I moved a step or two apart from her.

"I do not know," she said demurely, "that you use any great effort to prevent the mistake."

That I felt to be true. I wondered for a moment whether she had not a right to know, and I turned back to her. She was sitting with her head cocked on one side and glancing whimsically towards me from the tail of her eye. The glance became, on the instant, the blankest of uninterested looks. I plumped down again on the grass.

"That evening," I began, "when I left the candle burning in the stables, I rode into Keswick. There was something I should have done before I came hither," and I stumbled over the words.

She took me up immediately with a haughty indifference, and her chin very high in the air.

"Nay, I have no desire to pry into your secrets—not the least in the world."

"Oh," said I, "I fancied you were curious."

"Curious?" she exclaimed, with a flash of her eyes. "Curious, indeed! And why should I be curious about your concerns, if you please?" And she spoke the word again with a laugh of scorn, "Curious!"

Said I, "The word gains no force from repetition."

Dorothy Curwen gasped with indignation.

"A very witty and polite rejoinder, upon my word," she said slowly, and began to repeat that remark too, but broke off at the second word.

For a little we were silent. Then she plucked a reed of grass and bit it pensively.

"No!" she said indifferently, "since my father has lived quietly at Applegarth, I have lost my interest in politics."

"It was no question of politics at all!" I exclaimed, and—

"Oh!" she exclaimed, swinging round to me with all her indifference gone.

"No," I went on, but reluctantly, for I was no longer sure that I ought to tell her, and quibbled accordingly. "There was some one in Keswick for whom I had news which would not wait."

"News of your escape?" she interposed, with a certain constraint in her voice.

"Partly that," I replied, and continued, "and from whom I most heartily desired news."

She sat for a moment with her face averted and very still.

"And what is she like?" she asked of a sudden.

The question startled me so that I jumped and stared at her open-mouthed. But by the time I had fashioned an answer, she had no longer any need for it For "No! No!" she exclaimed. "I have no wish to hear;" and she fell unaccountably to talking of Jervas Rookley, at first in something of a flurry, and afterwards in a tone as though she found great comfort in the thought of him. "He is not so black as he is painted," was the burden of her speech, and she played many variations on the tune.

Now, I had in my pocket a certain letter from Lord Derwentwater, which was a clear disproof of her words, and, to speak the truth, her manner stung me. For whatever part of my misfortunes I did not owe to myself, that I owed to Mr. Jervas Rookley.

"And I never could bring myself to believe that story of the wad-mines," she said. "Never! Ah, poor man! What will he be doing now? It is a thought which often troubles me, Mr. Clavering. Doubtless he is somewhere tossed upon the sea. It is a very noble life, a sailor's. There is no nobler, is there?" and she asked the question as if she had no doubt whatever but that I should agree with her.

"I know nothing of that," I replied in some heat, "but as for the wadmines I know that story to be true, for I have seen the shaft."

She shook her head at me with an air of disappointment. It seemed she thought I was slandering the man after slipping into his shoes. I whipped the letter out of my pocket and thrust it before her.

"There, Madam, there!" I exclaimed. "The thought of Mr. Rookley need no longer trouble you. I am glad, indeed, to have the opportunity of disposing of your trouble. It will be the one moment's satisfaction the man has given me. He is nowhere tossed upon the sea, in that noblest of all lives, as you will be able to perceive for yourself, if you will glance through this letter, but, on the contrary, sitting quietly in an armchair in whatever room at Blackladies pleases him best."

"I am not so short of sight," she observed sedately, "that I need the paper to be rubbed against my nose."

She took it and read it through once and a second time. I told her the story of my dealings with Mr. Rookley, from the moment of his coming to me at the Jesuit College in Paris, to the morning when I fled from Blackladies, and so much of his dealings with me as I was familiar with. It was, in fact, much the same story that I had told to my Lord and Lady Derwentwater, and contained little mention of Mr. Herbert, except the fact that he was painting my portrait, and no mention whatsoever of Mr. Herbert's wife. For I found that the whole account of my proceedings since I had come to England, fell very naturally into two halves, each of which to all seeming was in itself complete. She heard me out to the end, and then in low, penitent voice, for which it seemed to me there was no occasion—

"I knew nothing of this," she said, "or I would never so much as have uttered Mr. Rookley's name. I could not know. You will bear me out in this; I could not know." And she turned to me with the sweetest appeal in her grey eyes and a hand timidly outstretched.

"Indeed," said I, earnestly, "I will. You could not know, and I can well believe Mr. Jervas Rookley's conduct was very different to you." With that I took her hand, and again took it gingerly by the finger-tips. Thereupon she snatched it away, and got quickly to her feet.

"And for whom——" she began, and stopped, while she very deliberately fastened a button of her glove which was already buttoned.

"For whom—what?" said I.

"It is no matter," she said carelessly, and then, "For whom was the picture intended?" and as though she was half-ashamed of the question, she ran lightly down the hillside without waiting for an answer.

"For no one," I cried out after her. "It was intended to hang in the great hall of Blackladies." But she descended into the house, and I—I passed through the orchard and up the hillside behind it, and over the crest of the fell, until ridge upon ridge opened out beneath the overarching sky, and the valleys between them became so many furrows drawn by a giant's plough. And coming into that great space and solitude where no tree waved, no living thing moved, no human sound was heard, I dropped upon the ground, pressing a throbbing face down among the cool bracken, and twining my fingers about the roots of ferns. It was the blackest hour that had ever till then befallen me; mercifully I could not know that it was but a foretaste of others yet blacker which were to follow. Something very new and strange was stirring within me; I loved her. The truth was out that afternoon. I think it was her questioning which taught it me. For it brought Mrs. Herbert into my thoughts, and so I learned this truth by the bitterest of all comparisons. I saw the two faces side by side, and then the one vanished and the other remained. Here, I thought, was my life just beginning to take some soul of meaning; here was its usual drab a-flush with that rosy light, as of all the sunrises and all the sunsets which had ever brightened across the world— and I must give it up, and through my own fault. There was the hardest part of the business—through my own fault! The knowledge stung and ached at my heart intolerably. There was nothing heroical in the reparation which I purposed; here was no laying down of one's life at the feet of one's mistress, with a blithe heart and even a gratitude for the occasion, such as I had read of in Mr. Curwen's romances—and how easy that seemed to me at this moment!—it was the mere necessary payment for a sordid act of shame.

It was drawing towards night when I rose to my feet and came down the mountain-side to Applegarth, and, as the outcome of my torturing reflections, one conviction, fixed very clearly in my mind before, had gained an added impulsion. I must needs hasten on this reparation. It was not, I am certain, the fear that delay in the fulfilment would weaken my purpose, which any longer spurred me; but of those two faces which had made my comparison: one, as I say, had vanished from my thoughts, the other now occupied them altogether, and it seemed to me that if by any chance I missed the opportunity of atonement, I should be doing the owner of that face an irreparable wrong.

Miss Dorothy Curwen came late from her room to supper, and the moment she entered the parlour where Mr. Curwen and I were waiting, it appeared that something had gone amiss with her, and that we were in consequence to suffer. Her face was pale and tired, her eyes hostile, and asperity was figured in the tight curve of her lips. From the crown of her head to the toe-tips, she was panoplied in aggression, so that the very ribands seemed to bristle on her dress.

It was plain, too, that she did but wait her opportunity. Mr. Curwen provided it by a question as to her looks, and a suggestion that her health was disordered.

"No wonder," says she, and "Not a doubt of it." She snatched the occasion with both hands as it were, and said, I think, more than she intended. "I am much troubled by an owl that keeps me from my proper sleep."

"An owl?" asked Mr. Curwen, with an innocent sympathy.

"An owl?" I asked in a sudden heat.

Her eyes met mine, very cold and blank.

"O-w-l," she answered, spelling the word deliberately.

I could not think what had caused this sudden change in her.

"But, my dear," said Mr. Curwen in perplexity, "are you certain you have made no mistake?"

"Oh no, sir, there will be no mistake," says I, indignantly, or ever she could open her lips. But, indeed, I do not know whether in any case she would have opened them or not. For her face was like a mask.

"But I did not know there was an owl at Applegarth," says he.

"He is a new-comer," says I; "but you may take my word for it, there is an owl at Applegarth—a tedious, solemn owl."

Miss Dorothy nodded her head quietly at each epithet, and her action much increased my anger.

"Then you have heard it, Mr. Clavering," says Mr. Curwen; and "Indeed I have," I cried in a greater heat than ever, for I noticed a certain contentment begin to steal over the girl's face at each fresh evidence of my rage. "Indeed I have—under the eaves at my bedroom window."

"But, my dear Mr. Clavering," expostulated Mr. Curwen, "what sort of an owl is it?"

"A very uncommon owl," said I.

"Oh dear no, not at all," said Miss Curwen, stonily, with a lift of her eyebrows.

"Well, we will have him out to-morrow," says the father.

"No, sir, to-night," says I, "this very night"

Dorothy gave a start and looked at me with a trace of anxiety.

"Yes," I repeated significantly, wagging my head in a fury, "to-night— no later."

"Oh, but I like owls," cried she of a sudden. "That can hardly be," I insisted, looking hard at her, "since they keep you awake o' nights."

At that she coloured and dropped her eyes from my face.

"Perhaps I exaggerated," she said weakly, and sat smoothing the table-cloth on each side of her with her fingers. She glanced up at me. I was still looking at her. She glanced from me to her father. He was waiting for her answer, utterly at a loss.

"But I like owls," she said again in a queer little, high-pitched, plaintive voice; and somehow I began to laugh, and in a moment she was laughing too. "You make too much of the trouble," said she.

"We will have him out to-morrow," said Mr. Curwen; and again she laughed, but with something of mischief, so that though for that night there the matter dropped, I suspected she had devised some plan by which I was to suffer a penalty for her present discomfiture. And that suspicion I found to be true no later than the next morning.

For while we were yet at breakfast, Mr. Curwen returned to the subject, and was for sending out Mary Tyson to fetch in one of the shepherds in order to oust the bird.

"Yes, indeed," cries Dorothy, with a delighted little clap of the hands and a quick meaning glance at Mary Tyson.

The shepherds were all on the hillside; not one of them was within reach, said Mary, with suspicious promptitude.

"But we have a ladder," said Dorothy, speaking at me, and her eyes sparkling and dancing.

I made as though I had not heard the suggestion.

"Then I will myself hunt him out," said Mr. Curwen, with a ready eagerness to make proof of his activity.

"Father, that cannot be," says she. "It would put us to shame. Rather I will take it in hand;" and again she looked at me.

There was no escape.

"It is a duty which naturally falls to me," said I, not with the best grace in the world.

"Nay," said she, "we cannot admit of duties in our guests. It must be a pleasure to you before we allow you to undertake it."

"Then it will be a pleasure," I agreed lamely.

"We will endeavour to make it one," she replied, with a malicious nod of the head.

I tried, you may be sure, to defer this chase for an owl which I knew did not exist, and hoped by talking very volubly upon other topics to drive the thought of it from their minds, and to that end lingered over my breakfast, even after the rest had for some while finished. But the moment we did rise from the table: "There is no time like present," hinted Dorothy, plainly; and Mr. Curwen warmly seconding her—for he began to show something of excitement, like a child when some new distraction is offered to it—I fetched the ladder from an outhouse and reared it against the wall of Applegarth, at a spot she pointed out close to my window. Accordingly I mounted, the while Mr. Curwen and his daughter remained at the foot—he quite elated, she very sedate and serious. But no sooner had I reached the topmost rungs, than Dorothy discovers the nest a good twenty feet away; and I must needs descend, like the merest fool, shift the ladder, and mount again. And when once more I was at the top, she discovers it at a third place, and so on through the morning. I know not how many times I ran up and down that accursed ladder, but my knees ached until I thought they would break. Once or twice I stopped, as if I would have no more of it, whereupon she covered me with the tenderest apologies and regrets.

"But it is a farce," said I, laughing in spite of myself.

"Of course you are very tired," said she, reproachfully. "It is a shame that I should put you to so much trouble;" and she pops her foot upon the lowest rung of the ladder. So there was no other course, but up I must go again, until at last she was satisfied, and I beaten with fatigue.

"It is a strange thing," said Mr. Curwen, scratching his forehead, "that we cannot discover it."

"I fancy Mr. Clavering was right," says she, with a bubble of delight, "and it is a very uncommon owl."

And I was allowed to carry the ladder back to the outhouse.

CHAPTER XIV
I DROP THE CLOAK

The lesson, however, was lost on me, or rather, to speak by the book, had the very reverse effect to that it aimed at. For my solemnity was increased thereby. I reflected that Dorothy would never have played this trick upon an enemy, or even upon an unconsidered acquaintance, but only upon one whom she thought of as a friend. And there was the trouble. I held her in that reverence that it irked me intolerably to masquerade to her, though the masquerading was to my present advantage in her esteem. I had, of course, no thought that ever I could win her, since I saw myself hourly either doomed to the gallows, or, if I failed of that, to a more disgraceful existence. But I was fain that she should know me through and through for no better than I was; and so I wore her friendship as a stolen cloak.

Now, a thief, if the cloak galls him, may restore it. That I could not do without telling her the whole story; and the story I could not tell, since it was not I alone whose honour was concerned in it, but a woman with me. Or the thief may drop the cloak by the roadside without a word, and get him into the night. Over that alternative I pondered a long, dreary while.

But while I was yet tossed amidst these perplexities, news came to hand which quite turned the current of my thoughts. It was the 18th day of September, and Mr. Curwen, I remember, had left Applegarth early that morning on horseback, and, though it was now past nightfall, had not yet returned; the which was causing both his daughter and myself no small uneasiness at the very time when Tash rapped upon the door. He brought me a letter. I mind me that I stood in the hall staring in front of me, holding the open letter in my hand. It seemed that I saw the lock fall from a door, and the door opening on an unimagined dawn.

"What is it?" cried Dorothy, and for a second she laid a gentle hand upon my arm.

"It is," I exclaimed, drawing in a breath, "it is that the Earl of Mar—the duke, God bless him! for now one may give him his proper title—has raised King James's standard at Kirkmichael in Braemar."

Dorothy gave a cry of delight, and I joined in with it. For if the duke did but descend into England, if England did but rise to welcome him—why, there would be the briefest imprisonment for those lying under charge, whether true or false, of conspiring for King James.

Through the open doorway sounded the tramp of a horse.

"My father!" said Dorothy.

I crammed the letter into my pocket without a glance at its conclusion, and ran down the pathway to the gate. As I opened the gate Mr. Curwen rode up to it.

"I am glad to have this chance of speaking to you alone," said he, as he dismounted. "I have been to-day to Whitehaven. My ship, the *Swallow*, is fitting out I have given orders that the work should be hurried, and the crew shipped with the least delay. The Swallow will sail the first moment possible, and lie off Ravenglass until you come. It is an arduous journey from here to Ravenglass, but safe."

A farm-servant came up and led away the horse.

"The *Swallow* should be at Ravenglass in six weeks from to-day," he continued.

"But, sir," said I in a whisper, though I felt an impulse to cry the news out, "there will be no need, I trust, for the *Swallow*. There is the grandest news to tell you;" and I informed him of the contents of my letter.

Mr. Curwen said never a word to me, but dropped upon his knees in the pathway.

"God save the King!" he cried in a quavering voice, and the fervour of it startled me. His hands were clasped and lifted up before him, and by the starlight I saw that there were tears upon his cheek. Then he stood up again and mopped his face with his handkerchief, leaning against the palings of the garden fence. "Mr. Clavering, I could add with a full heart, 'Now lettest Thou Thy servant depart in peace,' but that there is work even for an arm as old and feeble as mine." At that he stopped, and asked, in a very different tone of trepidation, "Does Mary Tyson know?"

"Miss Dorothy does."

"Ah, of course, of course," he said with resignation, "It is all one;" and he walked slowly up the path. At the door he turned to me, and set a hand on my shoulder. "There is work, Mr. Clavering, for the feeblest arm?" he asked wistfully.

Now, all my instincts urged me to say "Yes," but, on the other hand, I remembered certain orders which had been given to me in a very decided voice, so that I stood silent. With a sorrowful shake of the head, Mr. Curwen passed through the door.

"Maybe you are right," said he, disconsolately; and then, "But the question is worth proving"—this bracing his shoulders and making a cut in the air with an imaginary sabre. However, Mary Tyson bustled forward to help him off with his great-coat, and scolded all the boldness out of him in the space of a minute, drawing such a picture of the anxiety into which his early outgoing and late home-coming had thrown the household, as melted him to humility.

"It was to do me a service," said I, interposing myself.

"And the more shame to you," says she, bluntly; "white hairs must wait on young legs!" and off she flung to the kitchen.

It was not until the following morning that Dorothy made allusion to his absence.

"I went on business to Whitehaven," he replied with a prodigious wink at me, which twisted the whole side of his face—his daughter could not but have observed it—"though the business might have waited;" and he added hurriedly, "However, I bring a message for you, my dear, for I chanced to meet old Mr. Aislabie in the street, and he sent his love to Miss Cherry-cheeks."

"Cherry-cheeks!" cried she, indignantly, "Cherry-cheeks! How dare he? Is it a bumpkin, a fat country milk-maid he takes me for?"

"My dear," said Mr. Curwen, with the gentlest spice of raillery, "you certainly deserve the charming title now."

She said no more concerning the journey to Whitehaven, being much occupied with her indignation. Once or twice I heard her mutter, "Cherry-cheeks!" to herself, but with a tone as though her tongue was too delicate for the gross epithet, and, as if to disprove its suitability, she sailed in to dinner that day with her hair all piled and builded on the top of her head under a little cap of lace, and a great hoop petticoat of silk, and the funniest little shoes of green and gold brocade with wonderful big paste buckles and the highest heels that ever I saw. Nor was that the whole of her protest. For though, as a rule, she was of a healthy, sensible appetite, now she would only toy with her meat, protesting that she could not eat a bit.

"I have no doubt," says I, "but what you are troubled with the vapours," and got a haughty glance of contempt for my pains. And after dinner what does she do but sit in great state in the drawing-room, with her little feet daintily crossed upon a velvet cushion, fanning herself languidly, and talking of French gowns, as the latest Newsletter represented them, and the staleness of matrimony, and such-like fashionable matters.

"But no doubt," says she with a shrug of the shoulders, and a pretty voice of insolence, "Mr. Clavering will marry;" she paused for a second. "And what will the wife be like?"

I was taken aback by the question, and from looking on her face, I looked to the ground or rather to the velvet cushion by which I happened to be sitting. It was for that reason, that not knowing clearly what I should say, I answered absently—

"She must have a foot."

"I suppose so," she replied, "and why not two?"

"Yes!" I continued slowly, "she must certainly have a foot."

"And maybe a head with eyes and a mouth to it," says she; "or does not your modesty ask so much?"

"I wonder you can walk on them at all," said I.

The heels were popped on the instant demurely under the hoop petticoat.

"Owl," she said in a very soft, low, reflective voice, addressing the word in a sort of general way to the four walls of the room.

"Miss Cherry-cheeks," said I, in as near the same tone as I could manage.

She rose immediately, the very figure of stateliness and dignity, swam out of the room, without so much as a word or a nod, and, I must suppose, went hungry to bed; for we saw no more of her that night.

For the next few days, as may be guessed, we lived in a great excitement and stress of expectation at Applegarth. Mr. Curwen would get him to his horse early of the morning, now rather encouraged thereto than dissuaded, and ride hither and thither about the country side, the while his daughter and I bided impatiently for his return. I cannot say, however, that the information which he gleaned was a comfort to compensate us for the impatience of our waiting. From Scotland, indeed, the news was good. We heard that the Earl of Mar was gathering his forces at the market-town of

Moulin, and that the sixty men who proclaimed King James at Kirkmichael were now swelled to a thousand. But of England—or rather of those parts of it which lay about us—it was ever the same disheartening story that he carried back, a story of messengers buzzing backwards and forwards, betwixt a poor handful of landlords, and, for the rest, of men going quietly about their daily work. Once or twice, indeed, he returned uplifted with a rumour that the towns of Lancashire were only waiting for the Scottish army to march into England, before they mounted the White Cockade; on another occasion he satisfied us with a fairy-tale that the insurgents had but to appear before the walls, and Newcastle would forthwith open its gates; and at such times the old panels of the parlour would ring with laughter, as doubtless they had rung in the old days after Atherton Moor, and I would sit with a heart unworthily lightened by a thought that I might escape the payment which was due. But for the most part I had ever in my mind Lord Derwentwater's word about the pawns, and those yet earlier forebodings of my kinsman Bolingbroke. It seemed to me, indeed, that in this very rising of the Earl of Mar's, I had a proof of the accuracy of his forecasts. For he had sent word that the rebellion would be deferred, and here were the orders reversed behind his back. Moreover, we heard that the French King had died upon September 1st, and that I counted the most disheartening of calamities.

In this way, then, a week went by. On the evening of the eighth day, being the 25th September, I was leaning my elbows on the gate of the little garden, when I heard a heavy step behind me on the gravel. I turned, and there was Mary Tyson. It seemed to me that she was barring the path.

"Good-evening, Mary," said I, as pleasantly as possible.

"I am wishing for the day," said she, "when I can say the same to you, Mr. Clavering."

"And why?" said I, in astonishment. "It is no doing of mine that Mr. Curwen rides loose about the country-side."

"It is not of the father I am thinking," she interrupted; and I felt as though she had struck me.

"What do you mean?" I asked shortly.

"I know," she said, "this is no way for a rough old serving-body to speak to the likes of you. But see, sir," and her voice took on a curiously gentle and pleading tone, "I remember when she couldn't clinch her fist round one of my fingers. It's milk of mine, too, that has fed her, and it's honey to my heart to think she owes some of her sunshine to it I've seen her here at Applegarth grow from baby to child, and from child to woman. Yes, woman, woman," she repeated; "perhaps you forget that."

"No, indeed," said I, perplexed as to what she would be at; "it was the first thought I had of her."

"Then the more blame to you," she cried, and speech rushed out of her in a passion. "What is it that you're seeking of her—you that's hunted, with a price on your head? What is it? what is it?" And she stretched out her great arms on either side of her as though to make a barrier against myself. "Ah, if I were sure it would bring no harm on her, you should have the soldiers on your heels to-morrow. Many and many's the time I've been tempted to it when I've spied you in the orchard or on the lake. I have been sore tempted to it—sore tempted! What is it you want of her? It's the brother's clothes you are wearing, but is it the brother's heart beneath them?"

"Good God, woman!" I cried, dumfounded by her words.

She stood in the dusk before me, her grotesque figure dignified out of all knowledge by the greatness of her love for Dorothy. The very audacity of her words was a convincing evidence of that, and at the sight of her the anger died out of my heart. If she accused me unjustly, why, it was to protect Dorothy, and that made amends for all. Nay, I could almost thank her for the accusation, and I answered very humbly—

"I am like to get little good in my life, but may I get less when that is done if ever I had a thought which could disparage her."

"And how will I be sure of that?" asked Mary Tyson.

"Because I love her," said I.

An older man would have made, and a more experienced woman would have preferred, perhaps, a different answer; but I suppose she gauged it by the depth of her own affection. It struck root in a responsive soil.

"Ay, and how could you help it!" she cried, with a little note of triumph in her voice. But the voice in an instant deadened with anxiety. "You will have told her?"

"Not a syllable," says I. "I am, as you say, a man with a price on his head. I may be mated with an axe, but it is the only mate that I can come by."

She drew a deep breath of relief, and hearing it I laughed, but with no merriment at my heart She took a step forward on the instant.

"Well, and I am sorry," said she, "for you are not so ill-looking a lad in the brother's clothes." It was a whimsical reason, but given in a voice of some tenderness. "Not so ill-looking," she repeated, and at that her alarm reawakened. "But there's a danger in that!" she cries. "Miss Dorothy has lived here alone, with but a rare visitor once or twice in the twelvemonths. Maybe you speak to her in the same voice you use to me."

"Nay," I interposed, and this time my laugh rang sound enough. "Miss Curwen treats me with friendliness—a jesting friendliness, which is the very preclusion of love."

She bent forward a little, peering at me.

"Well, it may be," said she, "though I would never trust a boy's judgment on anything, let alone a woman."

Dorothy's voice called her from the house. She looked over her shoulder, and went on, lowering her tone—

"Look," said she, "at these boulders here," and she pointed to the darkening hillside. "They are landmarks to our shepherds in the mist But when the snow lies deep in winter, they will cross them and never know until they come to something else that tells them. It's so with us. We cross from this friendliness into love, thinking there are landmarks to guide us; but the landmarks may be hid, and we do not know until something else tells us we have crossed. And with some," and she nodded back towards the house, "there will be no retracing of the steps. Suppose you left your image with her. A treasure she will think it. It will prove a curse. You say you care for her?"

I saw what she was coming to, and nodded in assent.

"There is the one way to show it—not to her. No, not to her. That is the hardest thing I know, but the truest proof, that you will be content, for your love's sake, to let her think ill of you."

Dorothy's voice sounded yet louder. She came out into the porch. Mary Tyson hurried towards her, and receiving some order, disappeared into the house. Dorothy came slowly down the path towards me.

"You were very busy with Mary Tyson," said she.

"She was talking to me of the landmarks," said I.

"But one cannot see them," said she, looking towards the hillside.

I stood silent by her side. It was not that Mary Tyson's words had so greatly impressed me. I believed, indeed, that she spoke out of an overmastering jealousy for the girl's welfare. But I asked myself, since she had said so much, knowing so little of me, what would she have said had she known the truth? The temptation to set the sheriff on my path would long ago, I was certain, have become an accomplished act. Nor could I have blamed her. I was brought back to my old thought that I was wearing this girl's friendship as a thief may wear a stolen cloak.

"There is something I ought to tell you," said I suddenly, and came to a no less sudden stop, the moment that the sound of the words told me whither I was going. "But at this time," I continued in the lamest of conclusions, "I have no right to tell it you," and so babbled a word or two more.

She gave a little quiet laugh, and instead of answering me, began to hum over to herself that melody of "The Honest Lover." In the midst of a bar she broke off. I heard her breath come and go quickly. She turned and ran into the house.

That night, at all events, I acted upon an impulse of which I have never doubted the rectitude. Since I could not restore to her the stolen cloak, I took that other course, and dropped it by the wayside. I wrote a brief note of thanks to Mr. Curwen, and when the house was quiet, I crept from my room along the passage, and dropping out of that window which my host had shown me on the night of my coming to Applegarth, betook me under the star-shine across the fells.

CHAPTER XV
I REVISIT BLACKLADIES

That night I lay in the bracken on the hillside looking down into Ennerdale. Far below I could see one light burning in an upper window at the eastern side of Applegarth. It burned in Dorothy's chamber, and its yellow homeliness tugged at my heart as I lay there, the lonesome darkness about me, the shrill cry of the wind in my ears. The light burned very late that night. The clouds were gradually drawn like a curtain beneath the stars, and still it burned, and it was the blurring of the rain which at the last hid it from my sight.

For the next three days I hid amongst the hills betwixt Borrowdale and Applegarth. I was now fallen upon the last days of September, and the weather very shrewd with black drenching storms of rain which would sweep up the valleys with extraordinary suddenness, impenetrable as a screen, blotting out the world. The wind, too, blew from the north, bitter and cold, moaning up and down the faces of cliffs, whistling through the grasses, with a sound inimiably desolate, and twisting to a very whirlpool in the gaps between the mountain-peaks. To make my case the harder, I had come away in that haste, and oblivion of all but the necessity of my departure, that I had made little provision in my dress to defend me against the lashing of the wind and rain. I had picked up a hat and a long cloak, it is true, but for the rest, I wore no stouter covering than that suit of white which Mary Tyson had laid out for me so reluctantly. It was an unfit garb for my present life, and one that was to prove a considerable danger to me. But it was the cold discomfort of it which vexed me now. I had occasion enough to reflect on the folly of my precipitation, as I lay crouched in some draughty cave of boulders, watching the livelong day the clouds lower and lift, the battalions of the rain trample across the fells, and seeking to warm myself with the thought of that army in Scotland marching to the English borders. At nightfall I would creep down into Borrowdale, procure food from one of my old tenants who was well-disposed to me, and so get me back again to some jutting corner whence I could look down Gillerthwaite to Applegarth. But I looked in vain for the lights of the house. On the night of my departure, I saw them, but never afterwards, even when the air was of the clearest, so that I knew not what to think, and was almost persuaded to return to the house, that I might ascertain the cause of their disappearance.

So for four days and nights, whilst an old thought shaped to a resolve. For in the pocket of my coat, I had carried away not merely the button I had discovered in the garden at Blackladies—that never left my person—but the letter Tash had brought to me from Lord Derwentwater. I had been interrupted in the reading of it by Mr. Curwen's return, and so crammed it into my pocket with some part of it unread. However, I gave very careful heed to it now.

"My own affairs," it ran on, "have come to so desperate a pass that I dare not poke my nose into the matter of Herbert's disappearance; I live, indeed, myself, in hourly expectation of arrest. Your servant came again to me from Blackladies the other day, and told me a watch was no longer kept upon the house."

And since I had no knowledge that England was stirring in support of the rebellion, I determined to hazard an interview with my cousin, and so late on the fifth night climbed into the garden of Blackladies and let myself into the house as I had once seen Jervas Rookley do. I stood for a little in the parlour, feeling the darkness throb heavily about me with all the memories of that fatal night which had compassed my undoing.

Then I crossed towards the hall, but, my cloak flapping and dragging noisily at a chair as I passed, I loosed it from my shoulders and left it there. No lamp was burning in the hall, and since the curtains were drawn close over the lower windows, only the faintest of twilights penetrating through the upper panes made a doubtful glimmering beneath the roof; so that one seemed to be standing in a deep well.

The dining-room lay to my right on the further side of the hall. I made towards it, and of a sudden came sharply to a halt, my heart fairly quivering within me. For it seemed to me that the figure of a man had suddenly sprung out of the darkness and was advancing to me, but so close that the next step would bring our heads knocking against each other. And he had made no sound. As I stopped, the figure stopped. For a moment I stood watching it, holding my breath, then I clapped my hand to my sword, and the next moment I could have laughed at my alarm. For the figure copied my gesture. It was, moreover, dressed in clothes of a white colour from top to toe, and it was for that reason I saw its movements so distinctly. But I was likewise dressed in white. The one difference, in fact, between us which I noted was a certain black sheen in which it stood framed. I reached out a hand; it slid upon the polished surface of a great mirror.

The dining-room, I knew, opened at the side of this mirror, and I groped cautiously for the handle of the door, but before I found it my hand knocked against the key. With equal caution I opened the door to the width of an inch or so. A steady light shone upon the side of the wall, and through the opening there came the sound of a man snoring. I put my head into the room; and there to my inexpressible relief was Jervas Rookley. He was dressed in a suit of black satin, stretched to his full length upon a chair in front of a blazing fire, his head thrown back, his periwig on the floor, his cravat loosened, his shoes unbuckled off his feet.

I closed the door behind me; then opened it again and pocketed the key against which my hand had struck. The truth is that now that I was come into the man's presence, which I had before considered the most difficult part of the business, I now, on the contrary, saw very clearly that it was the easiest. I had not merely to come into his presence; I had to win out of it afterwards; and moreover I had somehow or other to twist from him the information about Mr. Herbert's whereabouts, for which I had adventured the visit.

I stepped on tiptoe across the carpet and seated myself in a chair facing him at the corner of the fireplace. Then I sought to arrange and order the questions I should put to him. But in truth I found the task well-nigh beyond my powers. It was all very well to tell myself that I was here on behalf of my remnant honour to secure the enlargement of Mr. Herbert. But the man was face to face with me; the firelight played upon his honest face and outstretched limbs; and I felt hatred spring up in me and kindle through my veins like fire. Up till now, so engrossed had I been by the turmoil of my own more personal troubles, I had given little serious thought to Jervas Rookley: I had taken his treachery almost callously as an accepted thing, and the depths of my indignation had only been stirred against myself. Now, however, every piece of trickery he had used on me crowded in upon my recollections. I might cry out within myself, "Anthony Herbert! Anthony Herbert!" Anthony Herbert was none the less pushed to the backward of my mind. That honest face was upturned to the light, and my thoughts swarmed about it I scanned it most carefully. It was more than common flushed and swollen, for which I was at no loss to account, since a bottle of French brandy stood on a little table at his elbow, three parts empty, and a carafe of water three parts full. I reached over for the bottle, and rinsing out his glass, helped myself, bethinking me that after my exposure of the three last days, its invigoration might prove of use to me.

But as I sat there and drank the brandy and watched Jervas Rookley's face, my fingers ever strayed to the hilt of my sword; I moved the weapon gently backwards and forwards so as to satisfy my ears with the pleasant jingle of the hanger; I half drew the blade from the sheath and rubbed my thumb along the edge until the blood came; and then I sat looking at the blood, and from the blood to Jervas Rookley, until at last an overmastering desire grew hot about my heart It was no longer the edge or the point of the sword which I desired to employ. I wanted to smash in that broad, honest face with the big pommel, and I feared the moment of his awakening lest I should yield to the temptation.

Fortunately, his first movement was one that diverted my thoughts. For as he opened his eyes he stretched out his hands to the brandy bottle. It was near to my elbow, however, on the mantelpiece, and I refilled my own glass. It was, I think, the sound of the liquor tinkling into the glass more than the words I spoke to him which made Rookley open his eyes. He blinked at me for a moment.

"You?" said he, but blankly with the stupor of his sleep still heavy upon him.

"Yes!" said I, drinking the brandy.

He followed the glass to my lips and woke to the possession of some part of his senses.

"I had expected you before," says he, and sits clicking his tongue against the roof of his mouth and swallowing, as though his throat was parched.

"So I believe," I returned. "You had even gone so far as to prepare for me a fitting welcome."

He was by this time wide awake. He picked up his peruke, clapped it on his head, and stood up in his stocking feet.

"Your servants, sir," says he with inimitable assurance, "will always honour their master with a fitting welcome, so long as I am steward, on whatever misfortunes he may have declined."

"I meant," said I, "a welcome not so much fitting my mastership as that honesty of yours, Mr. Rookley, which my Lord Derwentwater tells me is all on the outside."

I bent forward, keeping my eyes upon his face. But not a muscle jerked in it.

"Ah!" said he, in an indifferent voice. "Did Lord Derwentwater tell you that? Well, I had never a great respect for his discernment;" and he stood looking into the fire. Then he glanced at me and uttered a quiet little laugh.

"So you knew," said he, easily, "I had it in my mind, but I could not be certain."

"I have known it — —" I cried, exasperated out of all control by his cool audacity; and with a wave of the hand he interrupted me.

"You will excuse me," he said politely; and then, "There is no longer any reason why I should stand, is there?" and he resumed his seat and slipped his feet into his shoes. "Now," said he, "if you will pass the bottle."

"No," I roared in a fury.

"Well, well," he returned, "since there seems some doubt which of us is host and which guest, I will not press the request. You were saying that you have known it — —?"

"Since one evening when you showed me a private entrance into Blackladies," I cried; and bending forward to press upon him the knowledge that he had thereby foiled himself, I added in some triumph, "I have great reason to thank you for that, Mr. Jervas Rookley."

He leaned forward too, so that our heads were close together.

"And for more than that," said he. "Believe me, dear Mr. Clavering, that is by no means all you have to thank me for;" and he very affectionately patted my knee.

"And that is very true," says I, as I drew my knee away. "For I have to thank you for the fourth part of a bottle of brandy, but I cannot just bring to mind any other occasion of gratitude."

"Oh, gratitude!" says he, with a reproachful shake of the hand. "Fie, Mr. Clavering! Between gentleman and cousins the word stinks—it positively stinks. Whatever little service I have done for you, calls for no such big-sounding name."

His voice, his looks, his gestures were such as a man notes only in a friend, and a friend that is perplexed by some unaccountable suspicion.

"But you spoke of honesty," he continued, throwing a knee across the other and spreading out his hands. "It is very true I played a trick on you in coming to Paris as your servant But it is a trick which my betters had used before me. Your Duke of Ormond got him into France with the help of a lackey's livery. And your redoubtable Mar — —"

At that name I started.

"It is indeed so," he said earnestly. "The Earl of Mar, I have it on the best authority, worked his passage as a collier into Scotland."

It was not, however, that I was concerned at all as to how the Earl of Mar had escaped unremarked from London. But it suddenly occurred to me, as an explanation of Rookley's friendly demeanour, that the insurrection might be sweeping southwards on a higher tide of success than I had been disposed to credit. If that was the case, Mr. Jervas Rookley would of a certainty be anxious still to keep friends with me.

"So you see, Mr. Clavering," he went on, "I have all the precedents that a man could need to justify me."

"Well," said I, "it is not the trick itself which troubles me so much as your design in executing it."

"Design?" says he, taking me up in a tone of wonderment "You are very suspicious, Mr. Clavering. But I do not wonder at it, knowing in what school you were brought up;" and rising from his chair he took a pipe from the mantel-shelf and commenced to fill it with tobacco, "The suspicion, however, is unjust."

He bent down and plucked a splinter of burning wood out of the fire. "You do not smoke, I believe, but most like you do now, and at all events you will have grown used to the smell."

I started forward and stared at him. He lighted his pipe with great deliberation.

"Yes," said he nodding his head at me, "the suspicion is unjust." He tossed the splinter into the fire and sat down again.

"And how is little Dorothy Curwen?" he asked, with a lazy, contemptuous smile.

I sprang out of my seat, stung by the contempt rather than the surprise his words were like to arouse in me. And this, I think, he perceived, for he laughed to himself. Whereupon I felt my face flush; and that too he noted, and laughed again.

"Then you knew," I exclaimed, recovering myself—"you knew where I was sheltered!"

"A gentleman riding down Gillerthwaite at three o'clock of the morning is a sufficiently rare a sight to attract attention. I believe that, luckily, the shepherd who saw you only gossiped to a tenant of Blackladies."

I remembered the flock of sheep which I had seen scared up the hillside across the valley. But it was on my return from Keswick that I had been remarked—no later than a day after Rookley had striven to encompass my arrest.

"The news," said I, very slowly, "came to you in a roundabout fashion, and took, I suppose, some time in the coming. I infer, therefore, that it came to your ears after the Earl of Mar had risen in Scotland."

I was leaning upon the mantelpiece, looking down into his face, on which the fire shone with a full light; and just for a moment his face changed, the slightest thing in the world, but enough to assure me that my conjecture was right.

"There are inferences, my good cousin," he said sharply, "which it is not over-prudent for a man so delicately circumstanced as yourself to draw."

There was a note of disappointment in his tone, as though he would fain have hoodwinked me still into the belief that he stood my friend. And it suddenly occurred to me that there was a new danger in this knowledge of his—a danger which threatened not so much me as the people who had sheltered me. I resumed accordingly in a more amicable tone:

"It was not, however, of my whereabouts that I came hither to speak to you, but of the whereabouts of Mr. Herbert."

"Mr. Herbert?" says he, playing surprise. "What should I know of Mr. Herbert? Now, if I was to ask you the whereabouts of Mrs. Herbert, there would be some sense in the question, eh?" and he chuckled cunningly and poked a forefinger into my ribs. I struck the hand aside.

"What, indeed, should you know of Mr. Herbert," I cried—"you that plotted his arrest!"

"Arrest?" he interrupted, yet more dumfounded. "Plot?"

"That is the word," said I—"plot! a simple word enough, though with a damned dirty underhand meaning."

"Ah," he returned, with a sneer, "you take that interest in the husband, it appears, which I imagined you to have reserved for his wife. But as for plots and arrests—why, I know no more of what you mean than does the Khan of Crim Tartary."

"Then," said I, "will you tell me why you paid a visit to Mr. Herbert the night before he was arrested? And why you told him that if he came to Blackladies on the afternoon of the next day he would find Mrs. Herbert and myself in the garden?"

It was something of a chance shot, for I had no more than suspicion to warrant me, but it sped straight to its mark. Rookley started back in his chair, huddling his body together. Then he drew himself erect, with a certain defiance.

"But zounds, man!" he exclaimed, like one exasperated with perplexity, "what maggot's in your brains? Why should I send Herbert—devil take the fellow!—to find you in the garden when I knew you would not be there?"

"And I can answer that question with another," said I. "Who were in the garden at the time Mr. Herbert was to discover us?"

"The gardeners, I suppose," said he, thrusting his wig aside to scratch his head.

"It is a queer kind of gardener that wears buttons of this sort," said I; and I pulled the button from my pocket, and held it before his eyes in the palm of my hand.

He bent forward, examined the button, and again looked at me inquiringly.

"I picked it up," I explained, "on a little plot of trampled grass in the Wilderness on the next morning."

Rookley burst into a laugh and slapped his thighs.

"Lord! Mr. Clavering," he cried, and rising from his chair he walked briskly about the room, "your button is something too small to carry so weighty an accusation."

"Nay," I answered, smiling in my turn, "the button, though small, is metal solid enough. It depends upon how closely it is sewn to the cloth of my argument. It is true that I picked up the button on the morning that the soldiers came for me, but I was in the house on the afternoon before, and I saw——"

Jervas Rookley stopped in his walk, and his laughter ceased with the sound of his steps.

"You were in the house?" His mouth so worked that he pronounced the words awry. "You were in the house?"

"In the little parlour which gives on to the terrace."

Had I possessed any doubt before as to his complicity, the doubt would have vanished now. He reeled for a moment as if he had been struck, and the blood mottled in his cheeks.

"The house-door may be left open for one man, but two men may enter it," said I.

"You saw?" He took a step round the table and leaned across the corner of it. "What did you see?"

I took up a lighted candle from the table.

"I will show you," said I, and walked to the door.

He followed me, at first with uncertain steps. The steps grew firm behind my back.

They seemed to me significant of a growing purpose—so in the hall I stopped.

"We are good cousins, you and I," said I, holding the candle so that the flame lighted his face.

"Without a doubt," says he, readily. "You begin to see that you have mistaken me."

"I was thinking rather," said I, "that being good cousins, we might walk arm-in-arm."

"I should count it an honour," said he, with a bow.

"And it will certainly be a relief to me," said I. And accordingly I took his arm.

We crossed the hall into the parlour. The window stood open, as I had left it, with the curtains half drawn. Rookley busily pushed them back while I set the candle down. The sky had cleared during the last half hour, and the moon, which was in its fourth quarter, hung like a globe above the garden.

"I met Mr. Herbert in the hall," said I, "just outside this room. We had some talk—of a kind you can imagine. He went down the steps with his sword drawn. There he dropped his cloak, there he slashed at the bushes. Between those two trees he passed out of sight. I stepped out into the terrace to follow him, but before I had reached the flight of steps, I heard a pistol crack and saw a little cloud of smoke hang above the bushes there. I found the button the next morning at the very spot, and near the button, the pistol. It was Mr. Herbert's pistol. That," said I, "is my part of the story. But perhaps if we go back to the warmer room you will give me your part. For I take it that you were not in the house, else you would have heard my voice, but rather in the garden. You made a great mistake in not looking towards the terrace, my cousin." And again I took his arm, and we walked back.

I was, indeed, rather anxious to discover the whereabouts of Rookley during that afternoon, since so far I had been able to keep Mrs. Herbert's name entirely out of the narrative. If Jervas Rookley had been in the garden during the afternoon, and had only returned to the house in time to intercept Lord Derwentwater's letter concerning the French King's health, and had thereupon ridden off to apply for a warrant against me, why, there was just a chance that I might save Mrs. Herbert from figuring in the business at all.

Rookley said nothing until we were got back into the dining-room, but walked thoughtfully, his arm in mine. I noticed that he was carrying in his left hand the cord by which the curtains in the little parlour were fastened. He stood swinging it to and fro mechanically.

"Your suspicions," said he, "discompose me. They discompose me very much. I gave you credit for more generosity;" and lifting up the brandy bottle, he held it with trembling hands betwixt himself and the candle.

"I am afraid that it is empty," said I.

"If you will pardon me," said he, "I will even fetch another."

He laid the cord upon the table, advanced to the door and opened it wide. I saw him slide his hand across the lock.

"The key is in my pocket," I said.

He looked at me with a sorrowful shake of the head.

"Your suspicions discompose me very much," and he came back for a candle. I noticed too that he carelessly picked up the cord again.

"I think," said I, "that I will help you to fetch that bottle;" and I went with him into the hall.

There was something new in the man's bearing which began to alarm me. He still used the same tone of aggrieved affection, but with an indefinable difference which was none the less very apparent to me. His effort seemed no longer to aim at misleading me, but rather to sustain the pretence that he was aiming to mislead me. It seemed to me that since he had become aware of what I knew concerning his treachery he had devised some new plan, and kept his old tone to hinder me from suspecting it. I noticed, too, a certain deliberateness in the indifference of his walk, a certain intention in the discomposure.

In the hall he stopped, and setting down the candle upon a cabinet, turned to face me.

"Why did you come with me?" he asked gently.

"I did not know but what you might call your servants, and, as you put it, I am delicately circumstanced."

He raised his hands in a gesture of pity.

"See what suspicion leads a man to! My servants hold you in so much respect that if I harboured designs against your safety, to call my servants would be to ruin me."

I was inclined to believe that what he said was in a measure true, for I remembered the interview which I had had with Ashlock in the steward's office, and the subsequent consideration which had been shown me.

Then, "Look!" I cried of a sudden, pointing my arm. Right in front of me on that vacant space of the wall amongst the pictures hung the portrait of Jervas Rookley.

Rookley started ever so little and then stood eyeing me keenly, the while he swung round and round in a little circle the tassel of the curtain cord.

"You prate to me of suspicions," I cried, "there's the proof of their justice. This estate of Blackladies I held on one condition—that you should receive no benefit from it. We jogged side by side, you and I, cousins with hearts cousinly mated in the same endeavour! You still profess it! Then explain to me: how comes it the Whigs leave you alone, you stripped of your inheritance because of the very principles which outlawed me? Explain that, and I'll still believe you. Prove that you live here without the Government's connivance, I'll forget the rest of my suspicions. I'll count you my loyal friend. Only show me this: how comes it that I make my bed upon the bracken, and you lord it at Blackladies? Your presence the common talk, your picture staring from the walls?" and in my rage I plucked my sword from the sheath, and slashed his portrait across the face, lengthwise and breadthwise, in a cross.

The tassel stopped swinging. His shoulders hunched ever so little, his head came forward, the eyes shone out bright like beads, and his face tightened to that expression of foxy cunning I had noted before in mid Channel between Dover and Dunkirk.

"It is a gallant swordsman," he said, with a sneer, "and a prudent too."

"He looks to the original," I cried, "to give him the occasion of imprudence;" and I faced him.

"There is a better way," said he, with the quietest laugh, and he sprang back suddenly to the cabinet on which the candle stood. "We will make a present of a Michaelmas goose to King George."

I saw his hand for an instant poised above the flame, red with the light of it; I saw his figure black from head to foot, and at his elbow another figure white from head to foot, the reflection of myself in the mirror by his side; and then his palm squashed down upon the wick.

The hall fell to darkness just as I made the first step towards him. I halted on the instant. He could see me, I could not see him! He had thrown off the mask; he had proclaimed himself my enemy, and he knew where I had been sheltered. It was that thought which slipped into my mind as the darkness cloaked about me, and made me curse the folly of my intrusion here. I had hazarded not merely myself, but Dorothy and her father. He could see me, I could not see him, and the outcome of this adventure struck at Dorothy.

I stepped backwards as lightly as I could, until the edge of a picture-frame rubbed against my shoulder-blades, and so stood gripping my sword-hilt, straining my ears. Across the hall I seemed to hear Rookley breathing, but it was the only sound I heard. There was no shuffle of a foot; he had not moved.

Above me the twilight glimmered beneath the roof; about me the chamber was black as the inside of a nailed coffin. If I could only reach the windows and tear the curtains back! But half the length of the hall intercepted me, and to reach them I must needs take my back from the wall. That I dared not do, and I stood listening helplessly to the sound of Rookley's breathing. In that pitch-dark hall it seemed to shift from quarter to quarter. At one moment I could have sworn I heard his breath, soft as a sigh, a foot's length from me; I could almost have sworn I felt it on my neck; and in a panic I whirled my sword from side to side, but it touched nothing within the half circle of its reach. My fears indeed so grew upon me, that I was in two minds whether or no to shout and bring the servants about me. It would at all events end the suspense. But I dared not do it. Jervas Rookley distrusted them. But how much more cause had I! I could not risk the safety of Applegarth upon their doubtful loyalty. And then a sharp sound broke in upon the silence. It set my heart fluttering and fainting within me by reason of its abruptness, so that for a moment I was dazed and could not come at the reason of it. It was a clattering sound, and, so far as I could gather, it came from the spot where I had last seen Jervas Rookley standing. It was like—nay, it was the sound of a shoe dropped upon the boards. I know not why, but the sound steadied, though it appalled me. It spoke of a doubled danger and cried for a doubled vigilance. Rookley could not only see my white figure; he could move to it noiselessly, for he was slipping off his shoes.

I listened for the creak of a board, for the light padding sound of stockinged feet, for the rustle of his coat; and while I listened, I moved my sword gently in front of me, but my sword touched nothing and my ears heard nothing. Yet he must be coming—stealthily stepping across the hall—-I felt him coming. But from what quarter would he come? During those seconds of waiting the question became a torture.

And then a momentary hope shot through me. When he put the candle out his sword was in the scabbard. He had not drawn it, since I had listened so strenuously that I must have heard. However carefully he drew it, a chain would clink; or if not that, the scabbard might knock against his leg;

or if not that, there would be a little whirr, a sort of whisper as the blade slid upwards out of the sheath.

There was still a chance, then. At that point of the darkness from which the sound should come I would strike—strike the moment I heard it, with all my strength, down towards the floor. I tightened my fingers about my sword-hilt and waited. But it was a very different noise which struck upon my hearing, a noise that a man may make in the dragging of a heavy sack. I drew myself up close to the wall, setting my feet together, pressing my heels against the panels. The sound filled me with such terror as I think never before or since I have known the like of. For I could not explain it to myself. I only knew that it was dangerous. It seemed to me to come from somewhere about midway of the room, and I held my breath that I might judge the better on its repetition. After a moment it was repeated, but nearer, and by its proximity it sounded so much the more dangerous. I sprang towards it. A sobbing cry leapt from my lips, and I lunged at a venture into the darkness. But again my sword touched nothing, and with the force of that unresisted thrust I stumbled forward for a step or two. My cry changed into a veritable scream. I felt the fingers of a hand gently steal about each of my ankles and then tighten on them like iron fetters. I understood; halfway across the room Rookley had lowered himself full-length upon the floor and was crawling towards me. I raised my sword to strike, but even as I raised it he jerked my feet from beneath me, and I fell face forwards with a crash right across his body. My sword flew out of my hand and went rolling and clattering into the darkness. My forehead struck against the boards, and for a moment I lay half stunned. It was only for a moment, but when that moment had passed, Jervas Rookley was upon me, above me, his arms twined about mine and drawing them behind me, his knees pressed with all his might into the small of my back.

"We will truss the goose before we send it to King George," said he.

CHAPTER XVI
ASHLOCK GIVES THE NEWS

Then I remembered the curtain cord. I felt that Rookley was trying to pass it from one hand to the other beneath my arms; I could hear the tassel bobbing and jerking on the floor, and I summoned all my strength to draw my arms apart. For if he prevailed, here was the end of all my fine resolve to secure Mr. Herbert's enlargement!

I had flattered myself with that prospective atonement, as though it was a worthy action already counted to my credit. I saw this in a flash now, now that I was failing again, and the perception was like an agony in my bones. It seemed to me that a woman's face rose out of the darkness before me, mournful with reproach, and the face was not the wife's who waited in Keswick, but Dorothy's. She looked at me from beneath a hood half thrown back from the head and across her shoulder, as though she had passed me, even as I had seen in my fancies a woman's face look at me, when I had watched the procession of my hours to come in the Rector's Library at the Jesuit College.

Meanwhile Rookley's knee so closely pressed me to the floor that my struggles did but exhaust myself, and delay the event. I was no match for him in bodily strength, and he held me, moreover, at that disadvantage wherein a weak man might well have triumphed over a strong.

I could get no purchase either with hand or foot, and lay like a fish flapping helplessly on the deck of a boat, the while he pressed my arms closer and closer together.

It is not to be imagined that this unequal contest lasted any great while. The thoughts which I have described raced through my mind while my cry seemed still to be echoing about the walls, and as though in answer to that cry, a latch clicked as I felt the cord tighten about my elbows.

The sound came from somewhere on the opposite side of the hall, and I do not think that Rookley heard it, for now and again he laughed in a low, satisfied fashion as though engrossed in the pleasure of his task. I heard a shuffling of feet, and a light brightened in the passage which led to the steward's office. A great hope sprang up within me. There was one servant in the house whom I could trust.

"Ashlock!" I shouted at the top of my voice.

The footsteps quickened to a run.

"Damn you!" muttered Rookley, and he let go the cord. He had raised his hand to strike, but I did not give him time for the blow. With a final effort I gathered up my knees beneath me and raised myself on my forearms. Rookley's balance was disturbed already. He put out a hand to the floor. I got the sole of my foot upon the boards, jerked him off my back, and rolled over upon him with my fingers at his throat. Ashlock ran towards us with a lighted lamp in his hand. I let go my hold and got to my feet. Rookley did the same.

"You came in the nick of time," said Rookley, "My good cousin would have murdered me;" and he arranged his cravat.

"That's a lie," said I, with a breath between each word.

"It was Mr. Clavering's cry I heard," said Ashlock.

And while he spoke a commotion arose in the upper part of the house. Doors opened and shut, there was a hurry of footsteps along the passages, and voice called to voice in alarm. My cry had roused the household, and I saw Jervas Rookley smile. I crossed the hall and picked up my sword. As I returned with it, I saw here and there a white face popped over the balusters of the staircase.

"I have fought with you in your way," said I. "It is your turn to fight with me in mine."

Rookley crossed his arms.

"To fight with a hunted traitor!" said he. "Indeed, my cousin, you ask too much of me; I would not rob the gallows of so choice a morsel. Burtham, Wilson, Blacket!" and he lazily called up the stairs to the servants clustered there. "This is your work. Ashlock, do you carry the news to the sheriff."

I glanced at Ashlock; he did not stir. On the staircase I heard a conflict of muttering voices, but as yet no one had descended. So a full minute passed, while my life and more than my life hung in the balance.

I kept my eyes on Rookley, debating in my mind what I should do, if his servants obeyed him. Every nerve in my body tingled with the desire to drive at him with my sword point; but he stood, quietly smiling, his arms folded, his legs crossed. I could not touch him; being unarmed he was best armed of all, and doubtless he knew it.

"Well!" he asked, as with some impatience. "Are my servants leagued against their master to betray his King?"

One man descended a couple of steps, and then Ashlock spoke.

"Sir," he said, "it is not for poor men like us to talk of kings. Kings are for you, masters are for us. And as it seems there are two kings for you to choose between, so there are two masters for the likes of us. And for my part," he raised his voice, and with his voice his face, towards the stairs— "for my part, I stand here;" and he crossed over to me and stood by my side.

I can see the old man now as he held up the lamp in his tremulous hand and the light fell upon his wrinkled face. I can hear his voice ringing out bold and confident. It was Ashlock who saved me that night. I saw the servants draw back at his words, and the mutter of voices recommenced.

"Very well," cried Rookley, starting forward. "Choose him for your master, then, and see what comes of it!" He shook his fist towards the servants in his passion. "One and all you pack to-morrow. Your master, I tell you, is the master of Blackladies."

"They have no master, then," I cried, for it seemed that at his words they again pressed forward. "For you have less right here than I."

Rookley turned and took a step or two towards me, his eyes blazing, his face white. But he spoke in a low voice, nodding his head between the words:

"They shall pay for this at Applegarth."

It was my turn to start forward.

"Dorothy Curwen shall pay for this—little Dorothy Curwen!"—with a venomous sneer. "Your friend, eh? But mine too. Ah, my good cousin, it seems your fortune always to come second."

At that I did what I had so much longed to do when I first saw him asleep. He was within two feet of me; I held my drawn sword in my hand. I made no answer to him in speech, but the instant the words were past his lips, I took my sword by the blade, raised it above my head, and brought the hilt crashing down upon his face. He spun round upon his heels and pitched sideways at my feet.

"Now, Ashlock," said I, "get me a horse."

"But there's no such thing, sir, at Blackladies," he replied. "They were seized this many a week back."

"How travels this?" and I pointed to Jervas Rookley.

"He travels no further than between the dining-room and the cellar."

And I crossed into the little parlour and picked up my cloak and hat. Then I returned to the hall. Burtham had raised Jervas Rookley's head upon his knee, and Wilson was coming from the kitchen with a bason of water and a towel. They looked at me doubtfully but said no word. I went to the hall door, unfastened the bolts, and started at a run down the drive. I had not, however, advanced many yards, when a cry from behind brought me to a halt; and in a little, old Ashlock joined me.

"I did but go for my hat, sir," he said, reproachfully. "A bald pate and an old man—they are two things that go ill with a night wind."

He was walking by my side as he spoke, and the words touched me to an extreme tenderness. He was venturing himself, without a question, into unknown perils, and for my sake. I could hear his steps dragging on the gravel, and I stopped.

"It must not be," I said. "God knows I would be blithe and glad to have a friend to bear me company, and it is a true friend you have been to me." I laid a hand upon his shoulder "But it is into dangers and hardships I shall be dragging you, and that I have no right to do without I can give you strength to win through them, and that strength I cannot give. These last days, the rain and hail have beat upon me by day, and the night wind has whistled through my bones in the dark. My roof-tree has been a jutting rock, my bed the sopping bracken, and so it will be still. It needs all my youth to bear it, it will mean death and a quick death to you. You must go back."

"Master Lawrence," he replied, catching at my arm, "Master Lawrence, I cannot go back!" and there was something like a sob in his voice.

"Had we horses," I continued, "I would gladly take you. But even this morning there is work for me to do that cries for all my speed."

Ashlock persisted, however, pleading that I should name a place where he could join me. Two things were plain to me: one that he had resolved to throw his lot in with me; the other that I must cross the fells to Applegarth without the hamper of his companionship. For Jervas Rookley, I felt sure, would seize the first moment of consciousness to exact his retribution. At last a plan occurred to me.

"You have crossed to Lord's Island already," I said. "Go to Lord Derwentwater again. Tell him all you have heard to-night, and make this request in my name: that he will keep you until I send word where you can join me."

"But Lord Derwentwater has fled," Ashlock exclaimed. "He fled north to Mr. Lambert, and thence goes to his own seat at Dilston, in Northumberland."

"He has fled! How know you this?"

"I was at Lord's Island this two days since, sir, seeking news of you. The warrant was out for him even then. He meets Mr. Forster at Greenrig, on the 6th of October. He told me he had sent to your hiding-place and bidden you join him there."

"At Greenrig with Mr. Forster? Then the country's risen." I could have gone down on my knees as I had seen my cousin do. "If only God wills, the rising will succeed;" and I cried out my prayer, from a feeling even deeper than that I cherished for the King. "Listen, Ashlock! The morning is breaking. Do you meet me by noon betwixt Honister Crag and Ennerdale Lake. There is a path; hide within sight of it;" and without waiting to hear more from him I set out at a run across Borrowdale. It was daylight before I had crossed the valley, and the sun was up.

But I cared little now whether or no I was seen and known. Since Jervas Rookley knew I had lain hidden those first weeks at Applegarth—why, it mattered little now who else discovered the fact. But indeed, Jervas Rookley was not the only one who knew.

For when I reached Applegarth, I found the house deserted. I banged at the door, and for my pains heard the echo ring chill and solitary through an empty house. I looked about me; not a living being could be seen. Backwards and forwards I paced in front of those blind windows and the unyielding door. I ran to the back of the house, thinking I might find an entrance there. But the same silence, the same deadly indifference were the only response I got. I know not what wild fears, what horrible surmises passed through my mind! It was because the house had sheltered me, I cried to myself, that desolation made its home there. I dropped on the grass and the tears burst from my eyes. For I remembered how Dorothy had sung within the chambers, how her little feet had danced so lightly down the stairs.

Ashlock was already waiting me when I retraced my steps to the Honister Crag, and, indeed, I was long behind the time.

"To Greenrig," I said. Towards evening, however, Ashlock's strength gave out, and coming to the house of a farmer, I procured a lodging. In truth, I was well-nigh exhausted myself. The next day, however, Ashlock was in no condition to accompany me, and leaving a little money which I had with me for his maintenance, I went forward on my way alone.

Sleeping now in a cottage, now in the fields, and little enough in either case, using such means of conveyance as chance offered me upon the road, I came early in the morning of the sixth to Greenrig in Northumberland, and while wandering hither and thither, in search of the place of meeting, and yet not daring to inquire for it, I came upon a cavalcade. It was Lord Derwentwater at the head of his servants, all armed and mounted. I ran forward to meet him.

"What is it, lad?" he asked, reining in his horse. I do not wonder that he had no knowledge of me. For my clothes hung about me in tatters. No dirtier ragamuffin ever tramped a country road.

"How is it they did not seize your horses?" I asked, with my wits wandering.

Lord Derwentwater laughed heartily.

"There is a saying of Oliver Cromwell's," he replied, "that he could gain his end in any place with an ass-load of gold. But who are you that put the question?" and he bent over his horse's neck.

I caught at the reins to save myself from falling.

"I am Lawrence Clavering," I said; "you bade me meet you here." And with that I swooned away.

CHAPTER XVII
THE MARCH TO PRESTON

It was more from the exhaustion of hunger than any other cause that I fainted, and being come to myself, I was given food and thereafter accommodated with a horse; so that without any great delay the calvacade proceeded to its rendezvous. We fell in with Mr. Forster at the top of a hill, which they call the Waterfalls, and swelled his numbers to a considerable degree, there being altogether gathered at this spot, now that we were come, near upon sixty horse, gentlemen and their attendants, and all armed. After a short council it was decided that we should march northwards and meet Brigadier Macintosh at Kelso. Besides, argued Mr. Forster, there was great reason to believe, that if we did but appear before the walls, Newcastle would open its gates to us; in the which case we should not only add largely to our forces but secure that of which we stood most in need—I mean ordnance and ammunition. "For," said he, "Sir William Blackett, whose interest is very considerable in the town, has armed and enlisted in troops all the colliers and keelmen and miners in his pay, and does but wait for us to set them in motion."

Accordingly, in the height of confidence and good spirits, the little band set out towards Plainfield on the river Coquett, though for my part I could but ponder in the greatest distress upon the deserted aspect of Applegarth. Nor was Lord Derwentwater in any way able to relieve my fears, seeing that he had himself been seeking refuge from one place to another. I was driven therefore to persuade myself, as the best hope which offered, that Mr. Curwen and his daughter had embarked in the *Swallow* and were now come safely to France. Yet, somehow, the while I persuaded myself, my heart sank with the thought of the distance that was between us.

We came that night to Rothbury, and sleeping there, marched the next morning to Warkworth, where, the day being Saturday, the 7th of October, Mr. Forster resolved to lie until the Monday. It was in the parish church of Warkworth that Mr. Buxton, our chaplain, first prayed publicly for King James III., substituting that name for King George, and it was in Warkworth too that King James was first of all in England proclaimed King of Great

Britain. I remember standing in the market-place listening to the huzzaing of our forces and watching the hats go up in the air, with how heavy a heart! So that many chided me for the dull face I wore. But I was picturing to myself the delight with which Dorothy would have viewed the scene. I could see her eye sparkle, her little hand clench upon her whip; I could hear her voice making a harmony of these discordant shouts.

On Monday we rode out of Warkworth, and being joined by many gentlemen at Alnwick and other places, and in particular by seventy Scots Horse at Felton Bridge, marched into Morpeth, three hundred strong, all mounted. For we would entertain no foot, since we had not sufficient arms even for those we had mounted, and moreover were in a great haste to surprise Newcastle. To this end we hurried to Hexham, where we were joined by some more Scots Horse, and drew out from there on to a moor about three miles distant It was there that we sustained our first disappointment. For intelligence was brought to us from Newcastle that the magistrates having got wind of our designs, had gathered the train-bands and militia within the walls, and that the gates were so far from opening to receive us that they had been walled up and fortified with stone and lime to such a degree of strength that without cannon it was useless to attempt them.

Accordingly we marched chapfallen back to Hexham and lay there until the 18th, with no very definite idea of what we should do next However, on the 18th a man came running into the town crying that General Carpenter with Churchill's Dragoons and Hotham's foot, and I know not what other regiments, had on this very day arrived at Newcastle from London, and without an instant's delay had set about preparing to attack us. The news, you may be sure, threw us into a pretty commotion, and the colour of our hopes quite faded. Messengers sped backwards and forwards between General Forster and Lord Derwentwater and Captain Shaftoe; councils were held, broken up, reformed again; the whole camp hummed and sputtered like a boiling kettle. I passed that day in the greatest despair, for if this rising failed, every way was I undone. It was not merely that I should lose my life, but I should lose it without securing that for which I had designed it—I mean Mr. Herbert's liberation. In the midst of this flurry and confusion, however, Mr. Burnett of Carlips rode into Hexham, with a message that Viscount Kenmure, and the Earls of Nithsdale, Carnwath, and Wintoun had entered England from the western parts of Scotland and were even now at Rothbury. Mr. Forster returned an express that we would advance to them the next morning; the which we did, greatly enheartened by the pat chance of their arrival, and being joined together with them marched in a body to Wooler on the following day and rested the Friday in that village.

We crossed the Tweed and entered Kelso on the 22nd of October, and about an hour after our entry the Highlanders, with their outlandish bagpipes playing the strangest skirling melodies, were led in by old Mackintosh from the Scots side. The joy we all had at the sight of them may be easily imagined, and indeed the expression of it by some of the baser followers was so extravagant that a man can hardly describe it with any dignity. But I think we all halloo'd them as our saviours, and so even persuaded our ears to find pleasure in the rasping of their pipes.

The next day being Sunday, Lord Kenmure ordered that Divine Service should be held in the great Kirk of Kelso, at which Papists and Protestants, Highlanders and Englishmen attended very reverently together; and I believe this was the first time that the rubric of the Church of England was ever read on this side of the Forth in Scotland. Mr. Patten, I remember, who after turned his coat to save his life, preached from a text of Deuteronomy, "The right of the first-born is his." And very eloquent, I am told, his sermon was, though I heard little of it, being occupied rather with the gathering of men about me, and wondering whether at the long last we had the tips of our fingers upon this much-contested crown. For the Highlanders, though poorly armed and clad, had the hardiest look of any men that ever I saw. My great question, indeed, was whether amongst their nobles they had one who could lead. For on our side, except for Captains Nicholas Wogan, and Shaftoe, we had few who were versed in military arts, and Mr. Forster betrayed to my thinking more of the incompetency of the born Parliament-man than the resourceful instinct of the born strategist; in which opinion, I may say, I was fully warranted afterwards by that fatal omission in regard to Ribble Bridge.

On the Monday morning the Highlanders were drawn up in the churchyard and marched thence to the market-place, in all the bravery of flags flying, and drums beating, and pipes playing. There they were formed into a circle, and within that circle another circle of the Gentlemen Volunteers, whereof through the bounty of Lord Derwentwater, in supplying me with money and arms, I was now become one; and within that circle stood the noblemen. Thereupon a trumpet sounded, and silence being obtained, the Earl of Dumferling proclaimed King James, and read thereafter the famous manifesto which the Earl of Mar sent from his camp at Perth by the hand of Mr. Robert Douglas.

We continued, then, in Kelso until the following Thursday, the 27th of October, our force being now augmented, what with footmen and horse, to the number of fourteen hundred. The delay, however, gave General Carpenter time to approach us from Newcastle, and he on this same Thursday came to Wooler and lay there the night, intending to draw out to Kelso and give us battle on the following day. No sooner was the intelligence received than Lord Kenmure calls a council of war, and here at once it was seen that our present union was very much upon the surface. For whereas Earl Wintoun was all for marching into the west of Scotland, others were for passing the Tweed and attacking General Carpenter. For, said they, "in the first place, his troops must needs be fatigued, and in the second they do not count more than five hundred men all told, whereof the regiments of Dragoons are newly raised and have seen no service."

Now, either of these proposals would in all probability have tended to our advantage, but when a multitude of counsels conflict, it is ever upon some weak compromise that men fall at last; and so it came about that we marched away to Jedburgh, intending thence to cross the mountains into England. Here it was that our troubles with the Highlanders began. For they would not be persuaded to cross the borders, saying that once they were in England they would be taken and sold as slaves, a piece of ignorance wherein it was supposed Lord Wintoun had tutored them. Consequently our plans were changed again, and instead of crossing into North Tynedale, we turned aside to Hawick, the Highlanders protesting that they would not keep with us for the distance of an inch upon English soil.

From Hawick we marched to Langholme, a little market-town belonging to the Duchess of Buccleugh; and there we made another very great mistake. For here the Earl of Wintoun strongly advised that we should make ourselves masters of Dumfries, and to that end, indeed, a detachment of cavalry was sent forward in the night to Ecclefechan. And no doubt the advice was just and the plan easy of accomplishment. Dumfries, he urged, was unfortified either by walls or trainbands; it stood upon a navigable river whereby we might have succours from France; it opened a passage to Glasgow; and the possession of so wealthy a town would give us great credit with the country gentlemen thereabouts, and so be the means of enlarging the command. All these arguments he advanced, as Lord Derwentwater, who was present at the council, informed me, with singular moderation of tone, but finding that they made no sort of headway with the English party:

"It is sheer folly and madness," he burst out. "You are so eager to reap your doubtful crops in Lancashire, that you will not stoop to the corn that lies cut at your feet. I tell you, there are many stands of arms stored in the

Tolbooth and a great quantity of gunpowder in the Tron Steeple, which you can have for the mere taking. But you will not, no, you will not. Good God, sirs, your King's at stake, and if you understand not that, your lives;" and so he bounced out of the room.

The truth is we of the English party were so buoyed up by the expresses we received from Lancashire that nothing would content us but we must march hot-foot into England. And though, of course, I had no part or share in the decision of our course, I was none the less glad that our side prevailed, nay, more glad than the rest, since I had an added motive. For so long as we remained in Scotland there would be no disturbance of administration in England. Examinations would be conducted, assizes would be held, and for all I knew, Mr. Herbert might be condemned and hanged while we were yet marching and countermarching upon the borders. The thought of that possibility was like a sword above my head; I raged against my ignorance of the place of Mr. Herbert's detention. Had I but known it, I think that in this hesitation of our leaders I would have foregone those chances of escape which the rebellion promised, and ridden off at night to deliver myself to the authorities. For it was no longer of my dishonour, if I failed to bring the matter to a happy event, at least for Anthony Herbert and his wife, that I thought. But the prospect of failure struck at something deeper within me. It seemed in truth to reach out sullying hands towards Dorothy. I held it in some queer way as a debt to her, due in payment for my knowledge of her, that I should fulfil this duty to its last letter. So whenever these councils were in the holding, I would pace up and down before the General's quarters, as a man will before the house in which his mistress lies sick; and when the counsellors came forth, you may be sure I was at Lord Derwentwater's elbow on the instant, and the first to hear the decision agreed upon.

From Langholme, then, we crossed into England. It is no part of my story to describe our march to Preston, and I need only make mention of one incident during its continuance which had an intimate effect upon my own particular fortunes.

This incident occurred when we were some ten miles out of Penrith. The whole army was drawn up upon a hill and lying upon its arms to rest the men. I was standing by the side of young Mr. Chorley, with my eyes towards Appleby, when Mr. Richard Stokoe, who acted as quartermaster to Lord Derwentwater's troop, suddenly cried out behind me—

"Lord save us! Who is this old put of a fellow?"

"He mounts the white cockade," said young Mr. Chorley, turning and shading his eyes with his hand.

"And moves a living arsenal," said the other with a laugh.

"Yet hardly so dangerous as his companion, I should think."

"Very like. We'll set her in front of the troops, and so march to London with never a shot fired. But, Clavering!" he cried of a sudden. "What ails the man?"

But Clavering was galloping down the hillside by this time, and did not draw rein to answer him. For the old put of a fellow and his companion were no other than Mr. Curwen and his daughter. A living arsenal was in truth no bad description of the old gentleman; for he carried a couple of old muskets slung across his shoulders, a pair of big pistols were stuck in his belt, another pair protruded from the holsters, a long straight sword slapped and rattled against his leg, while a woodman's axe was slung across his body.

When I was a hundred yards from the pair I slackened my horse's speed: when the hundred yards had narrowed to fifty, I stopped altogether. For I remembered my unceremonious departure from Applegarth, and was troubled to think with what mien they would accost me. I need, however, have harboured no fears upon that score. For Mr. Curwen cried out:

"I wagered Dorothy the sun to a guinea-piece that we should find you here."

"I did not take the wager," cries Dorothy, as she drew rein; she added demurely, "But only because he could not have paid had he lost."

They were followed at a little distance by some half a dozen shepherds and labourers mounted on ponies, which, to say the least, had long since passed their climacteric, and armed with any makeshift of a weapon which had happened to come handy. The troop drew up in a line, and Mr. Curwen surveyed them with some pride.

"They lack a banner," said he, regretfully. "I would have had Dorothy embroider one of silk for Roger Purdy, in the smock there, to carry—straighten your shoulders, Roger!—a white rose opening, on a ground of sky-blue, but——"

"But Dorothy had some slight sense of humour," says she, "and so would not."

"Then," said I, with a glance of perplexity towards the girl, "you are, indeed, come to join us?" For I could not but wonder that she who had so resolutely removed her father from the excitement of the preceding intrigues, should now second his participation in the greater excitement of the actual conflict.

"Indeed," he cries, "I am; and Dorothy has come so far to wish us a God-speed, but will return again with Dawson there. What did I tell you, Mr. Clavering? There is a work for the weakest arm. But you are surprised!"

"I am surprised," I answered, "that Mary Tyson is not here as well."

"Ah," said he, "do you know, Mr. Clavering, I fear me I have done some injustice to Mary Tyson. I thought her a poor witless body." Dorothy made a movement, and he hurriedly interposed, "The best of servants, but," and he glanced again defiantly at his daughter, "a poor witless body outside the household service. But since the messenger came with the constables to Applegarth, she has shown great good sense, except in the matter of simples. For, indeed, my pockets are packed with them."

"The constables came to Applegarth!" I exclaimed, bethinking me of Jervas Rookley's threat. "And when was that?"

Miss Curwen, I noticed, was looking at me with a singular intentness as I uttered the exclamation, and gave a little nod of comprehension as I asked the question. It was as though my asking it assured her of something which she had suspected.

"When?" echoed Mr. Curwen, with a smile. "Why, the morning you left us. You were right in your surmise, and I take it very kindly that you delayed so long as to scribble your gratitude, though that delay was an added danger."

"Oh, I was right?" said I, though still not very clear as to what it was that I had surmised correctly; and again Miss Curwen nodded.

"Yes!" said he, "but, indeed, it was early for travellers. But we were waiting for you at the breakfast-table when we first heard the sheriff's horses. I was not sure that you would hear them at the back of the house."

"But one of the windows looked down the road," said I, understanding why he had seen no discourtesy in my precipitate departure. I could not in any case give the real reason which had prompted me to that, and since here was one offered to me, why, I thought it best to fall in with it—"the window about which I hunted so long for the owl," I added, turning to Miss Curwen, For her manner of a minute ago warned me that she put no great faith in her father's explanation of my conduct, and I was desirous to test the point.

"You hunted vainly," said she, "because the owl flitted one night," and so left me in doubt.

"That is true," continued Mr. Curwen to me. "I did not think of the window, and indeed was somewhat puzzled by the quickness of your escape. For I sent Mary Tyson to warn you the while I barricaded the door and held a parley with the sheriff from the window. She came back to tell me you were gone."

"Would she had come back quicker!" exclaimed Dorothy with a shudder.

"Why?" I cried at the sight of her distress. "Was there—was there—any hurt done? Oh no, not to you. I could never forgive myself."

"No, not to us," replied Mr. Curwen. "Dorothy takes the matter too much to heart. Had she fired of a purpose she would have been right, or very little to blame. For I am old-fashioned enough to consider a guest sacred as an altar-vessel. But since she fired by mistake——"

"Miss Curwen fired!" I said.

"And shot the sheriff from behind my shoulder," continued Mr. Curwen.

"Father!" she entreated, covering her face with her hands.

"Nay, child," said he, reassuringly. "There was no great harm done. A few weeks with his arm in a sling."

"But I saw the blood redden through his sleeve!" cried she, drawing her hands down from her face and clasping them together. And as though to rid herself of the topic she jogged her bridle and rode forward.

I turned my horse and followed with Mr. Curwen, the while he gave me more precise account of what had happened.

"The sheriff took an absurd and threatening tone when he found the door barred, which suited me very ill. So I bade Dorothy load my pistols while I parleyed with the man. He threatened me in I know not how many Latin words and in a tone of great injury, whereupon, perceiving that, since he spoke a learned tongue and wore the look of a gentleman, it would be no derogation, I threw down my glove as a gage and challenged him to take it up."

I shot a glance at Mr. Curwen, but he spoke in a simple, ordinary voice.

"Instead of doing that," he continued, "he disappointed me greatly by a violent flow of abuse, which was cut short on the instant by Dorothy's pistol. She was standing behind me, who stood on a chair, and fired beneath my arm. 'Oh, the poor dear!' she cried, 'I have hurt him,' and plumped down in a faint. It was indeed the luckiest accident in the world, for the constables, seeing their chief wounded, were sufficiently scared to stay no longer than gave them time to pick him up."

"But all this occurred a month ago!" I exclaimed, "Surely the sheriff's men returned."

"In the evening; but they found no one at Applegarth. Dorothy and I with Mary Tyson were on our way to Carlisle. The other servants I sent to their homes. We have good friends at Carlisle, Mr. Clavering," he said, with one of his prodigiously cunning winks, "very good, safe friends. We said good-bye to them when your army had passed Carlisle, and so returned home."

"And Miss Curwen?" I asked. "What of her, since you come with us?"

"She will be safe at home now," said he, "and Mary Tyson is there to bear her company."

"She will be safe, no doubt," said I, "so long as we keep the upper hand."

We were by this time come to the top of the hill, and Dorothy was already talking to Lord Derwentwater.

"So," says he, coming forward and taking Mr. Curwen by the hand, "here are the four of us proscribed."

"We will wear our warrants for an order at St. James's Palace," cries Dorothy; and at that moment the trumpet sounded.

A brief leave-take between Dorothy and her father, and we were marching down the hill, Mr. Curwen joined to the Gentlemen Volunteers, his six henchmen enrolled in Lord Derwentwater's troop.

Dorothy remained behind upon the hilltop with the servant who was to convey her home, and though we marched away with our backs towards her, I none the less gathered, as we went, some very distinct impressions of her appearance. Nor can it be said that they were the outcome of my recollections. For when I first saw her riding towards the hill, I was only conscious that it was she riding towards me, and very wonderful it seemed. And afterwards, when I heard her voice, I was only conscious that it was she who was talking, and very wonderful that seemed too. But I did not remark the particulars of her appearance. Now as we were marching away, I gained very distinct impressions, as for instance of: item a little cocked hat like a man's, only jauntier; item a green riding-coat; item a red waistcoat, etc. The truth is, my head was turned backwards all the time, and we had not advanced more than a couple of hundred yards before my horse was turned in the same direction. For I let myself fall to the rear until I was on the edge of the troops, and then faced about and fairly galloped back to her.

She was looking with great intentness in the direction precisely opposite to that from which I came; and as I halted by her side:

"Oh!" said she, turning in the most perfect surprise, "I did not think that it would be you. I expected it would be my father."

"I gathered that," I replied, "from your indifference."

She answered nothing, but industriously stroked the mane of her horse.

"Now say 'owl,'" I added.

She began to laugh, then checked herself and looked at me with the chilliest stare.

"And if I did say 'owl,'" she asked in a puzzled simplicity, "would it rain?"

I began to wish that I had not spoken.

"Well?" she insisted, "what if I did say 'owl'?"

"I should say 'Robin Redbreast,'" I replied weakly.

"And a very delicate piece of wit, to be sure, Mr. Clavering," says she with her chin in the air. "You have learnt the soldier's forwardness of tongue. Let me pray you have learnt his——" And then, thinking, I suppose, from my demeanour that I was sufficiently abashed, she broke off of a sudden. "I would that I were a man," she cried, "and could swing a sword!"

She looked towards the little army which defiled between the fields, with the sun glinting upon musket and scabbard, and brought her clenched fist down upon the pommel of her saddle.

"Nay," said I, "you have done better than swing a sword. You have shot a sheriff, though it was by accident."

She looked at me with a certain timidity.

"You do not blame me for that?"

"Blame you. And why?"

"I do not know. But you might think it—bloodthirsty," she said, with a quaver in her voice, betwixt a laugh and a cry.

"How could I, when you swooned the instant afterwards?"

"My father told you that!" she exclaimed gratefully; and then: "But he did not tell you the truth of the matter. He said I fired by accident. But I did not; I meant to fire;" and she spoke as though she was assuring me of something incredible. "Now what will you say?" she asked anxiously.

"Why," said I foolishly, "since it was done to save your guest——"

"Oh dear, no," she interrupted coolly, and the anxiety changed to wonder in her eyes. "Indeed, Mr. Clavering, you must not blame yourself that it was on your account I fired." She spoke with the greatest sympathy. "You have no reason in the world to reproach yourself. It was because of my father. He threw down his glove from the window and challenged the sheriff to mortal combat, with whatever weapons he chose, and the sheriff called him—mad. It was that angered me. I think, in truth, that I was mad. And since the pistol was loaded and pointed at the man, I—I pulled the trigger." Then she turned to me impulsively, "You will have a care of my father—the greatest care. Oh, promise me that!"

"Of a truth, I will," I replied fervently.

"Thank you," said she, and the old friendliness returned to her face. "We could not keep him. From the day that he heard of the rising in Northumberland, he has been in a fever. And he meant to go without our knowing. You are familiar with his secrecies;" she gave a little pathetical laugh. "He was ever scouring his pistols and guns in the corner when he thought we should not see him. He meant to go. I feared that he would slip from the house one night, like——" She caught herself up sharply, with half a glance at me. "So it seemed best to encourage him to go openly. Besides," she added slowly, bending her head a little over her horse's back—she seemed to be carefully examining the snaffle—"I thought it not unlikely that we should find you here."

"Ah, you had that thought in your mind?" I cried, feeling my heart pulse within me. "Indeed, it turns my promise to a sacred obligation. What one man can do to keep your father safe, believe it, shall be done by me." I was looking towards the receding army as I spoke, and a new thought struck me. "You would have let me go," I exclaimed in reproach, "without a hint of your request, had I not come back to you?"

She coloured for an instant, but instead of answering the question—

"I knew you would come——" she began, and broke off suddenly. "Yes, why did you come back?" she asked in a voice of indifferent curiosity.

"I had not said good-bye to you. You gave me no chance, and it hurt me to part from you that way."

"But I thought that was your custom," she replied, with some touch of resentment underneath the carelessness. "It would not have been the first time. You were careful not to leave a light burning in the stables the last night you quitted Applegarth."

"I saw that you knew."

"Yes," said she, hurriedly. "I heard your foot upon the gravel."

"But I said good-bye to the candle in your window all that night, until the morning broke from a shoulder of High Stile. I had to go. There were reasons."

She interrupted me again in a great hurry, and with so complete a change of manner that I wondered for a moment whether Mary Tyson had related to her the conversation at the gate of the garden.

"I have no wish to hear them," she said with a certain pride.

"Nor I to tell you of them," I returned, and doubtless I spoke in a humble and despondent voice.

"I do not know the secret," she said gently; "but if I can help you at all——" she relapsed into gentleness. "Why, you are helping me, and I would gladly pay you in the same coin."

"Nay," said I, shaking my head, "no one can help me. It is my own fault, and I must redeem it by myself. It was a little thing in the beginning, only I did not face it. It grew into a trouble, still I did not face it Now the trouble has grown into a disaster, and I must face it."

She sat her horse in silence for a moment.

"I have known for a long while that there was some trouble upon you. But are you sure"—she turned her face frankly to me—"are you sure I cannot help? Because I am a woman, after all?" she said with a whimsical smile.

"Miss Curwen," said I, "if this was a case wherein any woman could fitly help me, believe me, I would come to you first in all this world. But——" I hesitated, feeling it in truth very difficult to say what yet remained. But I had already said too much. I had said too much when I told her I had watched the light in her window, and the consciousness of that compelled me to go on. "But the business is too sordid. I would have no woman meddle in it, least of all you. The trouble is the outcome of my own wilful folly, and my one prayer is that I draw the consequence of it solely upon my head." I gathered up the reins and prepared to ride away.

"Well," said she, in a voice that trembled ever so little, "we may at least shake hands;" and she held out her hand to me. "And observe, Mr. Clavering," she continued with a smile, "I say *hands*," laying some emphasis upon the word.

I could not take it.

"I have not even the right," I said, "to touch you by the finger-tips. But," and I drew in a breath, "if ever I regain that right——"

"You will," she interrupted, her voice ringing, her face flushing, her eyes bright and sparkling. "I am sure of that. You will."

The confidence, however misplaced, was none the less very sweet to me, and I felt it lift my heart for a moment. But then—

"Even if that comes true," I replied, "there will still be a barrier which will prevent you and me from shaking hands, and that barrier will be a prison-door."

She started at the word, as though with some comprehension; and since I had no heart to explain to her more concerning the pit into which I had fallen, I raised my hat and rode down the hill. It seemed to me that the prison-door was even then shutting between us in the open air. For these last days I had lost my hopes that in this rising we should succeed. The chessboard was spread open, and the chessmen ranged upon the board. We had no pawns, and only novices to direct the game. There was General Wills in front of us, and General Carpenter behind us; and, moreover, one question dinning in our ears, at every village where we halted, at every town where we encamped, "Where is the King?" With the King in the midst of us, who knows but what the country might have risen? But, alas! the King was not as yet even in Scotland, and since he delayed, what wonder that our lukewarm friends in England tarried too?

All this flashed through my mind as I rode down the hillside, and the reflection brought with it another thought I turned in my saddle. I could just see Miss Curwen disappearing on the further side of the hill, and again I rode up to the top and descended with a shout towards her.

"Should we fail," I cried hurriedly—"should the usurper hold his own——"

"And you think he will, I know," she answered. "You told me so a minute ago, when you spoke of the prison-door."

Her words fairly took my breath away. I stared at her, dumbfoundered. Did she know my story, then?

"But if we fail, what then?" And her question brought me back to her own necessities.

"Why, there will be a great danger for you at Applegarth."

She turned to me very solemnly.

"If we fail," she said, "keep that word you pledged to me. I shall treasure the pledge, knowing you will not break it, Guard my father!"

"But it is of you that I am thinking."

"Of me?" she said; "why, if needs be, I suppose I—I can shoot another sheriff;" and with a plaintive little laugh she set the spur to her horse.

I rode across the hill, and, once upon the flat, galloped after our regiments. The expression of her confidence was as a renewal of my blood. It sang in my ears sweet, like a tune dimly remembered, and heard again across a waste of years. "I would fulfil that double trust," I cried with a leaping heart, and then in more humility fell to a prayer that so I might be permitted.

For it was a double trust I felt. It was not merely that I was pledged to the safeguarding of her father, but it seemed to me that I was no less firmly pledged to bring about that other and more difficult result. I must regain the right to hold her hand in mine, even though I might win no advantage from the right.

CHAPTER XVIII
AT PRESTON AND AFTERWARDS

The siege of Preston forms no part of this story, and fortunately so for me, since I saw and understood of its brief and fatal enactment no more than was done under my own nose. Why General Wills and his dragoons were allowed to pass the Ribble Bridge and the narrow lane which leads to it without so much impediment as a single shot might cause; why Mr. Forster made no attempt to break out down the Fishergate Street into the marshes beyond the town when General Carpenter closed in upon our rear; by what persuasions the Highlanders were finally induced to lay down their arms— these are questions for historians to dispute and find answer to, if they can. For my part, I fought at Macintosh's barrier a little below the church, where the first attack was made, with one eye upon Preston's regiment of foot in front and the other upon Mr. Curwen at my side; and what with the enemy and my friend, my hands were full.

The attack was made about eleven of the forenoon. I remember very distinctly the extraordinary hush that fell upon us when our friends from the windows of the houses above us signalled that the troops were approaching. In front stretched the empty street, so still, so bare in the sunlight, and taking on of a sudden an appalling significance. Half an hour before, messengers had ridden hither and thither with resounding hoofs, patrols tramped upon the footway, citizens peeped timorous from casement and door. We had glanced down it as we looked to our weapons with a matter-of-fact word: "This way they will come." Now it seemed to wait in a conscious expectation, the responsible agent of destiny. France, Scotland, England, every country in Europe had a stake to be played for in this street, and it was as though it had been new-swept and garnished for the game. I know that every cobble throughout its length seemed to gleam in the sunlight distinct and separate from its fellows. And then, whilst we stood silent behind the barrier, while from the windows the Highlanders bent forward craning their necks, grasping their muskets, the deadly silence was broken by the ringing tramp of a single horse, and from a passage at the side betwixt two houses in the middle distance, an officer rode out into the open causeway with his drawn sword in his hand. For a moment, every man of us, I think, held his breath. The officer looked up the street to the barrier and again down the street and at the windows to see how our men were posted. Then a shout went up, loud, unanimous, like a single voice; with a single movement every musket was raised to the shoulder, and in a second the air whistled with bullets and flashed in a hundred tiny flames. But it seemed the officer bore a charmed life. No bullet struck him then, and cantering back within the shelter of the passage, he presently led out and ranged his men. The men were Preston's regiment; the officer, their Lieutenant-colonel, the Lord Forrester, and with their appearance the battle was begun in earnest. I have hinted that I had some difficulty in restraining Mr. Curwen's ardour, and Lord Forrester gives me an instance pat to the point. For during that moment's silence, when the colonel stood alone in the street, Mr. Curwen climbs unsteadily to the top of the barrier, and with his white hair blowing from his shoulders, his dreamy eyes ablaze with I know not what fancies of antique chivalry, calls upon the colonel to settle then and there with him in single combat the succession to the Crown. Or, rather begins to call, I should say, for the moment at which he began to speak was precisely that moment at which I saw the muskets go up to the shoulders, and leaping after him I pulled him unceremoniously down.

And here we found the value of our cannon. For we had two pieces at our barricade, and though they failed at first, it was owing to a sailor who professing skill and experience was entrusted with the management of them, and who aiming at Preston's regiment in the street, with great ingenuity brought down a chimney from the tops of the houses. The truth is the man was full with ale, but having got rid of him, we fared better, and firing securely from behind the barrier, did so much execution as made our adversaries draw off.

That night we remained at the barrier firing platoons whenever a light appeared in those houses which we knew to be occupied by our opponents, and getting such sleep as we could to fit us for the morrow.

The next morning, however, we heard that General Carpenter by forced marches had come upon our rear so that the town was invested about, and there was no way for us except by the gates of death. And at the same time many rumours of a capitulation were spread abroad which drove the Highlandmen into a frenzy. All the morning then we remained in the greatest uncertainty, but about three of the afternoon Colonel Cotton rode up the street with a dragoon and a drum beating a chamade before him, and then we knew that these rumours were indeed the truth. He alighted at the Mitre, whither we presently saw Lord Kenmure, Mr. Forster, and Lord Widdrington making haste to join him; and in a little came a messenger to us seeking Lord Derwentwater. He was at the moment digging in a trench to deepen it, with his waistcoat off; and slipping on his clothes:

"Curse the fellow!" he cried, and so turned to me, "Lawrence! never trust a Tory! If you outlive this misfortune never speak to one! They are damned rogues in disguise. Here's Lord Widdrington, good tender man that cannot travel without his soup in a bottle! Curse the fellow! All yesterday, while you and I, and the rest of my good friends here, were pleading the cause with the only music our enemies will dance to, what was my Lord Widdrington doing, but sitting in an alehouse, licking his bottle of soup? The gout he blames! Well, well, the gout is a very opportune complaint;" and so striking his hands together to remove the mud from them, off he goes to the Mitre.

It was some little while before he returned to me, during which I bethought me not so much of the pass into which I had fallen, as the means by which I might extricate myself. For extricate myself I must. There was Mr. Herbert in the first place. Here was the end of our insurrection, and I thrown back upon my first plan of delivering myself to the authorities; and in the second, I must needs get Mr. Curwen to some spot in which he could lie safely, until such time as the matter had blown over; and furthermore, to these two duties was yet added a third and new obligation. Yet, I think it was this last which enheartened me to confront the other two, for there was something very sweet in the mere notion of it, which leavened all my distress.

In about two hours came Lord Derwentwater back, and drawing me aside:

"It is not a capitulation," he said, "but a mere surrender. Forster is given till seven of the morning to reconcile his troops to it. Meanwhile, I go with Colonel Cotton as a hostage." He pulled out his purse as he spoke, and rummaging in his pockets, added to it such coins as he had loose about him.

"We will divide them," said he. "Nay, they will be of more service to you than to me. I was quartered with an apothecary—you know the house—a man very discreet and loyal. Doubtless he will do for you what he can if you add my recommendation to your request. It may be that you can escape, since you are hampered with no companions and are little known."

"Nay," I replied, "I have Mr. Curwen to safeguard, if by any means I can. He gave me shelter and every kindness when I was at my wits' ends. Besides——" And then I came to a stop and felt myself flushing hot, but hoped the grime of the gunpowder would hide my confusion.

"Well?" he asked shrewdly—"Besides?"

"Besides," I stammered, "I promised his daughter."

"Ah!" said he, "I told you it would be Dorothy Curwen;" and with that he shook me by the hand. But at the touch I realized of a sudden all the love and friendliness which he had shown to me from my first coming into Cumberland. I had a picture before my eyes of the house on Lord's Island—my Lord and his Lady in the cosy parlour; the children in their cots above. I looked into his face; it was bravely smiling. The chill November evening was crowding upon us as we stood there in the street; the lights began to shine in the windows; close to us a soldier was cursing Mr. Forster; beyond the barrier, down the street, one of Will's dragoons was roaring out a song; and before the Mitre door under the lamp Colonel Cotton was sitting on his horse. I could say nothing to Lord Derwentwater but what would point his misfortunes, and so—

"My lord," I cried simply, "God send that you and I may meet again."

"God send no answer to that wish, Lawrence," he replied solemnly.

He walked lightly to the Mitre door, as lightly as a man to his wedding. He mounted his horse; his face shone clear for a moment beneath the lamp, and that was the last glimpse I had of it. He rode down the street with Colonel Cotton; I made my way in all haste to the apothecary with whom he had lodged.

I had some talk with the apothecary, of which the purport will appear hereafter, and returned for Mr. Curwen, whom I found immediately, and my servant Ashlock, whom I did not find until late in the evening. For he had been employed in carrying gunpowder from barrier to barrier, so that I knew of no fixed spot where I could lay my hands on him. However, as I say, I found him at the last, and when General Wills marched into Preston Market-place at seven o'clock of the Monday morning, Mr. Lawrence Clavering, with a blue apron about his waist, was taking down the shutters from the apothecary's shop, while Mr. Curwen, much broken by fatigue and disappointment, lay abed in an attic of the house, with Ashlock to tend on him.

All that day, which was Monday the 14th of November, I lived in a jumping anxiety. For the shop from morn to night was beset with people seeking remedies for the wounded. These people, however, for the most part, belonged to General Wills' force; and luckily the citizens of the town had so much to distract them in the spectacle of the troops and of the prisoners—now ranged in the market-place, now marched off and locked up in the church—and in their own joy at escaping from the siege with so little damage, that they forgot those trivial ailments which bring them to the apothecary's. So the new journeyman, pounding drugs in a corner as far from the window as he could creep, escaped notice for that day and lay down to sleep beneath the counter with a mind a thought easier than his aching arm.

In something less than a minute, it seemed to me, I felt a tug at my coat. I started up with a cry, and looking to see the red coat of a soldier, beheld the homely brown of my friend the apothecary. His hat was on his head, the door of the shop stood open, and the full daylight poured into it.

"Thomas," he said, with a whimsical glance through his spectacles, "I cannot do with an idle apprentice. I must cancel your indentures."

"What do you mean?" I asked.

"Willy nilly I must keep you for to-day, since I have a little journey to take and I cannot leave the shop untended. But to-morrow, Thomas, you must go." With that he grew more particular, and informed me that General Carpenter intended to lead his troops to Wigan no later than this very morning, since they could not be housed in Preston, and were, moreover, in sore need of rest from the rapidity of their march.

"General Wills," he continued, "is left to guard the prisoners, and that doubtless he can do—but he cannot watch the streets as well."

Thereupon he gave me some directions as to what answers I should give to his customers, and went off upon his errand. And as a result of this errand, on the Wednesday evening the apothecary took a walk. He walked down the Fishergate Street, and every now and again, when a watchman or an officer going his rounds approached, he knocked twice upon the pavement with a heavy cane he carried, and maybe loitered for a little until the officer had passed. There were three men following him, whereof one I can affirm kept his hand beneath his great-coat tightly clasped about the butt of a loaded pistol; and whenever that double knock sounded, the three men dived into the first alley that presented. The apothecary's walk led across the marsh to the river's bank. The marsh itself might be deemed an unlikely spot for a comfortable citizen to take the air in when the night mist was smoking up from it to a November moon. But the rest of his peregrination was more extraordinary still. For he chose that point of the bank at which the river shallows and makes a ford, and without hesitation waded across. On the opposite side he waited for the three who followed to come up with him; which they did with a little delay, since two of them were old and the footing not the steadiest in the world. Half a mile along the bank the apothecary went forward and whistled. A boat slipped out from a clump of alders and the fugitives stepped on board. There was a hurried whisper of thanks from the boat, a bluff pooh-poohing of them from the bank, and the boatman pushed off. We kept down the stream for some two hours, and disembarking again, after once more re-crossing the river, struck slantwise over the fields, and so towards morning came to a fisherman's cottage set amongst the sand-hills by the sea. It was here that my apothecary was wont to come upon his holidays and spend the time fishing; and he could have hit upon no refuge better suited to my purpose.

My first thought, however, when the boatman admitted us into his cottage, was for Mr. Curwen. It was now some hours since he had waded through the ford, and what with his wet limbs and the weary tramp across the fields, I was afraid lest he might fall into some dangerous fever. I was the more inclined to credit this fear from a perception that he was more troubled and downcast than I had seen him even after our submission and defeat. Accordingly, I asked the boatman to lend him some woollen stockings and other dry garments, which the man very readily did, and set before us thereafter a meal.

Mr. Curwen, however, eat little or nothing, but sat shaking his head, as though the world had crumbled about his ears. I made an effort therefore to rally him into the recovery of his good spirits, though with the heaviest heart. "All was not lost," I said, "for here were we with whole skins, in a secure retreat, while, on the other hand, the Earl of Mar might be winning who knows what victories in Scotland."

"It is not of the King," he replied regretfully, "nor of myself that I was thinking. It was of my daughter. I fear me, Mr. Clavering, I have given too much thought to a cause in which I was of the smallest use, and too little to Dorothy, with whom my duty lay."

He spoke in a breaking voice and with a gleam of tears in his lack-lustre eyes.

"Mr. Curwen," said I, changing my note on the instant, "on the Sunday afternoon at the barricade I bethought me with all humility of the path which I must take through this tangle of our misfortunes; I saw very clearly that there were three duties enjoined on me. The first was, to help you to security, if by any means I could. Nay," I said, as he raised a hand in deprecation, "it was a promise I made to your daughter, and, believe me, it is one of the few comforts left to me in what remains of life that I see some prospect of carrying that promise to a successful issue. The second duty was, to bring your daughter Dorothy," and it was my voice now which broke upon the word, "safely to you. That I have promised to myself, but I hold it no less sacred than the first."

He reached out a hand to me across the table.

"And the third?" he asked timidly.

"It is the payment of a debt," I replied—"a debt incurred by me to be repaid by me, and I put it last, not because it is of less incumbency than the other two, but because it ends my life, and with my life such poor service as I can do my friends."

"It ends your life!" he exclaimed.

"So I do hope," I replied, and since I meant the words, I can but trust there was no boastfulness in the expression, "for it is my life alone that can now set the tally straight God knows, my trouble lies not in the payment, but in the means of payment. For there are matters which I do not know, and it may be that I shall waste my life."

This I said, thinking of my ignorance as to where Mr. Herbert lay imprisoned. I had a plan in my head, it is true, which offered me some chance of accomplishing this duty, but it only offered me a chance. Mrs. Herbert had promised me that she would remain in the lodging at Keswick, and during the interval since I had last set eyes on her, she might well have received news of her husband's whereabouts. But would she keep the promise—she had every reason in the world to distrust me—would she keep the promise I had so urgently besought of her?

"Mr. Clavering," said my friend, "I told you just now I was afeared I had thought too much of the King and too little of my Dorothy, but these words of yours put even that better thought to the blush. You have been at my elbow all the last days protecting me; you have brought about my escape; you are planning how to save my daughter; and all this while you have seen—you, young in the sap of your strength—you have seen the limits of your life near to you, as that barrier by the church was near to us at Preston. And not a word of it have you spoken, while we have bemoaned ourselves and made no secret of our misery. Not a word have you spoken, not a hint has your face betrayed."

"Mr. Curwen, I beg of you," I replied quickly, for the praise jarred on me, as well it might. "A man does not speak what it shames him even to think of. But to my plan."

I drew from my pocket a sheet of paper and a pencil, with which I had provided myself before I quitted the apothecary's shop.

"Your sloop the *Swallow* should be lying now off the mouth of the Esk by Ravenglass."

Mr. Curwen started at my abrupt remark. Was it merely that, amidst the turmoil and hurry of the last weeks, he had clean forgotten his design to set me over into France? Or was it that he had countermanded his order since that night when I had fled from Applegarth?

"It should be cruising thereabouts to pick me up," I said, feeling my heart drumming against my breast. I did not dare to put the question in its naked directness. "It should have reached Ravenglass by now." Mr. Curwen sat staring at me. "The ship—the ship I mean! Oh, answer me!" I cried. "Answer me!"

"Yes!" he said slowly. "The *Swallow* should be now at Ravenglass. That is true." He seemed to be assuring himself of the fact and speculating on its import.

"You sent no message to prevent it sailing, after I left you?"

"None!" said he.

I drew a breath of relief.

"But we are now at the fifteenth of November. How long did you bid the captain wait?"

Mr. Curwen seemed of a sudden to grasp my design, though, as he showed me in a moment, he had got no more than an inkling of it.

"Until you hailed him," he replied, rising from his chair in some excitement "He was to wait for you. That was the top and bottom of his orders. There was no time fixed for your coming."

"Then," said I, in an excitement not a whit less than his, "the *Swallow* will be waiting now up the coast?"

In the little room we could hear the surf booming upon the sand. I flung open the window. The sound swelled of a sudden, as though the music of a spinet should magically deepen to an organ-harmony.

"Your *Swallow*," I exclaimed, "lifts and falls upon the very waves which we hear breaking on the sands."

Mr. Curwen stepped over to my side. The sandhills stretched before us, white under the moon, and with a whisper from the grasses which crowned them. I found a cheering comfort in their very desolation. Beyond the sandhills, the sea leaped and called, tossing to and fro a hundred jewelled arms. I felt my heart leaping with the waves, answering their call, and the fresh brine went stinging through my veins.

"Northwards," I cried, reaching out an arm, "round the point there, up the coast, beyond Morecambe Bay the *Swallow* waits for us. It is no great distance, Mr. Curwen. God save Lord Bolingbroke, who betrayed the Catalans!" I heard my voice ring with an exultation I had not known for many a day. I strained my eyes northwards along the sea. It seemed to my heated fancies, that the barrier of the shores fell back. My vision leaped over cape and bay, and where the Esk poured into the sea by Muncaster Fell I seemed to see the *Swallow*, its black mast tapering across the moon; I seemed to hear the grinding of its cable as it strained against the anchor.

Then very quickly Mr. Curwen spoke at my side.

"There is my daughter. In this great hope of ours, are we not forgetting her?"

"Nay," I replied, "it is of your daughter I am thinking. You trust your captain, you say? You trust your captain will be waiting now? If so, he will be waiting a fortnight's time; he waits until I come." I drew Mr. Curwen back to the table.

"Look you, Mr. Curwen, I marched with Mr. Forster from the outset of the rising. We crossed from the Cheviots into England on the 1st of November; we proclaimed King James in Preston Market-square upon the 10th. Nine days enclosed our march, and we marched in force. There were other necessities beyond that of speed to order our advance. There was food to be requisitioned, towns to be chosen for a camp wherein our troops could quarter. At Penrith, at Appleby, we drew up for battle. All this meant delay. Some of us rode, no doubt, but our pace was the pace of those who walked. And, mark, nine days enclosed our march. A man alone and free to choose his path would shear two days from that nine, maybe three. I cannot choose my path, there will be hindrances. I must travel for the chief part by night. But I have not so far to go. Grant me nine days, then! It is the sixteenth—nay, the seventeenth. On the twenty-sixth I should be knocking at the door of Applegarth."

"Nay," said he, "you will be captured. You have risked enough for us, more than enough. Mr. Clavering, I cannot permit that you should go."

"Yet," said I, with a smile, "you will find that easier than to prevent me. You told me of a safe route between Applegarth and Ravenglass," I continued. "How long will it take a woman to traverse it?"

"I called it safe," he answered doubtfully, making dots upon the paper with the point of his pencil, "because it stretched along the watersheds. But that was in September. Now it may be there will be snow."

The winter indeed had fallen early that year. Yes, the snow might be deep on the hills. I had a picture before my eyes of Dorothy struggling through it.

"Then we will add another day," I answered, and strove to make the answer light. "Given that other day, how long shall we take from Applegarth to Ravenglass?"

"Three days," said he, "or thereabouts."

"Nine days and three, twelve together. Your daughter, Mr. Curwen, shall be on board the *Swallow* by the twenty-ninth. Meanwhile I think you can lie safely here with Ashlock. From Ravenglass the sloop shall sail directly here, and, taking you up, make straight for France. So sketch me here the way from Applegarth!"

Mr. Curwen drew a rough outline on the paper while I bent over him.

"You will mount to the top of Gillerthwaite," he said, "then bear to the right betwixt Great Gable and the pillar. Descend the grass into Mosedale. Here is Wastdale Church; strike westwards thence to the great gap between Scafell and the Screes. This is Burnmoor—five miles of it, and there is no water; after you pass Burnmoor tarn until you have come down to Eskdale. Cross Eskdale towards the sea. The long ridge here is Muncaster Fell. Keep along the slope of it, and God send you see the *Swallow*!"

He gave me the paper. I folded it carefully and thrust it into my pocket. Then I took up my hat and held out my hand to him. He took it, and still clasping it came to the door with me, and out into the open.

"Mr. Clavering," he said, "when you first came to Applegarth I told you that I had lost a son. To-night I seem to have found another, and it would be a great joy to me if, when the *Swallow* puts in here, I could see that second son upon its deck."

I stood for a moment looking at him, his words so tempted me! The difficulties of the adventure which lay before me became trivial in my eyes as the crossing of a muddy road. My fancy, bridging all between, jumped to the moment when the *Swallow* should loose its sails with Dorothy on board. I saw myself in imagination standing by her side, watching the Cumberland Hills lessen and dwindle, the while we streamed down the coast towards the sandbanks here.

"Then you shall see me," I longed to cry. But the thought of another woman weeping by a lonely lamp in Keswick crept into my heart, and thereafter the thought of a man lying somewhere kennelled in a prison.

CHAPTER XIX
APPLEGARTH AGAIN

I travelled along the beach until I reached the southern cape of Morecambe Bay, and only now and again swerved inland when I espied ahead of me the smoke and houses of a village. This I did more for safety's sake than for any comfort or celerity in the act of walking. Indeed, the sand, which, being loose and dry, slipped and yielded with every step I took, did, I think, double the labour and tedium of my journey. But on the other hand, the country by the sea-coast was flat, so that I could distinguish the figures of people and the direction of their walk at a long distance—a doubtful advantage, you may say, and one that cut both ways. And so it would have been but for the grassy sand-hills which embossed the wide stretch of shore. It was an easy thing to drop into the grass at the first sight of a stranger and crawl down into the hollows betwixt the hillocks; and had such an one pursued me, he would have had the most unprofitable game of hide-and-seek that ever a man engaged in. I had other reasons besides for keeping near the sea. For since I travelled chiefly by night and in the late and early quarters of the day, I had need of a resting-place when the day was full. Now so long as I kept to the coast I had ever one ready to my hand amongst these lonely and desolate sandhills, where I was easily able to scoop out a bed, and so lie snug from the wind. For another thing, I had thus the noise of the sea continually in my ears. I did not know in truth what great store I set on that, until a little short of Lancaster I turned my back on it. The sea sang to me by day and by night, lulling me like a cradle-song when I lay cushioned among the sand-hills, inspiriting as the drums of an army when I walked through the night. It was not merely that it told me of the *Swallow* swinging upon its tides, and of the great hopes I drew therefrom, but it spoke too with voices of its own, and whether the voices whispered or turbulently laughed, it was always the same perplexing mystery they hinted of. They seemed to signify a message they could not articulate, and it came upon me sometimes, as I sat tired by the shore, that I would fain sit there and listen until I had plucked out the kernel of its meaning. I used to fancy that once a man could penetrate to that and hold it surely, there would be little more he needed to know, but he would carry it with him, as a magic crystal wherein he could see strangely illuminated and made plain, the eternal mysteries which girded him about.

From Morecambe Bay I turned inland towards the borders of Yorkshire, and passing to the east of Kirby Lonsdale, that I might avoid the line of Forster's march, curved round again towards Grasmere. Here I began to redouble my precautions, seeing that I was come into a country where my face and recent history might be known. For since I had left the coast I had voyaged in no great fear of detection, taking a lift in a carrier's cart when one chanced to pass my way, and now and again hiring a horse for a stage. The apothecary at Preston, in addition to his other benefactions, had provided me with an inconspicuous suit of clothes, and as I had money in my pockets wherewith to pay my way, I was able to press on unremarked, or at least counted no more than a merchant's clerk travelling upon his master's business.

From Grasmere, I mounted by the old path across Coldbarrow Fell, which had first led me to Blackladies, and keeping along the ridge crept down into Keswick late upon the seventh day. There was no light in Mrs. Herbert's lodging as I slipped down the street, and for a second I was seized with a recurrence of my fear that she had left the town. It was only for a second, however. For that conviction which I had first tasted when I rode down Gillerthwaite in the early morning, had been growing stronger and stronger within me, more especially of late. I was possessed by some instinctive foreknowledge that the occasion for which I looked would come; that somehow, somewhere I should be enabled to bring forward my testimony to the clearing of Mr. Herbert from the imputation of disloyalty. It was a thought that more and more I repeated to myself, and each time with a stouter confidence. It may be that these more immediate tasks to which I had set my hand—I mean the rescue of Mr. Curwen and his daughter from the consequence of participation in the rebellion—hindered me from looking very closely into the difficulties of the third and last. It may be, too, that this conviction was in some queer way the particular message which the sea had for me—that I had received the message unconsciously while pondering what it might be. I do not know; I only know that when I repeated it to myself, it sounded like nothing so much as the booming of waves upon a beach.

I slept that night under a familiar boulder on the hillside above Applegarth, and in the early morning I came down to the house, and without much ceremony roused the household. Mary Tyson poked her head out of a window.

"Miss Dorothy?" I cried

"She is asleep."

"Wake her up and let me in!"

So I was in time. Mary Tyson came down and opened the door; and in a little, as I waited in the hall, I heard Dorothy's footsteps on the stairs.

"You have escaped!" she cried; "and my father—you bring bad news of him?"

"No; I thank God for it, I bring good news."

And the blood came into her cheeks with a rush.

I told her briefly how we had escaped from Preston. She listened to the story with shining eyes.

"And all this you have done for—for us?" she said with a singular note of pride in her voice.

"It is little," I replied, "even if what's left to do crowns it successfully. But if in that we go astray, why, it is less than nothing." Thereupon I told her of the plan which I had formed with regard to the *Swallow*, and of the journey which she and I must take. She listened to me now, however, with an occupied air, and interrupted me before I had come to a close.

"It is you who have done this?" she repeated in the same tone which she had used before.

"I did but keep my promise. It was made to you," I answered simply.

"I am your debtor for all my life."

"No," I cried. "It is the other way about."

"I do not feel the debt," she said very softly, and then raising a face all rosy: "Ah, but I let you stand here!" she exclaimed. "You shall tell me more of your plan while we breakfast, for I am not sure that I gave a careful ear to it;" and taking me by the arm she led me towards the dining-room. "You have come from Preston in all this haste. My poor child!" She spoke in a quite natural tone of pity, and I doubt not but what my appearance gave a reasonable complexion to her pity. It was the motherliness, however, which tickled me.

"What is it you laugh at?" she asked suddenly, her voice changing at once to an imperious dignity.

"I was thinking," said I, "that your head, Miss Curwen, only reaches to my chin."

"If God made me a dwarf," said she, with a freezing stateliness, "it is very courteous of you to reproach me with it—the most delicate courtesy, upon my word."

She was in truth ever very sensitive as to her height, and anxious to appear taller than she was; for which anxiety there was no reason whatever, since she was just of the right stature, and an inch more or less would have been the spoiling of her; which opinion I most unfortunately expressed to her, and so made matters worse. For said she—

"Your condescension, Mr. Clavering, is very amiable and consoling;" and with that she left me alone in the room, until such a time as breakfast should be ready. I went out, however, in search of Mary Tyson, and finding her, explained my design, and asked her to put together in a bundle the least quantity of clothes which would suffice for Dorothy until she reached France. Mary fell in with the plan immediately, and began to regret her age and bulk that would hinder her from keeping pace with us. But I cut short her discourse, and bidding her hasten on the breakfast, made shift with a basin of water and a towel to hurriedly repair the disarray of my toilet.

For now every instant of delay began to drag upon my spirits. Once upon the hillside, it would be strange, I thought, if we did not contrive to come undetected to Ravenglass. We had to cross two valleys, it is true, but they were both rugged and bleak, with but few dwellings scattered about them, and those only of the poorer sort, inhabited by men cut off from the world by the barrier of the hills, who from very ignorance could not, if they would, meddle in their neighbours' affairs. The one danger of the journey that I foresaw lay, as I have said, in the great fall of snow.

But here within the walls of the house it was altogether different. Danger seemed impending about me. Every moment I looked to hear the beat of hoofs upon the road, and a knocking on the door. It was, I assured myself, the most unlikely thing that on this one day the officers should come for Dorothy Curwen, but the assurance brought me little comfort I tasted in anticipation all the remorse which I should feel if the girl should be taken at the very moment of deliverance.

I was the more glad, therefore, when, on coming into the garden, I found Dorothy already dressed for the journey, in a furred waistcoat and a hood quilted and lined with a rose-coloured taffety.

"That is wise," said I, "for I fear me, Miss Curwen, we shall have it cold before we get to our journey's end."

She said never a word, but stood looking at me, and if glances could make one cold, I should have been shivering then.

"But let me be quick," I continued. "Is it known that you are at Applegarth? Have you ridden far abroad?" And in my anxiety I went over to the window and gazed down the road. Neither did she answer my questions, but, standing by the fireplace, in an even, deliberate voice she began to read me a lecture upon my manners.

"Miss Curwen!" I cried; "do you understand? Every moment you stay here, every word you speak, imperils your liberty."

She waited patiently until I had done, and continued her lecture at the point where I had interrupted her, as though I had not so much as spoken at all.

"This is the purest wilfulness!" I interrupted again, being indeed at my wits' end to know how I should stop her. I think that I showed too much anxiety, with my bobbings at the window, and exclamations, and that, seeing my alarm, she prolonged her speech out of sheer perversity to punish me the more. At last, however, she came to an end, and we set ourselves to the breakfast in silence. However, I was too hot with indignation to keep that silence wisely.

"The most ill-timed talk that ever I heard," I muttered.

She laid her knife and fork on the instant, and quietly recommenced. I rose from the table in a rage, and by a lucky chance hit upon the one argument that would close her lips.

"You forget," said I, "that your father's safety depends on your escape. If you and I are taken here, how shall he get free?" And in a very few minutes after that I took up the bundle Mary Tyson had made ready, and we crossed the threshold of Applegarth and made our way up Gillerthwaite.

It was still early in the morning, but I pushed on with perhaps greater urgency than suited my companion, since I was anxious that we should lie that night in Eskdale. Dorothy, indeed, walked more slowly than was usual with her, and there seemed to me to be an uncertainty in her gait, at which I was the more surprised, since the wind blew from the east, and we, who were moving eastwards, were completely sheltered from it by the cliffs of Great Gable, towering at the head of the valley. The steeper the ascent became, the greater grew the uncertainty of movement, so that I began to feel anxious lest some sickness should have laid hold upon her. I thought it best, however, to say nothing of my suspicion, but contented myself with glancing at her stealthily now and again. There was no hint of sickness discoverable upon her face, only she pursed her lips something sullenly, as though she was persisting in what she knew to be wrong; and once I thought that her eyes caught one of my troubled glances, and she coloured like one ashamed. At last, just as we had topped the summit of the pass, and were beginning to descend the broad, grassy cliffs between that mountain and the Pillar, she spoke, and it was the first time she had opened her lips since we had left Applegarth.

"It is an apology you need, I suppose," said she, with a singular aggressiveness, and my anxiety increased. For since I could not see that I had given her any occasion to take that tone, I was inclined to set it down to some bodily suffering.

"An apology?" I asked, with an effort at a careless laugh. "And what makes you fancy I need that?"

"It is so," she insisted, "else you would not be glowering at me in this ill-humour."

"Nay," I answered seriously, "I am in no ill-humour."

"You are," she interrupted almost viciously. "You are in the worst ill-humour in the world. Well, I do apologize. I should not have kept you waiting at Applegarth."

And I do not think that I ever heard an apology tendered with a worse grace.

"And now that I have begged your pardon," she continued, "I will carry my own bundle, thank you;" and she held out her hand for it.

"No indeed, and that you will not do," said I, hotly, "if you beg pardon from now to Doomsday."

"It is perfectly plain," said she, "that you mean to pick a quarrel with me."

Now, that I took to be the most unjust statement that she could make. And—

"Who began it?" I asked. "Who began the quarrel?"

"It is a question," she replied, with the utmost contempt, "that children ask in a nursery;" and very haughtily she marched in front of me down the hillside.

We had not gone more than a few yards before I stopped, only half stifling the cry which rose to my lips. I plumped down on the grass and fumbled in my pockets. Dorothy paused in her walk, turned, and came back to me.

"What is it?" she cried, and, I must suppose, noting my face, her tone changed in an instant "Lawrence, what is it? What is the paper?"

The paper was that on which Mr. Curwen had sketched the line of our journey. We were come to the curve in our descent into Mosedale from which that line was visible, as plainly marked on the face of the country as on the paper which I held in my hand. On the ridge of the horizon I could see the long back of Muncaster Fell, but it was not that which troubled me. We could keep on the western flank of Muncaster Fell. It was that gap between Scafell and the Screes which leads on to Burnmoor! I looked east and west. This gap that I see, I said to myself, is not the gap which Mr. Curwen meant; there will be another—there will be another! But all the time I knew most surely that this was the gap, and that over it stretched our path. Slantwise across Wastdale, and bearing to the right, Mr. Curwen had said. Well, Wastdale lay at my feet, its fields marked off by their stone walls, like the squares on a chessboard. Yes, that indeed was our way. Why, I could see Burnmoor tarn, of which he had made particular mention, and—and it lay like a pool of ink upon a sheet of white paper. There was the trouble! The wind had blown from the south-east this many a day, and with the wind, the snow; so that while in Gillerthwaite, in Ennerdale, in Newlands, through which I had come to Applegarth, I had seen the snow only upon the hilltops, and had not been troubled with it at all; there on Burnmoor it was massed from end to end. And Burnmoor was five miles across. I looked at Dorothy. Could she traverse it—she that was ailing? Five miles of snow, and the wind sweeping across those five miles like a wave! For there was no doubt but we should have the wind. If I looked upwards towards Scafell, I could see, as it were, the puff of a cannon's smoke rising up into the air. That was the wind whirling the snow. If I looked downwards into Wastdale, I could see the yew-trees by the church tossing their boughs wildly this way and that. I could hear it rushing and seething in Mosedale bottom. I looked at Dorothy, and my anxiety grew to alarm.

"What is it troubles you?" she said again.

Well, somehow or another this line had to be traversed. I should serve no end by increasing her suffering with an anticipation of the evils before us.

"Nothing," I answered, thrusting the paper back into my pocket "I was wondering whether or no I had mistaken our road." And I rose to my feet.

I could perceive from her face that she knew I was concealing some obstacle from her. She turned abruptly from me, and led the way without a word. I followed, noticing, with an ever-increasing dismay, how more and more she wavered as the descent grew steeper. And then all at once I caught sight of something which set me laughing—loudly, extravagantly, as a man will at the sudden coming of a great relief. Dorothy stopped and regarded me, not so much in perplexity, as in the haughtiest displeasure.

"Good lack!" I cried; "nay, don't stare at me. I cannot but laugh. For I believe it was the beginning of a fever troubled you, and now I know it to be a pair of heels."

She flushed very red and turned herself to face me, so that I could no longer see more than the tips of her toes.

"I know too the cause of your anger against me. It was a mere consciousness that you should not be wearing them."

"Oh, what a wiseacre!" says Dorothy, confiding her opinion to the rocks about her. "What a wonderful perceptive wiseacre! how Miss Curwen is honoured with his acquaintance!" All this in a tone of quiet sarcasm, which would have been more effectual had she not stamped her foot upon the ground. For on stamping, the heel slipped upon a loose stone, and had I not been near enough to catch her, the next instant she would have been lying full-length on the ground.

She gave something of a cry as I caught her, and sitting down, panted for a little. We both contemplated the heels. Then I drew out the paper again from my pocket.

"It was this I was considering;" and I handed it to her. "Mr. Curwen sketched it for me, and it is the way we have to go."

I pointed out the gap and the snow upon Burnmoor. She followed the direction of my gaze with a shiver, and again, but this time with equal melancholy, we fell to contemplating the heels.

"I put them on," she explained, with a touch of penitence, "before you said that about my father."

"But you could have changed them afterwards," I rejoined foolishly; and for my pains saw the penitence harden into exasperation.

"Besides, I cannot walk at all without heels," says she, briskly making a catch at her assurance.

"You cannot walk with them, I know, that's a sure thing," I persisted.

She turned to me very quietly—

"In spite of this great knowledge of yours, Mr. Clavering, of which, during the last minute, I have heard so much," she began deliberately, "there is one lesson you have yet to learn and practise. I have remarked the deficiency not only on this but on many occasions. You lack that instinct of tact and discretion which would inform you of the precise moment when you have said enough——"

How much longer she would have continued in this strain I do not know. For I sprang to my feet.

"If it is to be another lecture," I cried, "I accept the conclusion before it is reached. I can guess at it. Heels are your only wear, and the taller the better. Sailors should be enjoined by law to wear them, and they alone preserve the rope-dancer from a sure and inevitable death."

"A wiseacre first," says she, ticking off my qualities upon her fingers, "and now a humorist! Well there! a salad bowl of all the estimable virtues estimably jumbled. And meanwhile," she asked innocently, "are we not wasting time?"

I well-nigh gasped at her audacity; for who was to blame, if not she with the heels? However, this time I was sufficiently wise to keep silence, leaving it to experience to reprove her, as it most surely would. In which conviction I was right, for more than once she tripped on the grass as we descended; halfway down she reluctantly allowed me to assist her with a hand, and as we two moved along the side of Mosedale Beck at the entrance into Wastdale, she wrenched her ankle. The pain of the wrench luckily was not severe, and lasted no great while. She was in truth more startled than hurt, for we were treading the narrowest steep path, and at the side the rocks fell clear for about twenty feet to the torrent.

Thereupon she gave in and allowed me to go forward to a farmhouse lying at no great distance in Wastdale, and procure for her foot-gear of a more suitable kind. And comical enough it looked when she put it on, but I dared not laugh or so much as give hint of a smile, since I saw that her eyes were on the alert to catch me; for the worthy housewife hearing a story that I made up about a young girl who was travelling in a great haste across Ennerdale to visit a father who lay sick beyond there, which story was altogether a lie, though every word of it was truth, made me a present of a pair of her own boots and would take no money for them.

These Dorothy put on. I slipped those she had been wearing into the pockets of my great-coat, and making a hurried meal off some provisions which Mary Tyson had added to the bundle, we again set out.

I was now still more inclined to push forward at our topmost speed, for it was well past midday, and the tokens of foul weather which I had noted in the morning had become yet more distinct. The clearness had gone from the day, the clouds, woolly and grey, sulked upon the mountain-tops and crept down the sides; the wind had suddenly fallen; there was a certain heaviness in the air, as of the expectation of a storm. We went forward into the valley. When we were halfway to the church, a puff of wind, keen and shrewd, blew for an instant in our faces, and then another and another. But that last breath did not die like the rest; it blew continuously, and gathered violence as it blew.

The yew-trees in the churchyard resumed their tossing; we were so near that I could hear the creaking of their boughs. I looked anxiously towards the gap through which we were to pass to Eskdale. It was still clear of the mist, but where a shrub grew, or a tree reached out a branch on the slope beneath the gap, I saw the wind evident as a beating rain; and even as I looked, the gap filled—filled in a second—not with these slow, licking mists, but with a column of tempest that drove exultant, triumphing, and now and again in the midst of it I perceived a whirling gleam of white like foam of the sea.

I looked forwards to the church, backwards to the house. The church was the nearer. I took Dorothy by the elbow.

"Run!" I cried.

"I cannot," she replied, lagging behind.

I pressed her forward.

"You must."

"These shoes——" she began.

"Devil take the shoes!" cried I; and thereupon, with a perversity which even I would not have attributed to her, she slipped a foot out of a shoe, and stepped deliberately into a puddle.

"There," says she, defiant but shivering, "I told you they were too wide."

"You did it of a set purpose," said I. I looked towards the gap: it was no longer visible. The storm was tearing across the valley. I picked up Miss Dorothy Curwen in my arms, and ran with her towards the church. I got to the stone wall of the churchyard; a little wicket gave admittance, but the wicket was latched.

"Let me down!" says Dorothy.

"No!" says I, and I pushed against the wicket with my knee. It yielded; a few flakes of snow beat upon my face; I ran through the opening.

The churchyard, like the church, was the tiniest in the world; the walls about it reached breast high, and within the walls the yews were planted close in a square: so that standing within this square, it seemed to me that the storm had lulled. I carried Dorothy to that side of the church which was sheltered from the wind. I tried the door of the church, but it was locked. I set Dorothy down under the wall, slipped off my great-coat, and wrapped it warm about her.

"Look!" said I, shortly.

Just past the angle of the church the snow swirled forwards—down in the valley here it was rather sleet than snow—lashing the fields through which I had run.

"Where are you going?" said Dorothy, as perhaps with some ostentation I buttoned my coat across my breast.

"To pick up your shoe," said I; and I walked out through the wicket.

"I never met a man of so wicked a perversity," said she from behind me.

CHAPTER XX
A CONVERSATION IN WASTDALE CHURCH

When I returned with the shoe, I found Dorothy sitting huddled against the church wall in a very doleful attitude.

"Oh!" she cried remorsefully, as she took the shoe from me, "you are drenched through and through, and it is I that am to blame."

"It matters nothing at all," I replied. "I have been out upon the tops of these ridges, and of nights. It would be strange if I were not inured to a little cold."

"You will take your coat, however."

I had the greatest difficulty in persuading her to keep it; for since I was drenched already, the coat would not dry me, but I should wet the coat. This was the argument I employed to her, though I had another, and a more convincing, to satisfy myself—I mean the sight of her wrapped up in it. It was a big, rough, heavy frieze coat and made a nest for her; she had drawn the collar of it close about her ears, and her face, rosy with warmth and the whipping of the wind as we came across the fields, peeped from the coat, like a moss-rose at the budding.

We sat for a while in silence—for the whistling of the storm was grown so loud, that we had need to shout, and even then the wind snatched up the words out of hearing almost before they had passed our lips.

In front of us the tempest roistered about the valley, twisting the sleet and snow this way and that, shrieking about the bases of the hills, whistling along the invisible ridges; now and again, however, there came a momentary lull, and during one of these intervals the clouds broke upon our left and disclosed the peak of Great Gable. Rising in that way, from the mists that still hid its flanks, the peak seemed so high that you thought it must be slung in mid-air; it stood out black against the grey clouds, barren, impregnable. Dorothy shuddered at the aspect of it.

"You were out upon those heights," she shouted into my ear, "night and day, after you left Applegarth?"

"Yes!" I nodded. Doubtless I should have pointed out that I did not make my bed upon the pinnacles, and that there was all the difference in the world betwixt rain and snow. But, to tell the truth, her anxiety on my account was of that sweetness to me that I could not lightly bring myself to dispense with it. I was debating the matter in my mind, when a tile, loosened by the wind, slid from the roof of the church and smashed upon the ground, a couple of feet from Dorothy. It turned the current of my thoughts effectually. The door of the church I knew to be locked; I crept round to the east end of the building. There was a great window with the panes set in lead, which reached from the roof to within three feet of the ground. And in that window a second window was made by the lowest of these leaded panes. Inserting my knife, I was able to force up the latch which fastened this second window, and found that, with some squeezing and compression, a body might crawl through the opening. I went back to Dorothy. "It will be safer in the church," said I. I climbed through the window by the side of the altar, and turned to help Dorothy in after me. But as I was in the act of helping her, I heard a clatter on the ground without. She was halfway through the window at the moment, and slipped back with a laugh.

"This time," said she, as she appeared again, and set her hands upon the sill—"this time I did not drop it on purpose." And I helped her in.

The church was barely furnished with perhaps a dozen of rough deal pews, and had not even a vestry, so that the parson's surplice lay neatly folded upon a chair in the chancel. Into one of the pews we entered, and since Dorothy was warm within my coat, I took and wrapped the surplice about my shoulders. So we sat side by side, silent, in the gloom of the church, the whitewashed walls glimmering about us, the sleet whipping the windows and tearing at the door. Somehow the sound of the storm had now become very pleasant to me, since it seemed to shut us off, as upon an island, more securely from the world.

It is strange how a man may walk again and again along a quite familiar path with companions who have grown familiar in his thoughts, and then on some one day, in a twinkling, and for no reason that he can afterwards discern, let him think never so hard, the companions with whom he has fared will lose their familiarity, will become, as it were, transfigured, and the spot to which he has come will take on a magical aspect and a magical light He seems to have come thither for the first time on that day; and let him con over the landmarks to prove the fancy wrong, the fancy will none the less abide with him, solid as truth. He recognizes the spot as in some way intimately concerned with him; it seems to have been waiting for him, and for the conjunction of this one particular hour with him. And the picture which he has of it, thus suddenly revealed, becomes henceforth part and parcel of his being, imperishably treasured within the heart of recollection. So, at all events, it was with me.

A picture of this valley in which we were, of this church in which we sat, sprang up before my eyes, and I viewed it with a curious detachment. It was as though I stood upon the rim of the mountains and looked down into the hollow. I saw the desolate hills ringing it about, made yet more desolate by the blurring snow. I saw the little white church set within its stunted, beaten yews, apart in the mid-centre of the valley. It was, too, as though I saw, by some strange clairvoyancy, through the walls, and beheld the two fugitives securely sheltered, side by side, in the dusk of the pew. And the picture has remained clamped in my memory ever since, so that I have but to close my eyes, and not merely do I see it vividly as I did then, but I experience again that vague sense of a voice crying somewhere out of Nature's heart, "This spot has been waiting for you twain, and for this one hour."

It was a movement which Dorothy made, brought me to myself. For she suddenly clasped her hands together with a shudder.

"You are cold?" I cried.

"No," she replied in a low voice. "I was thinking of that peak we saw and the horror of it by night," and her voice trembled for an instant, "and of your watching from the darkness the lights of Applegarth. We were comfortably in our beds; and it rained that night I remember the patter of the rain against the windows."

"Nay," said I, "there was little harm done. I am no snow-man to be washed away by a capful of rain."

She turned to me very quickly.

"Tell me," she said, in a voice no less quick. "The evening that you went from us—you were talking for a long while at the gate with Mary Tyson, you will remember. I interrupted your talk."

"Yes! I remember," I answered, staring straight in front of me.

"Well," she continued, "I have often wondered," her voice sank yet lower, "whether that going of yours was not a flight—flight from—from us at Applegarth. For, after all, it was something Mary Tyson said to you that made you go."

I turned towards her with a start.

"You know what Mary Tyson said?"

She looked at me in silence, her eyes shining out of the dusk. Then she lowered her head.

"I guessed it," she said in a whisper. "I guessed it then, for I know Mary's care for me. And the next morning when we sent her to warn you that the sheriff was at the door, I read it in her face. I mean," said she, recovering herself hastily, "I read your departure in her face, and I knew it was what she had said to you had driven you out, and not your own necessities."

She paused; I did not answer.

"The knowledge has troubled me sorely," she said, "for you were our guest."

"It made but the one night's difference," I urged, "for on the morrow came the officers."

"Ah! but that was the accident," she answered shrewdly. "They might not have come—they might never have come—and still you would have fled. I have said this much to you," she went on with a change of tone, "because I would have you look on me just as a friend, who trusts you, who has great cause to trust and thank you, and who would count it a very real happiness if she could, in any small way, repay you. I told you when we met on your march that I knew there was some great trouble."

"And the answer I gave to you then, I must give now. I am bound to face that trouble by myself. It was my sin brought it about."

"Ah! but one never knows whence help may come," she replied; and the gentle earnestness with which she spoke so tempted me to unbosom myself, that instinctively I drew away from her. "You think it is just a woman's curiosity which prompts me," she cried, mistaking my movement. "Ah! no. Acquit me of that fault! I am not sure, but it may be that I can help you."

Did she know? I wondered. My thoughts went back to that last meeting near Penrith. I had spoken then of a prison-door which must close between us twain, and she had made an answer which seemed to hint a suspicion of the truth.

"And even if I cannot, the mere telling sometimes helps," she continued, "so long as one tells it to a friend. I mean"—and here she began to speak very slowly, choosing her words, and with a certain difficulty in the utterance—"I mean I was afraid that something Mary might have said checks you. There are things one does not confide to an acquaintance, or, again, to one whom you think to look upon you as ever so much nearer than an acquaintance.

But to a friend, yes! A friend is a halfway house between, where one can take one's ease;" and she drew a breath, like one that has come to the end of a dangerous task.

As for me, I sat listening to that word "friend." The walls seemed to retain it, and whisper it again to me after she had ceased, and in the changing tones which she had used. For now Dorothy had spoken it with an earnest insistence, as though anxious—almost over-anxious—I should just accept the phrase as the true definition of what she felt towards me; and now her voice had faltered and stumbled at the word. It may have been a lack of modesty—I cannot tell—but I think it would have been the falsest modesty in the world had I affected to neglect the manner of the speech, while considering the matter of it. But be it as it may, the one thought which rose in my mind, engrossing me, distinct, horrible in distinctness, was this: What if that word "friend" cloaked and concealed another—another which, but for those few weeks at Blackladies, I might—who knows!—perhaps have persuaded her to speak? Why then, if that was true, here was I implicating, in distress, the one woman who was chiefest in the front of my thoughts.

How that sin of mine reached out, making me a ban and a curse, bearing its evil fruit in unimaginable ways! And in the agony of my heart I cried—

"Would to God I had never come to Applegarth!"

The cry rang fierce and sharp through the little church. Silence succeeded it, and then—

"That is not very kind," said Dorothy, with a tremulous reproach, "It pains me."

"Ah! don't mistake," I went on. "For myself, I could not hope to make you understand what my visit there has meant to me. I came to Applegarth on an evening. The day I had passed waiting upon the hillside, and while I was waiting there, I made a resolve to repair, under God's will, a great wrong. Well, when I first saw you, I had but one thought—a thought of very sincere gladness that I had come to that resolve or ever I had had speech with you. And during the weeks that followed, this resolve drew strength and vigour from your companionship. That vigour and that strength it keeps, so that my one fear now is, lest chance may bar me from the performance. That is your doing. For until I came to Applegarth, all my life behind me was littered with broken pledges."

She laid her hand for an instant upon my sleeve.

"But what return have I made to you," I continued, "except a pitiful hypocrisy? I came to Applegarth an outlaw—yes, my one fault my loyalty!

So you believed; so I let you believe. I wore your brother's clothes, and he died at Malplaquet. There was hypocrisy in the wearing of them!" And I turned suddenly towards her. "There was a picture I once saw—the picture of a dead man speaking. Even then it seemed to me an image of myself."

"A dead man speaking!" interrupted Dorothy, with a start.

"Yes!" said I, and I told her of the picture which Lord Bolingbroke had shown to me at the monastery of the Chartreux in Paris, and of the thought which I had drawn from it.

"A dead man speaking," she repeated, in a voice which seemed hushed with awe; "how strange!"

The storm had ceased to beat the window; the dusk was deepening to darkness; the silence was about us like a garment. I sat wondering at Dorothy's tone, wondering whether I should say what yet remained to say. But I had made use before of secrecy and deception. It would be best I should simply speak the truth.

"A dead man speaking," again said Dorothy.

"I had warning enough, you see," said I, "and I recognized the warning. The picture seized upon my thoughts. I knew it for an allegory, but made no profit of my knowledge. And so the allegory turns fact."

"What do you mean?" she asked, catching her breath.

"Oh, don't speak until I have done!" I cried "I find it hard enough to tell you as it is while you sit silent. But the sound of your voice cheats me of my strength, sets the duty beyond my reach. For it is a duty." I paused for a moment to recover the mastery of my senses. "I spoke to you once of a prison-door which would close between you and me. But that was not the whole of the truth. That prison-door will close, but it will open again; I shall come out from it, but upon a hurdle."

"Oh no!" cried Dorothy in such a voice of pain as I pray God I may never hear the like of again. I felt it rive my heart. She swayed forward; her forehead would have struck the rail of the pew in front. I put my arm around her shoulders and drew her towards me. I felt her face pressed against my bosom, her fingers twining tightly upon my coat.

"Yes, yes, it is true," I went on. "The allegory turns fact. Even in Paris, those months agone, I came to look upon myself as the figure in the picture, as the dead man speaking, meaning thereby the hypocrite detected. But now the words take on a literal meaning. It is a dead man who is speaking to you—no more than that—in very truth a dead man. You must believe it; and believe this too, that since my cup of life this long while back has overbrimmed with shame, and since it was I who filled it why, I could go very lightly to my death, but for the fear lest it should cause my little friend to suffer pain."

She disengaged herself gently from my clasp.

"I cannot take that fear away from you," she said in a broken whisper.

"And indeed I would not lose it," I replied. "In my heart of hearts I know that I would not lose it."

"What is it, then, you mean to do?" she asked.

"To travel with my friend as far as Ravenglass, to set her safe on board the *Swallow*, and then—somewhere there is a man in prison whose place is mine."

"You do not know where?" she exclaimed suddenly.

"No," said I, "but——"

She interrupted me with a cry.

"Look!" she said hurriedly, and pointed to a little window close beneath the roof. Through that window the moonlight was creeping like a finger down the wall, across the floor. "The storm has cleared; we can go."

She rose abruptly from her seat, and moved out into the chancel Something—was it the hurry of her movement, the tension of her voice?— made me spring towards her. I remembered that, when I spoke to her on the hillside near Penrith, it had seemed to me then that she had some inkling of the truth.

"You know!" I exclaimed—"you know where the prisoner is?"

"No," she cried, and her voice rose almost to a scream belying the word she spoke.

How she came by her knowledge I did not consider. She knew! I had no room for any other thought.

"Oh, you do know!" I implored, and dropping on my knee I seized the hem of her dress to detain her. I felt the dress drag from me; I held it the more firmly. "You do not know—oh, tell me! A man innocent of all wrongdoing, lies in prison—the charge, treason. Think you they will weigh his innocence after this rebellion? The fetters he wears are mine, his punishment is mine, and I must claim it. There's no other way but this plain and simple one. I must needs claim it. Oh think, ever since I have known you, the necessity that I should do this thing has grown on me, day by day, as each day I saw you. I have felt that I owed it to you that I should succeed. Do not you prevent me!"

She stood stock still; I could hear the quick coming and going of her breath, but in the uncertain twilight I could not read her face; and she did not speak.

"Listen!" I continued "If you do not tell me, it will make no difference. I shall still give myself up. But to the other it may make all the difference in the world. For it may be that I shall fail to save him."

Still she kept silence. So, seeing no other way, I stood up before her and told her the story from end to end, beginning with that day when I first rode over Coldbarrow Fell to Blackladies in company with Jervas Rookley, down to the morning when I fled from the garden where the soldiers searched for me.

I saw her head droop as she listened, and bow into her hands; yet I had to go on and finish it.

"But," said she, "you were not all to blame. The woman——"

"Nay," said I, "it can serve no purpose to portion out the blame; for, portion it as you will, you cannot shred away my share."

"Mr. Herbert," she objected again, "would have been taken in your garden, whether you had returned or no that afternoon."

"But my fault was the instrument used to ruin him. He was taken while he followed me. He was taken, too, because of me. For had I not ridden so often into Keswick, he would never have been suspected."

"It was his jealousy that trapped him, and Jervas Rookley provoked the jealousy."

"But I furnished him with the means."

The arguments were all old and hackneyed to me. I had debated them before, so that I had the answers ready. There was, besides, one final argument, and without waiting for her to speak again, I used it.

"And what of the wife waiting in Keswick?"

She turned away with a little swift movement, and again stood silent. Then she said—

"Yes! I too will face it bravely. Mr. Herbert lies in Carlisle Castle, waiting his trial. You know, after the message came to Applegarth, my father and I fled to Carlisle; we took refuge with friends—Whigs, but of my mother's family, and for her sake they gave us shelter. They knew the Governor of the Castle. He told them of a prisoner newly brought thither upon a warrant—a Mr. Herbert, who solaced himself night and day with the painting of the strangest picture ever known. You showed to me a letter at Applegarth, wherein a painter was mentioned and named, and I knew you had some trouble to distress you. I grew curious to see the prisoner; no one suspected I was in Carlisle, and so my friends consented to take me. I saw him. It is true I had no speech with him, but I saw the picture. It was a portrait of yourself, I thought, but I could not be sure. I was sure before you told me. I was sure when you spoke to me of that picture you had seen in Paris. For this portrait, too, that Mr. Herbert painted, was a portrait of yourself, as a dead man speaking."

I noticed that as she spoke her voice gained confidence and strength, and at the close it rang without a trace of fear or reluctance.

"Thank you," said I, simply. "Thank you with all my heart."

"Yes!" she replied, "it was right that I should tell you. You will go to Carlisle?"

"In truth I will;" and as she moved into a line with the window, the moonlight made a silver glory about her face. I saw with a great joy that her eyes, her lips were smiling. It seemed to me, indeed, that both our hearts were lighter. There was this one thing to do, and now here was the means revealed by which it might be done.

We climbed out of the window, and since it was too late for the continuance of our journey, we sought lodging for the night at that farmhouse which I had already visited. I remember walking across the fields in the star-shine and the moonlight, wondering at this vicarious revenge Herbert had taken on my picture, and at the strange destiny which had made this girl, so dear to me, the instrument of my atonement. And as we waited at the door, I said to her:

"I owed you much before to-night; but to-night you have doubled the debt."

"And I am proud to hear you say it," she replied.

From the farmer I borrowed a change of clothes, and coming down the stairs again, found Dorothy, to her evident satisfaction, in her own shoes, which she had taken from the pocket of my great-coat. We sat for a long while after our supper over the fire in the kitchen, talking of the days at Applegarth and laughing over that owl-hunt. Only twice was any reference made to our conversation in the church. For once I said:

"Do you remember when I came down to Applegarth, you were singing a song? It was called, 'The Honest Lover,' and I would fain have the words of it." And thereupon she wrote out the song upon a sheet of paper and gave it to me.

And again, when Dorothy had lit her candle, she stood for an instant by the door.

"That resolve you spoke of?" she said. "You had come to it on the day that you first reached Applegarth. It was the resolve to free Mr. Herbert at any cost?"

"Yes," said I.

"And it was that you were so glad you had determined on when you first saw me?"

"Yes," said I again.

"Well," said she, "it is the sweetest compliment that was ever paid to a woman."

The next morning we started betimes in the same cheerfulness of spirits, and making light of that dreaded snow as we crossed Burnmoor, descended into Eskdale about nine of the forenoon, and so reached Ravenglass before it was dusk. There, to my inexpressible delight, I saw the *Swallow* riding on an anchor a little way out. We crept down to the beach, and waited there until it was dark. Then I lighted a lantern which I had brought from the farmhouse for the very purpose, and lifting it up, swung it to and fro. In a little there was an answering flash from the sloop, and a little after that I heard the sound of oars in the water, and fell to wondering what sort of parting we should make, and, perhaps, in a measure, to dreading it. But the parting was of the simplest kind.

"It is good-bye, then," said Dorothy, "and we will shake hands, if you please."

This time I took her hand fairly within my palm, and held it clasped whilst it clasped mine.

"I am thanking God," said I, "for the truest friend that ever man had."

"Yes!" said she, nodding her head, "that is very prettily said, and no more than the truth."

"Ah!" said I, "you ever enjoyed a very proper notion of yourself;" and with that the boat grounded upon the beach, and, after all, we two parted with a laugh. I heard the song of the seamen at the windlass, coming across the water with an airy faintness, and then I set my face to the hillside.

CHAPTER XXI
I TRAVEL TO CARLISLE AND
MEET AN ATTORNEY

It was a lonely business whereto I now was set, but in truth it is lonelier in the recollection than it was in the actual happening. As I sit over my fire here on a winter's night, I begin at times to wonder how I went through with it. I remember the incessant moaning of the sea,—for I followed my old plan, only with a greater precaution, and kept along the coast until I was nigh upon Whitehaven—and discover a loneliness in the thought that it was carrying Dorothy from me to France; I find, too, an overwhelming desolation in the knowledge that she and I had spoken the last good-bye, and a melancholy atop of that in the cheerfulness of our parting. But these notions are but the moss that gathers upon recollections. The sea brought no loneliness home to me,—rather it crooned of Dorothy's safety, nor was I conscious then of any desolation in the knowledge that my eyes would not again rejoice in the sight of her, for that very parting raised me out of my slough more nearly to her level; and as for the cheerfulness—why, just in that way would I have had her part from me. I believe, indeed, that I was more sensible of her presence on that journey from Ravenglass to Carlisle than ever I had been, even when her voice was in my ears or the knocking of her shoes upon the stones.

Moreover, there were two very immediate questions which pressed upon me, and saved me from much unprofitable rumination about myself. Dorothy had spoken of Anthony Herbert "waiting his trial," when she herself was in Carlisle, and that was over a month ago. Was he still waiting, or was the trial over? I had no means of resolving that question, and many a night I lay awake in some barn or outhouse, blowing on my frozen fingers to keep them warm, and casting up the probabilities. I was thus in a perpetual fever lest, after all, my intentions should be thwarted by a too late arrival. And to make the matter worse, I was compelled to practise every precaution, lest I should be recognized. Of which there was, to my thinking, no small danger, for in the first place my flight from Blackladies had made, as I knew, some noise in these parts, and moreover I had ridden openly on the march to Preston.

So here was my second question: Could I reach Carlisle a free man? for that I deemed to be an altogether necessary and integral part of my design. Once a captive, I was foredoomed already upon my own account, and any plea that I might urge on behalf of Anthony Herbert would win the less credit, since it would be made at no cost whatever to me who made it. If, however, I could come undetected there, and so give myself up, why, the voluntary relinquishment of life might haply be taken as a guarantee and surety for my word. Consequently I was reduced to a thousand shifts to avoid attention; I went miles about to come upon a solitary inn, and more often than not, when I reached it, my heart would fail me, and I would take to my heels in a panic, or at best gulp down the hastiest meal, and pulling my coat about my ears, front the cold night again. It was then a good twelve days after the *Swallow* had lifted anchor and sailed down the coast, that I crept one dusky evening through the Botcher Gate into Carlisle; and what with the fear of capture and the fevers of delay, the endless fatigue to which during these many weeks I had been exposed and the inclemencies of the season, you may be sure I was in a sufficiently pitiable condition. I repaired at once to the market-place, and picking out the most insignificant tavern, learnt therein, over a glass of brandy from my host, that I was as much as a week in advance of my time. The news was an indescribable relief to me; and going out, I hired a mean lodging in a little street near the Horse Market, where I would lie that night, and determine on my course. For since I had yet a week, I thought that I might dispose of some portion of that time to the best advantage, by discovering the particulars of the charge which Anthony Herbert would have to meet. In which task I did not anticipate a very great difficulty, inferring, from what Dorothy had told me, that, what with the speculation his picture had given rise to, I should find his case a matter of common gossip. Accordingly, in the morning I bought at a dealer's a suit of clothes which would befit an apprentice, and tying my own hair in a cheap ribbon, which I was able to do, since I had discarded a peruke for convenience' sake after I left Blackladies, and changing my boots for a pair of shoes, I walked across the town towards the castle, in the hope that, either amongst the loiterers at the gates, or in the meadow by the river, I might discover something to my purpose.

In this Fortune favoured me, for though I learned little or nothing upon the first day, about three o'clock of the afternoon upon the second, while I stood in the open space betwixt the castle and the town, a little brisk gentleman came stepping from the gate-house and glanced at every one he passed with a great air of penetration, as who should say, "My friend, you have no secrets from me." He shot the same glance at me, though with more indifference, as though from habit he would practise it upon any who came in his way, be they mere apprentices. It was he, however, who was the one to be discomposed. For up went his eyebrows on the instant and his mouth gaped. He did not, however, stop, but rather quickened his pace and passed me. A few yards away he stopped to exchange a word with an acquaintance, but I noticed that he cast now and again a furtive glance towards me. My curiosity was fairly aroused, and being reluctant to lose any occasion that might serve me, I drew nearer and loitered in his vicinity until such time as the conversation should have ended.

Dismissing his acquaintance, he turned of a sudden.

"It is a disappointing place—Carlisle," he began abruptly; "the grass grows in the streets, which, I take it, are the dirtiest outside Bagdad, and the houses, what with their laths and clay and thatch, are as little reputable to the eye."

I knew not what in the world to make of this strange beginning, and so stared at the man in perplexity.

"You will have been sorely disappointed," he suggested, "for I am told that, on the contrary, the streets of Preston are very clean and spacious, and the houses built with some taste."

"It seems you know me," said I, starting forward.

"It has almost that air," he replied with a spice of mockery; "I have known more effectual disguises than an apron and a pair of brass buckles. But, indeed, had you dirtied your face, as you unwisely omitted to do, I should have known you none the less."

He stood with his head cocked on one side, enjoying my mystification.

"I have no doubt, sir, of your discernment and penetration," said I, thinking to humour him; "but since I cannot call to mind that you and I have ever met——"

He came a step nearer to me, and with a roundabout glance, to see that no listener was within earshot:

"There is a pretty unmistakable likeness of you yonder"—he jerked his head towards the castle—"though maybe the expression wants repose; moreover, I could not hear that you were taken prisoner, and so was inclined to expect you here."

"Then who in the world are you?" I exclaimed.

"Mr. Nicholas Doyle," said he, "and a lawyer of too much repute to be seen publicly hobnobbing with a rascally apprentice without questions asked. So if you please, you will just walk behind me until I come to my house, and when I go in at the front door you will slink round to the back."

These directions I followed, and was shown up the stairs to the first floor, whereupon Mr. Doyle locked the door and drew a screen before the keyhole.

"Now, Mr.—Mr. Whitemen, shall we say?—for though your face is little known, your name has been heard here—I may offer you a chair;" which he did, drawing it politely to the fire, and therewith offered me his snuff-box, but "without prejudice to his politics," as he said. For "none of your scatterbrained, romantical flim-flam for me," said he. "An honest Whig, my dear sir. By the way," and his eyes twinkled slyly, "I trust you did not find my staircase very dark?"

I was not in the humour to take any great pleasure in his witticism, as may be imagined, and I replied simply—

"You know the whole story, then?"

"Part the husband told me," said he, nodding his head, "part the wife. I pieced it together."

"The wife!" I exclaimed. "Then Mrs. Herbert is here—at Carlisle?"

"Doubtless," he returned; "where else?"

"I did not know," said I.

It was Mr. Doyle's turn to look surprised.

"But," said he, "she left word for you at Keswick. It was for that reason I told you I was not greatly surprised to come upon you."

"Nay," said I, "I have not been to Keswick. I learnt Anthony Herbert was here—well, from other sources. But," and I started forward eagerly in my chair, "Herbert must then have sent for her;" and I spoke joyfully enough, for of late, and in particular since I had known where Herbert lay, I had begun to reflect that, after all, his enlargement, could that be brought about, did not altogether patch up the trouble.

"No," answered Mr. Doyle; "Herbert only talked of her. I sent for her."

"I may thank you for that," said I. "They are reconciled?"

"It is a delicate point," said he, "how far. My client, it appears, was persuaded by that worthy gentleman, Jervas Rookley, that—well, that there were more solid grounds for his jealousy than actually existed. It is true Rookley has shown something of his hand, but not all of it. We are in the dark as to his motives, and Mr. Herbert—well, doubtless you have some notion of the whimsies of a man in love. Now he is in the depths of abasement, now he is very haughty on the summits of pride. A man in love! My dear sir, a man in love is very like a leg of mutton on my roasting-jack in the kitchen. First he spins this way, then he spins that, and always he is in the extremity of heat whichever way he spins. He is like the mutton, too, in his lack of sense, and in the losing of the fat; and very often, when he is roasted through and through, my lady serves him up for the delectation of her friends. Believe me, Mr. Clavering"—he checked himself, but the name was out of his mouth—"when next you figure on the jack, you will do well to bear in mind my simile. A leg of mutton, my dear sir."

Now, I had good reason to find his simile uncommonly distasteful, the more because I had a like reason for knowing it to be unjust; and, perhaps with more heat than was needed, I answered—

"For my part, I have no objection——"

"To a man in love!" said he, taking me up. "Nor I, indeed. On the contrary, I hold him in the greatest esteem, not so much, perhaps, for his falling in love, as for his consequent falling out of it, whereby comes much profitable litigation."

"Well," said I, anxious to put an end to his discourse, "your advice, Mr. Doyle, may be the best in the world; but you offer it to a man who will never find occasion for pursuing it." And at that his face became grave. "Let us get to the root of the matter. You tell me Jervas Rookley has shown his hand. In what way?"

"Why, he is to be the chief witness for the crown. It was he who laid the information against Herbert. And, you will observe, he is a strong witness. For what object had he in view, if he did not believe the information? What had he to gain?"

"I will not say that he did not believe it," I returned; "I will not say that he does not believe it. But I know very well what he has to gain, and that is, the estate of Blackladies."

And I told the lawyer of the double game which Rookley had played.

"One way or another, whichever king sat the throne, he was to recover the estate," I continued. "If the Hanoverian won, why, I was to be exchanged for it; but since he thinks I have slipped through his fingers, he will be eager to make Herbert my substitute."

"Yes," said the lawyer, thoughtfully; "but there will be only your bare word for this."

"But I shall have sacrificed my life to speak it," I said anxiously. For this very point had greatly troubled me.

"No doubt that will carry weight," he assented, "but enough—I do not know. It will, however, serve to bring about that reconciliation which seems so to weigh with you. Look! There is a copy of the indictment;" and running over to a bureau, he brought it back and thrust it into my hands.

I read it through carefully, from the beginning to the end.

"You will see," said he, "that no direct act is alleged beyond the possession of that medal."

"That is mine," said I.

"Can you prove it?" said he. "It was found in Mr. Herbert's apartments."

I thought for a moment, and with a cry sprang to my feet:

"Indeed I can," I cried; "I can prove it" And I told him how.

"Good!" he exclaimed, in a voice which topped my own; and then—

"Hush!" he whispered, in the greatest reproach; "you should have more discretion, you should indeed." And very cautiously he unlocked the door, and then flung it violently open. The landing, however, was clear.

"You see, Mr. Whitemen, there is much we have to fight against apart from the charges. There is the apparent honesty of Mr. Rookley, and moreover there is this rebellion which calls for examples, and you may add to our difficulties a Cumberland jury. You will remember that we marched out against you at Penrith, four thousand strong. That will teach you the temper of the county."

"I do not remember," I replied, "that your four thousand stayed to exchange opinions with us."

Nicholas Doyle laughed good-naturedly.

"It is a hit, I will not deny," said he. "But what if they hold to the plan, and decline to exchange opinions when they are in the jury-box, eh, my friend? what then? So you see there are dangers. With your help we may just save my client, but it will be by no more than the skin of his teeth. Without you we may as well submit to a sentence at the outset. But," and he spoke with a voice of the deepest gravity, "all this, which makes your evidence of the greatest value to us, renders it fatal to you. I do not mince words; I set the truth frankly before you. Your evidence may serve Mr. Herbert's turn,—but there is no more than a chance of that—it will most certainly send you to an ignominious death. Every word you will speak will be a plea of guilty. And mark you, there is but one punishment for treason. It will be no stepping on to a scaffold, and reading a few protestations, and kneeling down at the block, as though you just condescended to leave the world. No, you will be drawn through the streets, trussed hand and foot, on a hurdle. Then they will hang you—for a bit, but not until you are dead. Then they will light a fire and take a knife to you—and it will seem, I fear me, a weary while before the end is reached!"

"Good God!" I interrupted him, and snatched up my hat. "Do you wish me to leave your client precisely to that same fate?"

"Where are you going?" he asked in an incredulous tone, noticing my movement.

"To Carlisle Castle," said I.

"I thought as much," said he, and took me by the arm. "I doubt if I should have said so much to you, had I not felt certain it would not weigh with you. But you are young, Mr. Clavering, very young; and though I must count you a traitor, and deserving all this punishment, I could not send you to that fate without you had counted up the cost."

"That is kindly said," I replied, and offered him my hand, which he shook very cordially. "But less than a fortnight ago I stood upon the sea-shore with never a soul in view and a ship's boat on the beach and a ship spreading its sails to set me over into France. I am not like to be turned aside now."

He looked at me with a certain shrewdness in his eyes.

"This is a reparation which you purpose? A man of the world would tell you there was no necessity for it."

"But you do not say that?" I returned.

"I say," and he paused for a second—"I say damn women!" he cried, and brought his fist down upon the table.

"Even in that amiable sentiment I cannot agree with you," I answered with a laugh. "And so I will make a call upon the Governor of the castle."

But again he caught me by the arm.

"That would be the ruin of both of you. The Crown presses for an example to be made. And Jervas Rookley, I think, from what you yourself have said, will move heaven and earth to keep you out of court. If you go now to the castle, there is little likelihood of your giving evidence for Mr. Herbert; he must produce you at the trial, and not a moment before."

Thereupon he recommended to me to lie quietly in my lodging during the week, and come not out except to see him now and again of a night. At his bidding, indeed, I repaired to his house on the following evening, and found a tailor there waiting for me. "For," said Mr. Doyle, "we must make the most of our advantages, though my heart aches at dressing you up for the slaughter. But it will make a difference whether a lad in an apron and brass buckles gives himself up, or a proper young gentleman, with an air of means and dignity. Your word will gain credit with the jury. Lord! what a sight we shall have in the spectacle of Jervas Rookley's face. By the way," and he turned towards me with a certain customary abruptness, "Jervas Rookley's face has something changed since I set eyes on it before."

"Indeed," said I, indifferently; "and in what way?"

"It is marred by a scar."

"A scar!" I cried, with considerable satisfaction. "On the right side? It should stretch from the cheek bone to the chin."

"It does," answered Mr. Doyle, dryly. "I wonder how he came by it?"

"Yes, I wonder," said I, reflectively, and chancing to look at each other, our eyes met, and we laughed.

"I think it very wise," said he, "that you did not surrender yourself to the Governor of Carlisle Castle."

This week passed monotonously enough for me, cooped up in my little apartment. But I had a great hope to cheer me through its passage. For, I had come so near to the attainment of my one end, and in the face of so many difficulties, that I could not but believe that Providence had so willed it, and having willed so much, would will that final issue which should crown the work; moreover, two days before the trial, Mr. Doyle brought me news which enheartened me inexpressibly. It was a message of thanks from Anthony Herbert, and to that message was added another from the wife, which showed me that the reconciliation had become an actual fact.

On the eve of the trial I slept at the house of Mr. Doyle. Indeed, from his window I heard the trumpeters, and saw the judge's carriage go by; and so dressing myself the next morning in my new suit, with Mr. Doyle fluttering about me like a lady's maid, I made my way quickly to the Guildhall.

CHAPTER XXII
REPARATION

The Guildhall stands northwards of the cross in the market-place, and I remember that I paused when halfway up the steps betwixt the pavement and the portico, and turned me about for a second to glance down upon that open space, and men coming and going about it as they willed in the warm sunlight. Mean houses enclosed it, shambles disfigured it; but I noticed no more than its width and spaciousness. How wide and free it seemed! And of a sudden my thoughts flashed me away beyond these houses, and beyond the gates. The market-place vanished before my eyes like a mirage. I was once more marching from Kelso to Preston, across the moors with the merlins crying overhead,—between the hedges,—under the open sky; and it seemed to me so swift was the passage of my memories, that I traversed in that brief interval all the distance of our march.

But many of the townsfolk were mounting to the court, and one that passed jogged against me with his elbow, and so waked me. I raised my head. Well, here was the court-house, within sat the judge; and though the sunlight beat upon my face, the shadow of the building had already reached about my feet.

The little court was nigh upon full, and I pushed into a corner beneath the gallery, where I was like to escape notice, and yet command a view of what was done. There I stood for the space of ten minutes or so, watching the townsfolk enter by twos and threes in a trickling stream, thronging the floor, blocking the doorways; and I know not why, but gradually a great depression, a dull melancholy, overstole my spirits. It was just for this moment that I had lived for many a week back, I assured myself; my days had been one prayer for its coming, my nights one haunting fear lest it should not come. Yet the assurance, repeat it as I might, had little meaning at the outset, and less and less at each repetition. My blood would not be whipped; I felt inert, in some queer way disappointed. I was like one quit of a fever, but in the despondency of exhaustion. I saw the prisoner set in the dock. I noticed the purple hollows about his eyes, the thin, flushed cheeks, the nervous gripping of his fingers on the rail. But the spectacle waked no pity in me, though I was conscious I should feel pity; aroused no shame, though I knew I should be tingling with shame. And when Anthony Herbert sent his gaze piercing anxiously this way and that into the throng, I wondered for a moment who it was for whom he searched. I saw Jervas Rookley seated at a table; he turned his head so that the bruised scar upon his face was visible from cheekbone to chin—and I, for all I felt towards him, might have been looking at the face of an inanimate statue. I saw the judge take his seat, his robes catching the sunlight and glowing against the black panels of the wall, like some monstrous scarlet flower. I was as one who contemplates a moving scene through a spy-glass, knowing it to be very far away. The actual aspect of the court became dreamlike to me, and when the clerk of the Crown cried out "Anthony Herbert, hold up thy hand!" it seemed to me that the curtain was but now rung up upon a puppet-show.

In this listless spirit I listened while the indictment was read. It set forth that "Anthony Herbert, as a false traitor, not weighing the duty of his allegiance, did with other false traitors conspire, compass, and imagine the death of his Majesty, the subversion of the Government, and to introduce the Romish religion; and for the effecting thereof, the said Anthony Herbert did conspire to levy war upon the kingdom and bring in the Pretender."

Thereupon the indictment being read, the jury was empannelled, which took no short time, for of a sudden Herbert, doubtless primed for the work by Nicholas Doyle, challenges one of them—John Martin, I remember, the man was named.

"Are you a freeholder of forty shillings a year?" he asked; and the judge taking him up, he was allowed counsel to argue the point, which was done at great length and with much talk of a couple of statutes, one dating from Henry V., the other from Queen Mary. It seemed that they contradicted one another, but I do not know. I only know that the sunlight, pouring through a high window on the east side, shifted like the spoke of a slow-revolving wheel, and was already withdrawing up the wall beneath the window when Jervas Rookley was called to give his evidence.

To this evidence I lent a careful ear, and could not but perceive that though there was little fact in the recital, yet innuendo so fitted with innuendo that it might well have weight with a jury already inclined to believe. But even this observation I was conscious of making rather as a matter of general interest than as one in which I was so intimately concerned.

Rookley told of Herbert's coming to Keswick, how immediately he made Lord Derwentwater's acquaintance and was entrusted with the painting of Lady Derwentwater's portrait—a work which carried him daily to the house on Lord's Island. Then he proceeded to tell of his own journey to Paris, and how he found me a novice in a Jesuit College. The journey to Bar-le-Duc he omitted, but said that I had given him advice to wait for me in Paris and so had ridden off for close upon a week. The journey, said he, aroused his suspicions; on my return I had openly professed to him my adherence to the Stuarts, and had informed him that I had travelled to Commercy and had seen the Pretender. He went on to describe his discovery that I carried a letter and his failure to possess himself of it.

"Then you knew Mr. Clavering was a Jacobite so long ago as that!" interrupted Anthony Herbert. "How comes it you waited so long before you moved for his arrest, unless you had a finger in the Jacobite pie yourself?"

"The witness need answer nothing that would incriminate himself," interrupted the judge, quickly. "Besides, your turn will come. Let the King's Counsel finish!"

"There is no reason why I should shrink from answering it," said Jervas, readily. "There was some plot on foot, so much I knew. But what the plot was I knew not nor ever did; and had I laid the information against Lawrence Clavering then, I should myself have closed the avenues of knowledge."

"And what have you to say to that?" asked the judge of Herbert. "You will need more discretion if you are to save your neck." And he wagged his head at the prisoner.

"My Lord," answered Herbert, in a heat, "I shall not want for discretion so long as I do not go begging for justice."

I could see Mr. Doyle in the body of the court, nodding and frowning at his client in a great fluster. But it was already too late for his signs to have their effect.

"Justice!" roared the judge, turning to the jury. "Sirs, the fellow cries for justice as though it were a stranger to a jury of Englishmen. Nay, but justice he shall have, full measure. I am here to see to that;" and he sat glowering at the unfortunate prisoner.

For myself the outburst was no more than I expected, and I listened to it as to an oft-told tale.

Jervas took up his story again. It may have been the heat, it may have been sheer weakness, but though I saw his face flush from expression to expression, the sound of his voice seemed to me no more than a dull droning, duller with every word; and yet every word I heard and clearly understood.

He told of my coming to Blackladies, of Lord Derwentwater's suggestion to me concerning Herbert, of my daily visits to the painter's apartment, of my subsequent journeys about the country-side, and the inquiries I made as to troops and munitions.

Even to me hearing the story, it almost appeared that Herbert was inextricably linked in the business, with such ingenuity was it told. The faces of the jury already condemned the prisoner, people nudged one another about me as each detail was added, and Herbert himself seemed to lose hope at the sight of the tangle in which he was coiled.

"I am for nothing in all this," he cried, but now in a very wail.

"And this too I doubt not is for nothing," said Mr. Cowper, the counsel, with a mocking irony, as he held up the medal which King James had given to me at Commercy. He turned to Rookley—

"You have seen this before?"

"In the prisoner's lodging at Keswick."

"Will you describe it?"

I bent forward. Rookley began to speak again. He described the head of King James struck upon the one side, the British islands upon the other, and made mention of the two mottoes: "Cujus est?" and "Reddite!"

Rookley paused, and there was a buzz of voices from the gallery, from the doorways, from the floor of the court. The medal was passed up to the judge. He turned it over in his hands, and had it carried to the jurymen. I saw their heads with many a wise wagging come together over it I leaned yet farther forward, looking at Rookley. For the first time that day I felt a pulse of excitement. Had Rookley chanced to glance my way, he must have seen me, so openly did I crane my head over my neighbour's shoulders. But he stood with downcast eyes in the meekest humility—the very figure and image of unconscious merit. Had he more to say about that medal? Every second I fancied I saw his mouth open and frame the words I dreaded. The murmurs of the throng increased; I could have shouted "Silence! Silence!" I feared that he would speak and I miss the words; I feared that the very noise about him would remind him, would suggest to him, would disclose to him, anyhow would unlock his lips. But he had no further details to give, and it seemed to me that already the fresh air fanned at Herbert's face.

"You saw the medal in the prisoner's lodging?" resumed the counsel. "When?"

"More than once," replied Rookley, and took up his tale again, and again my excitement died away. I remarked with some curiosity that he made no mention whatever of Mrs. Herbert from first to last, and I remembered how I had noticed before that the story fell into two halves, whereof each seemed complete without the other. He spoke, it is true, of a pretext by which he had lured Herbert to Blackladies, but did not define the pretext, nor did the counsel examine him as to it; while I felt sure that Anthony Herbert would be the last to start that game.

"Now," said the judge, turning to the prisoner, "it is your turn, if you have any questions to ask of the witness."

Herbert gathered up his papers.

"You saw this medal in my lodging?"

"Yes!"

"Do you know the purpose for which I had it there?"

Rookley straightened his shoulders, and facing Herbert, said very deliberately—

"I suppose it was a token which would pass you as trustworthy amongst the Jacobites."

"Did you never see it before you saw it in my lodging?"

"Never! My lord, I swear it upon my oath—never. The prisoner has no doubt some cock-and-bull story, but that is the truth. Upon my oath—never."

"The prisoner has no cock-and-bull story," answered Herbert, leaning fiercely over the dock, "but only what he will prove with witnesses." And so he turned from the subject.

It seemed to me that Rookley turned a trifle pale and for the first time lost his assurance. He glanced anxiously round the court; I drew closer into my corner. He knew that story of his about the medal to be false; he must needs have expected Herbert would press him closely concerning it. But he did not—he did not. There was reason for alarm. I saw the alarm gather on Rookley's face.

"You were at great pains to effect my arrest secretly," continued Herbert "And why was that?"

"I would not alarm Lawrence Clavering and his friends," he replied, "until I had a riper knowledge of their plots."

"But you laid the information against me with Mr. Fuller the magistrate on August 21st, and against Mr. Clavering on the 23rd; what was it made you change your mind between those dates?"

"But this is nothing to the purpose," said the judge, testily.

"I pray you, my Lord," said Herbert, with a certain dignity, "all this goes to the witness' credit; I am here for my life. I am allowed no counsel to defend me. I pray you let me go on with my questions!" And he turned again to Rookley. "Did you intercept a letter from Lord Derwentwater to Mr. Clavering on the afternoon of the 23rd?"

"A letter?" asked Rookley, with the air of a man hearing the matter mentioned for the first time.

"A letter," continued Herbert, "wherein Lord Derwentwater wrote that the French King was dying, and that Lord Bolingbroke counselled all thought of a rising should be deferred. And did you not thereupon, that same day, lay the information against Mr. Clavering?"

"But to what end is this?" interrupted the judge. "Clavering is not here. Were he here I should know how to deal with him. But the indictment is not drawn against Clavering. It is drawn against you, and you had best look to it."

"My lord, it is all of a piece," replied Herbert

"I was an innocent, an unconscious instrument of Rookley's hatred of Mr. Clavering."

Thereupon he proceeded to question Rookley as to the reason why he had been disinherited, and if it was true that he had robbed his father and ever proved a troublesome and disloyal son. To these inquiries he got nothing but evasions for replies; but I observed that the witness' anxiety increased, as I could understand. For doubtless he little expected to have these facts arrayed against him, and began to wonder whence Herbert's knowledge came.

The Court rose at the conclusion of his evidence for a short space, so that when it returned, the sunlight was pouring on to the floor of the room through the western window.

Other witnesses were called, amongst them one or two Whig gentlemen who spoke to seeing Lady Derwentwater's portrait.

"You infer from that that I am a traitor?" said Herbert to the first.

"I thought it a strange thing an artist should come so far as to Keswick," he replied.

"But, my lord, is it a crime for a man to come to Keswick?" cried Herbert "I came thither for the landscapes."

"And therefore painted portraits!" sneered the judge.

"Nay, but a man must live," answered Herbert.

I noticed that Blackett, my servant from Blackladies, was summoned to give evidence as to messages which I had despatched him with to Herbert. But I cannot say that I paid great heed to what he said. For that spoke of sunlight moved upwards from the floor towards the roof, changing as it moved from gold to red, and my weariness gained on me. I felt my limbs grow heavy beneath me and my head nodding, and the words which were spoken came to me muffled and drowsy, as if through a woollen curtain. At last Herbert was enjoined to make his defence. The sunlight streamed in a level blaze through the windows at the height of the gallery.

"My lord and gentlemen," he began, "I have nothing but innocence to plead. I cannot take the jury or the Court with oratory, but I declare in the presence of Almighty God that what is sworn against me is all a fiction. For rebelling against the established Government or attacking that precious life of his Majesty King George—I never had such a thought. You have heard a great many innuendoes and suspicions but very little fact, and I cannot be condemned upon suspicions. Moreover, I shall call a witness to prove to you that Jervas Rookley had the best of reasons for fitting those suspicions together. It is Blackladies that he covets, the estate from which his father disinherited him, and he seeks to regain it as a reward for his zeal by pursuing me to my death, though it cost him perjury. There is but one fact alleged against me, my Lord, in all this, that I had possession of the medal. But it never belonged to me, and that Jervas Rookley knows. I shall call a witness to prove to you that it belonged to Mr. Clavering, and to explain why it was discovered in my room."

"Well, call your witness!" said the Judge.

"I do, my Lord," said Anthony Herbert. "I call Lawrence Clavering." There was a quick movement all through the court like a ripple upon still water, and then, absolute silence—the silence of a night frost-bound and empty. There floated into my mind a recollection of the street beyond the barricade at Preston. The sunlight blazed ruddy upon motionless figures.

Had a woman fainted, it seemed you might. have heard her breathing. Then quick and sharp rang out a laugh. I knew the voice; I understood the relief in it. It flashed upon me of a sudden that here was I failing again, and this time irretrievably. I shook off the weariness which hung upon my limbs, the mist which was wrapped about my senses; I pushed aside the man who stood in front of me.

"I call Lawrence Clavering," repeated Herbert, the certitude of his tone weakening to a tremor.

From somewhere in the gallery I heard a sob, half-stifled—a sob as though a heart was breaking, and I knew too the voice which uttered that.

"Here!" I shouted, and thrust against the shoulders in front of me. A lane was carved as though by magic, and I advanced to the table.

"My lord, he is a rebel and a papist," said Rookley, starting up, his face livid, his eyes starting from their sockets.

"Doubtless I shall answer for both those crimes," said I, "in the law's good time. I am here this day to prevent a wrong."

Thereupon I was sworn and bidden to take my stand in the witness-box, which I did, being so placed that my back was towards the windows and the setting sun.

"My lord, the witness laughs," said Mr. Cowper; "I pray your lordship warn him that he swear truly."

But the witness was not laughing with any levity for the task to which his hand was set, and composed his face upon the instant. The gallery ran round the three sides of the hall; the sunlight, as I say, poured in from behind me and beat upon the gallery in front. I was looking to that part of it over against me from which I had heard a sob; and a face looked out from the rosy glow of the sunlight and smiled at me. It was at that face—the face of Dorothy Curwen that I smiled back. For my heart was lifted within me, exultant, rejoicing. I did not think then of the danger she ran, though the thought pressed heavily enough upon me afterwards; I did not even consider by what means she had come here. She *was* here. And this time I had not failed.

My musings, however, were interrupted by the judge, who warned me very outrageously that since nothing now could save my body, so I need not trust the saints would save my soul, if they caught me prevaricating from the truth.

"My lord," I replied humbly, "I was at Preston, and escaped. I could have fled out of England and got me safe to France; I am not like to have thrown away my life that I might tell a lie."

I shall not be particular to recount all the questions which Herbert put to me. He put many, and I answered them truthfully. I saw the judge's face cloud and grow sterner and sterner, for every word I spoke was a link to fetter me the more closely to my death; but the face up there in the gallery grew brighter and brighter; or so at least I imagined. It was to the gallery I looked for my judge, and there I saw myself acquitted.

"You have seen this medal?" asked Herbert.

"It belongs to me," said I.

"Belongs to you?" said the judge.

"It was given to me at Commercy by him whom I must ever regard as my King."

"How came it, then, in the prisoner's lodging?"

"I took it there myself that it might be painted in my picture."

"We shall need proof of all this," said the judge; "and prithee, friend," said he, with a biting irony, "consider the oath thou hast taken!"

"Proof there is, my lord," I cried, "and a sure proof—the picture itself."

Thereupon the portrait was exhibited. And since the court-house was now falling to darkness, a couple of candles were brought and set in front of it that it might be the better seen. It was the horridest picture that ever was seen; and the glare of the candles made it start out from the gloom like a thing alive. It was not, however, at the face I looked for any great while.

"There, my lord," I cried in excitement "On the breast! There the medal hangs."

And to his good fortune Anthony Herbert had painted that medal with all his minute elaboration. From where I stood I could distinguish the head of King James, and when the picture was held close one could read the motto, "Cujus est?"

I looked up to the gallery while the judge and the jury were inspecting the picture. The last rays of the sun glowed tenderly about Dorothy's face and died off it whilst I looked.

"But the face!" exclaimed Mr. Cowper. "My lord, this is no simple portrait. We are not at the bottom of the matter."

"The face I have painted since I was in prison," replied Herbert; and explained in some confusion, "I blamed Mr. Clavering for my arrest."

"Then," said the judge, "we shall need proof that the medal was not painted in when you were in prison too."

But that proof he had, and subsequently produced in the person of his landlord and the landlord's wife with whom he had lodged at Keswick.

Meanwhile he continued his questioning of me.

"You have heard Jervas Rookley describe the medal?"

"Yes."

"Is it the true description?"

"But incomplete," I answered, "for there are marks upon the medal. Upon one side is the face, but there are scratches upon that face, when it fell one day upon the stones. The forehead is indented, there is a mark lengthening the curve of the mouth, there is a scratch where the cravat meets the neck beneath the ear."

"How came these scratches?" asked Herbert.

"I dropped the medal out of my fob," said I, "when I was thrown from my horse on Coldbarrow Fell, the first time I came to Blackladies, and Jervas Rookley picked it up and gave it back to me."

There was a murmur amongst the spectators.

"It is not true," said Rookley, but in a voice so shaken that it belied the words.

The judge took the medal and examined it.

"I cannot see," he said. "Bring more candles."

The candles were brought; the judge examined the medal, and handed it to the counsel.

"My lord, the jury would like to see it," and the voice was that of the foreman.

How eagerly I watched their faces while they clustered once more about it!

"The marks are there," said the foreman, "as the witness has described them."

"I should know," said I. "I tried to rub them off so often."

"And Jervas Rookley picked it up?" asked Herbert.

"He held it so long, turning it over in his hand, that I had to ask him thrice before ever I could get it back."

I spoke with all the earnestness I had, and it seemed to me that the jury belied my words. But I could not tell, and I waited, while the judge summed up and the jury were away considering their verdict, in a fever of anxiety. How long they were! how slowly they filed into the court! I looked up to the gallery: a row of white faces bent on the rail, all gazing towards the jury-box, save one, and that one gazed at me as I sat by the table in the court I was indeed still returning that gaze when the verdict was announced, and I think it was Herbert's hand grasping mine which first informed me what the verdict was.

That night I slept in Carlisle prison, but as I came out upon the steps of the court-house between my guards, I saw, by the light of the lamp swinging above the door, Herbert and his wife standing side by side; and a few yards further, the sergeant who led the way turned his lanthorn on one side and showed me the little figure of a girl and a face which peeped from out a taffety hood.

CHAPTER XXIII
THE LAST

For, standing in the roadway there, she seemed to me the forlornest figure that ever a man set eyes upon. There was something more than a drooping sadness in the attitude, something strangely like remorse, as though unaccountably she blamed herself. But I was not so curious to unravel her thoughts at this moment, as I was fearful of the risk she ran. She had sat alone in the court-house; no one had so much as spoken to her, and she stood alone in the streets of Carlisle. The knowledge of her danger rushed in upon me, and I had but one hope to lighten it. I remembered that she had spoken to me of a Whiggish relative who had given her shelter, and I trusted that she would find a refuge with him.

And so it indeed proved. For I had not lain more than three days in the castle before this very gentleman was admitted to see me, and after a prosy exhortation on the nature of my crimes, he proceeded:

"I have thought it my duty to say this much to you, but I come at the instance of a poor misguided friend of yours, who is anxious you should have no fears for her safety." The worthy gentleman scratched his forehead in some perplexity. "I cannot repeat to you all that this friend said. A woman in tears—a man in delirium, they both say a great deal which is not to be repeated. But her messages were of the friendliest—of the friendliest. For the rest the *Swallow* lies off the mouth of the Eden, with your friend's father on board. It appears that the ship sailed up the coast from a spot you maybe know of better than I do. Our friend returns to it to-night, and it sails forthwith to France." At the door he stopped, and scratched his head again. Then he rapped for the turnkey to let him out.

"The messages were of the friendliest," he repeated, and as the door was opened at that moment, assumed a judicial severity, and so marched pompously out.

Left to myself, I fell straightway into a temper of amazing contradictions. For whereas I had before been moved by the thought of Dorothy's danger, now I was troubled that she should be in such haste to use her liberty.

"This very night must she go?" I asked of myself indignantly. "Well, there is no reason why she should stay. She will be safe in France," and so came perilously near to weeping over myself, who must remain behind in prison. But to that thought succeeded another, which drove the first clean from my head. Dorothy in tears! There was matter in that notion for an indictment against the universe; and the indictment I drew, and supported it with such arguments as I felt sure must enforce conviction. From that pursuit I came very naturally to a speculation, in the nature of those friendliest messages. I construed them by the dictionary of her looks, as she had sat in the gallery of the court-house. It was a task of which I did not tire, but drew great comfort from it, and found it very improving.

The next day, however, I was taken out of the castle and sent forward under an escort, to join my co-rebels who were being marched by easy stages to London. I caught them up at St. Albans, and coming to Barnet we had our hands tied, and halters thrown about our horses' necks, and so were carried through the streets of London to Newgate gaol. Such a concourse of people came to view us as I have never seen the like of. The town was dressed for a holiday; and what with the banging of drums, the hurrahing for King George, and the damning of the "Pretender," the air so rang with noise, that it was as much as you could to hear your neighbour speak. One sturdy Whig, I remember, planted himself in our way, and with many jeers and imprecations lifted up a jackdaw tricked out with white roses, which he carried on a warming-pan, and so paced backwards and in front of us, until a soldier cracked him on the chest with the butt of his firelock, and toppled the fellow into the gutter.

In Newgate, there I remained a weary while, though this period was made as light for us as well could be. We had the liberty of the Press yard, and were allowed to receive visitors and to visit one another—no inconsiderable privilege, one may think, if one counts up the number imprisoned there. There it came about that I saw much of Charles Ratcliffe, Lord Derwentwater's brother; and though he was not of his brother's amiable and endearing disposition, grew to some intimacy with him. He thought me, indeed, a great fool for running my head into the noose at Carlisle for a beggarly painter, and never scrupled to tell me so; but I think it was just that action which inclined his friendship my way. There were other consolations came to me, and one of them was lighted with a glimmering of hope; for one day came Sir William Wyndham to see me, and informed me that Lord Bolingbroke was very active in my behalf, urging upon his friends in England to make representations for my release, or, if that failed, to concert measures for my evasion. I set no great reliance upon either alternative, but Sir William Wyndham came again in March of the year 1716, after the rebellion had closed in Scotland, and Lord Bolingbroke had been dismissed from the service of King James.

"Mr. Secretary Stanhope encourages your kinsman," said he, "in the hope that he may be pardoned. In which event something might be done for you. Meanwhile, I have a message to deliver to you from him. 'Tell Lawrence,' he says, 'that here in Paris I am much plagued and pestered by a young friend of his, who tells me that unless I unlock Newgate, I do not deserve to be related to him. I am greatly humiliated by so much scolding, but will do what I can.'"

It was not very much, however, that he could do; and on the 8th of May I was arraigned with Charles Ratcliffe at the Exchequer Bar at Westminster, and tried there on the 18th, and taken back again a few days later to receive sentence.

"But we shall not be hanged," said Ratcliffe. "You will see."

Indeed, he ever had the greatest confidence that he would escape. I recollect that on the occasion when we were being carried from Newgate to receive sentence at Westminster, our coach was stopped in Fleet Street to make way for King George, who was setting out upon his first visit to Herrenhausen since he had come to the English throne. We stopped opposite a distiller's, and Ratcliffe, leaning from the window, very coolly called for half a pint of aniseed, and drank it off.

"There is some merit in the Dutchman, after all," he said with a laugh, "for I was in great need of that."

The events, however, justified his confidence. Never shall I forget the weeks which followed our condemnation—the intrigues with our friends outside, the timorous bribing of the gaolers within. One day the plan would be settled, the moment for its execution appointed, and the next thing maybe we saw was the countenance of a new gaoler, and so the attempt must needs be deferred and the trouble begin again. Or at another time news would be brought to us that we should receive the clemency of the Crown and only suffer transportation to the colonies; or, again, that we were to be granted a free pardon; or, again, that the sentence was to be carried out within a week. So that now we kicked our heels upon the pinnacles of hope, now we sank into a bog of despair, and either way we shivered with fever—all of us except Charles Ratcliffe.

It was with his usual serenity that when at last all arrangements had been made, he invited those of us who were in the plot to a grand entertainment in a room called the Castle, in the upper part of the prison.

"There are thirteen of us besides myself," said he, as soon as the supper was served and we were left alone. "The rest must shift for themselves. Mr. Clavering, do you help me with this file, and do you, gentlemen, be sufficiently ill-mannered to make as much clatter with the dishes and your talk as will drown the sound of it."

Whereupon he drew a file from his pocket, and I crossed over with him to a little door in the corner of the room; and while the others talked and clattered, I went to work with my file upon the screws of the plate which held the lock to the door. When I was tired and my fingers bleeding, Ratcliffe took my place, and after him another, until at last the plate came away.

"Now," said Ratcliffe, "the passage leads to the debtors' side. We have been to solace our good friend Mr. Tiverton, who has been most unkindly committed by his creditors. Mr. Tiverton—pray do not forget the name, gentlemen! For even the most obliging gaoler might cavil if we forgot the name."

We followed him quickly along the passage, across the yard to the porter's lodge.

"Poor man!" says Ratcliffe, "it is very barbarous and inhuman that a man of genius should go to prison for lack of money."

"For my part, sir," says the gaoler, throwing open the wicket, "I pity his tradesmen."

"But some men are born to be gulled," says Ratcliffe, with his tongue in his cheek. "And here's five guineas for you," and he stepped into the street.

We followed him quickly enough, and once there scattered without so much as a single word of farewell. Each man had his own plant, no doubt. For myself, I knew that a certain sloop was waiting for me on the Thames, and I hurried down to the water's edge below London Bridge. A boat was waiting by the steps.

"Lawrence," cried a voice which sent my heart leaping.

"Hush!" I whispered, and jumped into the stern.

Dorothy made room for me beside her.

"Push off," she said; and in a moment we were floating down the river, in and out between the ships.

"Give me the tiller," said I.

"No," said Dorothy; "it was my doing that you were brought into peril. Let me steer you out of it."

The number of ships diminished. Before they were about us like the trees of a forest, now they were the trees of an alley down which we passed; and ever the alley broadened and the trees grew scarce.

"I saw you that night at Carlisle," she began, "when you were taken to the castle;" and at that she broke off suddenly and her voice stiffened.

"My kinsman came to you at Carlisle. What did he say?"

"He said that he was charged with the friendliest messages from you."

"Is that all?"

Now, there was something more, but I thought it wise to make no mention of it.

"He did not repeat the messages," was all I said, and she sat up as though her pride was relieved, and for a little we were silent. A ship was anchored some way ahead of us, and a lanthorn swung on its poop.

"Is it the *Swallow?*" I asked.

"Yes," said she; and then, "before I left Carlisle I saw her."

For a moment I wondered of whom she was talking.

"I saw her and her husband."

Then I understood.

"She is very plain," said Dorothy in a whisper.

"Oh no," said I, "indeed she is not. You do her an injustice."

"But she is," repeated Dorothy, "she is."

It would have been better had I left the matter thus, but I was foolish enough to seriously argue the point with her, and so hot became the argument that we overshot the ship.

"That is your fault," said Dorothy, as she turned the boat

We rowed to the ship's side, a ladder was hoisted over, and a lanthorn held. By the light of it I could see Mr. Curwen, and behind him my servant Ashlock. I rose to give a hand to Dorothy, but she sat in the stern without so much as a pretence of movement.

"Come, Dorothy," said Mr. Curwen.

Dorothy looked steadily at me.

"She is very plain," she said, and then looked away across the river, humming a tune.

I was in a quandary as to what I should do. For I knew that she was not plain; but also I knew that Dorothy would not move until I had said she was. So I stood then holding on to the ladder while the boat rose and sank beneath my feet. I have been told since that there was really only one expedient which would have served my turn, and that was to tumble incontinently into the water and make as much pretence of drowning as I could. Only it never occurred to me, and so I weakly gave in.

Dorothy stepped on board. The boat was hoisted, the anchor raised, and in the smallest space of time the foam was bubbling from the bows. Overhead the stars shone steady in the sky and danced in the water beneath us, and so we sailed to France.

"Dorothy," said I, "there is a word which has been much used between us—friends."

"Yes!" said she in a low voice, "it is a good word."

And so it was many months afterwards before I came to her again in Paris and pleaded that there was a better.

"I would you thought with me," I stammered out.

Dorothy, with the sweetest laugh that ever my ears hearkened to, began to sing over to herself a verse of "The Honest Lover."

"Dear heart," she said, "I called you an owl, but it should have been a bat."

Jervas Rookley I never came across again. But I know that he did not win Blackladies, though whether a suspicion of his treachery is accountable or the avarice of the Hanoverians, I cannot tell. I have heard, too, that at one time he was the master of a ship trading in the South Seas; but of this, again, I have no sure knowledge.